TOWARDS A DEMOCRATIC DIVISION OF LABOUR IN EUROPE?

The Combination Model as a new integrated approach to professional and family life

Walter Van Dongen

  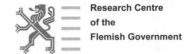

Research Centre
of the
Flemish Government

This edition published in Great Britain in 2009 by

The Policy Press
University of Bristol
Fourth Floor
Beacon House
Queen's Road
Bristol BS8 1QU
UK

Tel +44 (0)117 331 4054
Fax +44 (0)117 331 4093
e-mail tpp-info@bristol.ac.uk
www.policypress.org.uk

North American office:
The Policy Press
c/o International Specialized Books Services (ISBS)
920 NE 58th Avenue, Suite 300
Portland, OR 97213-3786, USA
Tel +1 503 287 3093
Fax +1 503 280 8832
e-mail info@isbs.com

© The Policy Press 2009

British Library Cataloguing in Publication Data
A catalogue record for this book is available from the British Library.

Library of Congress Cataloging-in-Publication Data
A catalog record for this book has been requested.

ISBN 978-1-84742-269-9 paperback
ISBN 978-1-84742-294-1 hardcover

Cover design by Qube Design, Bristol.
Printed and bound in Great Britain by MPG Books, Bodmin.

Contents

Acknowledgements

I would like to thank all the people who read the draft version and formulated their comments and suggestions. First of all, my thanks go to Professor Dr Emeritus Jaap Kruithof, my most important scientific mentor since 1980. Many thanks also to Professor Dr Eric Vanhaute of the University of Ghent, a personal friend since my first year in secondary school and a supportive colleague since 1990 with respect to the historical development of the division of labour between men and women in the western world. I would also like to thank Professor Dr Emeritus Robert Cliquet, director of the former CBGS until 2000, who always offered the space to develop the Combination Model and the different applications. Thanks also to Professor Dr Joris Ghysels of the University of Antwerp, Xavier Verboven, the former head of a large Flemish labour union and my colleagues Luc Deschamps, Josée Lemaître, Ronald Schoenmaeckers and Christine Van Peer for their comments and suggestions. Finally, I must mention Jonny Johansson (Eurostat), Kimberly Fisher (University of Oxford) and Jennifer Hook (Pennsylvania State University) for providing a number of specific datasets. Notwithstanding the helpful contribution of so many people, the contents of this study remain my sole responsibility.

List of figures

ONE

The division of professional and family labour

1.1 Societal background: towards a new basic model of society?

In recent years the issue of 'combining professional and family labour' has appeared centre-stage regarding daily life in all European countries. At the same time, this issue has received much attention in the science and policy fields. Most societal actors are increasingly realising that the daily combination of professional and family labour is the beating heart of societal life. All democratic policy organisations recognise the issue as a major policy challenge on a national and even European level since it concerns many societal actors (men and women, families, companies, clubs and governmental organisations) and many societal fields (employment, family life, labour organisation, childcare, education, mobility and so on).

Consequently, research, debate and policy relating to this issue must be placed within the overall development of society (and all its entities). This book examines the long search for a new integrated approach to the daily life of men and women within the different living arrangements of society (for example, families, clubs, companies, public organisations). In order to present this research clearly and effectively, different types of models have been used.

Each model is the combination of conceptual, empirical and normative dimensions. The *conceptual* dimension refers to the way we analyse or look at reality. The *empirical* dimension shows to what extent a (conceptual) model is actually (being) realised. The *normative* dimension refers to how society should be organised in the future. The permanent interaction between the three dimensions determines the actual overall development of society.

During a long period two basic models co-exist, the old model going downward and losing influence while the new one gains influence. A new basic model is partly a reaction against and a rejection of the previous model, but at the same time it is partly a continuation of the previous model, preserving a number of (positive and negative) elements.

In general, the development of western societies is illustrated by means of a number of successive *basic models*. Figure 1.1 shows three basic models for 1750–2150, each with a life span of about two centuries. The models vary, of course, from country to country.

A basic model of society is an overall framework of the structure and functioning of society and its different actors, representing different variants. So we can talk about the

Figure 1.1   Development of three basic models of society

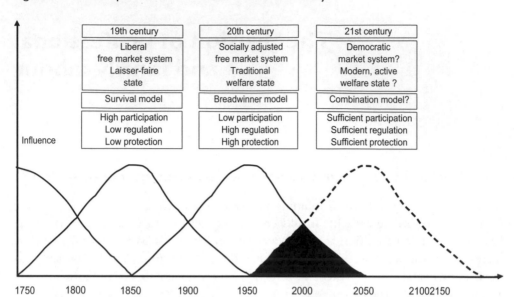

19th century	20th century	21st century
Liberal free market system Laisser-faire state	Socially adjusted free market system Traditional welfare state	Democratic market system? Modern, active welfare state ?
Survival model	Breadwinner model	Combination model?
High participation Low regulation Low protection	Low participation High regulation High protection	Sufficient participation Sufficient regulation Sufficient protection

19th-century model of the *liberal free market system* in most western countries, which started approximately in the middle of the 18th century, was dominant during the 19th century and vanished in the middle of the 20th century. This model stood explicitly for a strong liberal free market system, with its typical laissez–faire state that paid little attention to the daily professional, family and social life of men and women. The labour market participation of adult men and women and of children was fairly high, in a labour market and business world that was hardly regulated and that offered very few forms of social and financial protection. At the same time, there was a shortage of public provisions for social protection. In short, it was a *survival* model, with most individuals and families trying to survive with little means of subsistence (Lis, 1984; Seccombe, 1992, 1993; Smith and Wallerstein, 1992; Arrighi, 1994; Hopkins and Wallerstein, 1996; Vanhaute, 1997a, 1997b, 2002).

This model was countered and replaced by the 20th-century model of the *socially adjusted free market system*. This model appeared around the middle of the 19th century, was dominant in the period 1920-80 and will most probably disappear by the middle of the 21st century. As it was the dominant model during the previous period, we can now call it the 'traditional basic model' (without any negative connotation) or the model of the 'traditional welfare state'. The traditional welfare state emphasised the social correction of the free market by government and was much more concerned with the daily living conditions of men and women, with explicit and strong regulation of the labour market and increased 'social protection' for children and women, in particular married mothers. This resulted in a strong decline in the labour market participation of (married) women and children, compensated for by the extension of social provisions for breadwinner families. It is therefore also called the 'breadwinner model', with fathers taking on the role of breadwinner and mothers the role of housewife (household tasks and raising children). The traditional basic model was the foundation of all variants of the modern welfare state, as presented by the famous classification of Esping–Andersen (Esping–Andersen, 1990, 1999; see also Korpi, 2000; Schmid and Gazier, 2002; Gornick and Meyers, 2003).

The traditional welfare state, with all its variants, has increasingly come to a standstill during the past decades, largely due to its own contradictions. It is no longer able to provide sufficient adequate perspectives or solutions for the main problems society currently faces. This experience has forced society to search for another, more adequate conceptual and normative approach. During previous decades, many building stones for such a *new basic model* had already been created. During decades to come, this new basic model of society will be further developed and at a certain point it will become stronger than the traditional model. The main normative question here is to what extent the new basic model will stand for a fully *democratic society*, with a *democratic market system* and a *democratic division of labour* in families and organisations, using 'democracy' as the overall normative guideline for all actors and systems in society (Figure 1.1). This new concept will be explained in Chapter 3, as the basis for the normative future policy models for the division of labour. The transition to a new basic model influences all parts of society and implies that existing concepts are reformulated and combined with new concepts. It also demands other empirical data and adjusted normative starting points. As the title to this book states, this process is seen from the perspective of the daily division of professional and family work.

1.2   The Combination Model

1.2.1 Aims of the model

In the broad sense of the concept, the daily combination of professional and family life is a major motor of the daily life of all men and women, within the context of families and all other societal organisations. It expresses the complex interaction system between these domains, emphasising the need to deal with these interactions in an integrated way, conceptually, empirically and normatively. Consequently, an effective 'combination policy' must develop and realise an efficient integrated policy programme in all relevant societal fields, in line with the conceptual and normative approach and with actual development.

In this book we introduce a broad integrated approach to the *daily life and life course of men and women within different societal entities* (families, clubs, companies, public organisations, and so on). *Daily life* is seen as the daily division of activities or labour processes and their results. All activities are seen as productive labour processes that produce a valuable output and that are regulated by the general mechanism of human exchange. The *life course* is the inclusive concept for the development or change of daily life in time. The *development* of the daily life of men and women refers to societal changes in time, from the past to the future. The daily division or combination of professional and family labour is a major part of the overall division of activities. Using this approach, *professional labour* refers in the broad sense of the word to all paid occupational labour, that is, all labour that is being done as a profession or occupation in the labour market, with (normal) monetary payment. *Family labour* refers to all household tasks and caring activities within the family. These two basic activities are a major part of the overall division of time of all people, alongside other activities such as personal care, external education, social or voluntary labour and leisure activities.

The 'Combination Model' is presented in this book as a broad scientific instrument for developing an integrated policy for the division of professional and family work in democratic societies. It is a general concept for the integration of the conceptual, empirical and normative approach to this major societal issue. First, we formulate a broad interdisciplinary conceptual approach to understand the complex daily life of men and women in a complex society (Van Dongen, 1990, 1993). Next, several empirical models are used to show the actual development in a comprehensible way, largely supporting the conceptual model. Finally, some normative combination models are formulated, expressing how the division of labour can or should be reorganised on different levels of society, according to some relevant value systems. Starting from the criteria of desirability and feasibility, the 'Complete Combination Model' is selected as the most adequate policy model. This model is then used to formulate a consistent set of policy perspectives on the relevant societal fields.

This study aims to prove that the Combination Model is a useful instrument for all democratic societies, although it was originally developed mainly within Flemish and Belgian contexts.

1.2.2 Background

For science and policy the concept of the Combination Model was introduced for the first time in Flanders in 1999, in the context of the Flemish Round Table conference 'Professional and family life' (1998-99) (Van Dongen and Beck, 1999; Van Dongen and Franken, 1999; Van Dongen, Beck and Vanhaute 2001). The concept was largely inspired by scientific and policy debate on the 'combination scenario' in the Netherlands during 1995-2000 (Ministerie van Sociale Zaken en Werkgelegenheid, 1997, 1999a, 1999b, 2000; Commissie Dagindeling, 1998; Plantenga and Schippers, 2000). As a policy model, the combination scenario was the result of long scientific and policy debate on the desirable future division of labour in the Netherlands, which was largely the same in Belgium and in many other European countries. In general, it expressed the idea that the division of both professional and family labour between men and women should become much more equal in the next decades, albeit with sufficient diversity. However, it was largely presented by means of the new ideal family type with an equal division of professional and family labour between the two partners, as an alternative to the traditional breadwinner family that was dominant in the period 1950-80. As such, all attention went to promoting the one ideal family type, implicitly suggesting that in the longer run (almost) all (couple) families should follow this. So, the combination scenario was largely perceived as a dogmatic policy model, leaving insufficient space for gradual diversity among families. In other words, opponents argued that the combination scenario eliminated the free choice of people/families to choose another division of labour and that it led to maximum uniformity between men and women and among families. Although the theorists behind the combination scenario by no means had these 'goals' in mind, the practical presentation offered sufficient ground for this perception since it largely neglected the gradual character of both the actual and preferable future division of labour in the Netherlands (and other countries). Consequently, the combination scenario invoked strong resistance in different societal groups and, to a large extent, lost its political support, prohibiting any further elaboration, improvement and communication. As a result, after some years it almost completely disappeared from the Dutch scientific and political scene.

This development in the Netherlands motivated the desire to avoid an unproductive debate on this policy issue in Flanders/Belgium, where the policy discussion had the same ideological and emotional background and content. Therefore, a few normative combination models were introduced at the Flemish Round Table conference during 1998-2000, as possible policy models for the future combination of professional and family work (Van Dongen et al, 2001). The term 'model' is explicitly and intentionally used as a 'societal model' to emphasise the diversity of the actual division of labour within families and within society as a whole. We can therefore show that several relevant future models are possible according to the normative views in society. Every societal actor can develop a specific policy model and formulate specific policy proposals. By means of democratic decision making the most desired model can then be selected as a basis for the actual policy programme.

We started from an integrated conceptual approach to the division of labour and from the diversity of the actual division of labour in Flanders, the Netherlands and some other countries found in previous research (Van Dongen, 1990, 1993; Van Dongen et al, 1995). It could be observed that the *actual* division of professional and family labour was still fairly unequal and no longer reflected the (new) basic values of (a majority of the population in) most European countries. In other words, most European countries wanted to realise a more equal division of labour with *sufficient* equality between men and women in families, organisations and society as a whole. At the same time, all European countries wanted to offer individuals and families *sufficient* freedom to choose their specific division of labour. The central question, then, is how far the values of 'freedom' (diversity) and 'equality' can and should be realised in the daily division of labour. How equal should the daily division of labour be: very equal, moderately equal or only partly equal? In the same way, how much freedom should individuals and families have in order to realise their preferred division of labour? Consequently, the discussion about the relative weight of the values of freedom and equality demands a clear presentation of the gradual division of professional and family labour.

Following this process in a logical way, the *central scientific task*, then, was to develop *alternative gradual normative future models* (*policy models*) of the division of labour that were sufficiently in line with the actual development and with the normative views in society. To illustrate these models to a broader public we developed graphical presentations of the actual and desirable division of labour.

1.3   Other integrating models

During the past decade, similar integrating models have been developed in other parts of the world, largely reflecting specific societal and scientific backgrounds and orientation. These models have been developed separately to a large extent, although all researchers are influenced by general worldwide scientific and societal developments. These models helped us to further elaborate and improve the conceptual, empirical and normative approach of the Combination Model. Along with the combination scenario in the Netherlands, we discuss a few other relevant models.

First, we present the *transitional labour markets (TLM) model* that was originally launched by Günther Schmid, mainly from the perspective of transitional labour market research in economics and sociology (Schmid, 1997, 1998, 2002a, 2002b; Schmid and Gazier, 2002; Schmid and Schomann, 2004). Schmid's model had a fairly strong appeal and was the basis for an international scientific network during 2001-05, called TLM.NET (see www.siswo.uva.nl/tlm). The network brought together scholars from different social sciences from all over Europe. Their first goal was to compare research across the countries regarding basic labour market transitions and transitions into other spheres of social life. This led to proposals for the modernisation of the European social model; more specifically, new policy combinations were proposed that were more effective than traditional policies, for example unemployment insurance, lifelong learning, family and pension systems. These proposals should be placed within the comparative analyses of welfare regimes and social processes at the local, national and international (European) levels (Esping-Andersen, 1990, 1999; Korpi, 2000).

In the past 15 years, the scientific work and policy debate on the combination scenario and the TLM model was also linked to the development of the new *flexicurity model*, which has become quite attractive to a number of scientific research groups in Europe, especially in the Netherlands and Denmark. The attractiveness of this new model was shown during the international conference in Amsterdam in 2006: 'Innovating labour market policies: transitional labour markets and flexicurity'. The title of the conference strongly suggests the intrinsic link between the TLM model and the flexicurity model. The Dutch Institute for Labour Studies (OSA) and the Dutch Organisation for Scientific Research (NOW) have intensively scrutinised – both empirically and theoretically – the two approaches over the past few years (Muffels and Ester, 2004; Wilthagen and Tros, 2004; Wilthagen et al, 2004; Madsen, 2006; van den Heuvel et al, 2006).

Innovative labour market policies are necessary for the further preservation and development of our welfare states, to deal with two main trends or challenges: the internationalisation of the economy and the diversification of society. On the one hand, there is an urgent need, for the sake of competitiveness, to enhance the adaptability and flexibility of organisations, business processes and institutions. On the other hand, social cohesion appears to be at risk as large groups are being excluded socially and economically. European countries therefore need innovative policies that can increase labour force participation and the productivity of men and women as well as both flexibility and security. The main hypothesis is that the TLM model and the flexicurity model offered a good basis for innovating labour market policies.

In the US, many researchers have been working on this broad field of the division of professional and family labour of men and women, or, in US terms, the major issue of 'work and family'. For a number of years the Sloan Work and Family Research Network (http://wfnetwork.bc.edu) has offered a forum for researchers of all social sciences to promote and facilitate dialogue between academic researchers, employers and public policy makers.

Starting from this background, we would like to mention in particular the *dual earner/dual carer model* that was presented and clarified by Crompton (1999) as a possible normative answer to the more traditional historical models in the US. This policy model is further elaborated on and more broadly applied by Gornick and Meyers (2003, 2004a, 2004b). It clearly reflects the specific societal background, circumstances and normative views of the US.

The dual earner/dual carer model was, to a certain extent, inspired by the normative future models presented by Fraser (1994), mainly from a feminist political science perspective. Together with many other researchers and policy makers, Fraser observed that the actual division of professional and family work was still unequal in the US and in other western countries. This unacceptable situation was the basis for her idea that 'normative theorizing remains an indispensable intellectual enterprise for feminism, indeed for all emancipatory social movements. We need a vision or picture of where we are trying to go, and a set of standards for evaluating various proposals as to how we might get there' (Fraser, 1994, p 595). Starting from a critical evaluation of the ideal universal breadwinner model and caregiver parity model as two alternative policy models, she proposed a new integrating model that combined the positive aspects of these models and expressed a gender deconstructive vision based on real gender equity. Fraser (2006) calls this new model the *universal caregiver model*, which is quite similar to the *dual earner/dual carer model*.

Finally, we shall also mention the new approach recently introduced by Benko and Wesberg (2007) with the label '*mass career customization*'. This model is developed within the perspective of organisation of work in companies.

To show the development and meaning of the Combination Model in European countries and a few other OECD (Organisation for Economic Co-operation and Development) countries, we provide a brief comparison with the other models. While emphasising the similarities between the models, we also highlight the differences, according to societal background, scientific discipline and conceptual/normative approach. Each model is based on a few basic factors used to construct some typologies, which are the basis for the conceptual, empirical and normative societal models.

1.4 Development of the Combination Model in Flanders/Belgium

This study is based on our work during the past 15 years within the former Flemish Centre for Population and Family Study (CBGS), mainly dealing with the development of the Combination Model in Flanders/Belgium during 1950-2000, and placed within an international context.

Van Dongen (1993) has illustrated the development of an integrated, interdisciplinary approach to the division of labour within families and organisations and to the market system. This approach was the result of interaction between a broad education background (interdisciplinary ethical sciences and economic sciences), research experience during the first career stage and active participation in different societal organisations. The empirical research mainly shows the fairly positive development of the division of labour of women in the period 1950-90, emphasising increasing participation in the labour market and the changing division of household work. At the same time, Van Dongen (1993) visualises the societal thresholds for a more equal division of labour between men and women. Starting from the actual division of labour and the normative concept of a democratic division of labour, the major policy perspectives are formulated.

Van Dongen et al, in their 1995 study, present the main results of a broad survey on the daily combination of professional and family life in Flemish families in 1992, within a life course perspective. The study deals with the different aspects of the past and actual division of labour and their future choices or intentions. As such, it is largely the basis for the development of the empirical and normative combination models at a later stage. A central conclusion is that almost all Flemish women started their career with a paid job, but many gave up their jobs at a certain stage, temporarily or permanently, completely or partially. The gap increases during the first years with the arrival of children and mostly stabilises after the birth of the last child. The paid work of men and women must offer a good combination of personal, social, material and financial means, but for many the breadwinner motive is still quite influential. Another important conclusion is that the traditional idea of the 'double duty' of working women must be reformulated thoroughly: together with all working women almost all men have the double duty of daily combining professional and family work. The division of both tasks is still quite unequal and full-time working women have a more heavy daily duty than other groups. Moreover, the daily division of household tasks between partners is largely related to the relative division of the hours of professional labour. In future, more men and women would like a paid job, but at the same time a significant number of working men and women would like to have a job with less hours. Above all, they would like more time for family and personal activities.

Van Dongen et al, in their 1998 study, collect the analyses and views of some prominent Flemish and Dutch researchers, focusing on the decreasing influence of the breadwinner model in the two countries (and other European countries) and on the question of what the future division of professional and family labour could and should look like. The general conclusion is that the breadwinner model is clearly in decline in Flanders/Belgium, the Netherlands and all other European countries. Yet it still has a restraining influence on the division of labour in all sections of society. Therefore, democratic European societies must develop a new future policy view that can translate the central message of a democratic division of labour to a feasible policy model and a number of concrete policy perspectives.

These studies largely gave rise to the Flemish Round Table conference 'Professional and family life' (1998-2000), bringing different stakeholders together to formulate an answer to the basic question: which is the most suitable division of professional and family labour for democratic countries in the longer run? And which policy perspectives should then be followed? Largely inspired by the debate on the combination scenario in the Netherlands, the concept of the Combination Model was introduced during the conference, starting from a broad conceptual and normative approach to the division of labour. In 2001 Van Dongen et al integrated the main results of this previous work and that from the conference. The book officially presented the Combination Model to a broad public as a useful scientific instrument for studying the daily division of professional and family labour, integrating the combination perspective, the life course perspective, the family perspective and the organisation perspective. This refers to the permanent challenge of all men and women to realise the right combination of activities during different stages of the life course, within the context of their family and the organisation they work for. The Combination Model aims at an adequate empirical picture of the gradual division of labour between men and women, with sufficient attention paid to the relevant characteristics. The central policy question, then, implies the search for *another diverse division of labour* that is seen as the most desirable one in a democratic society, starting from a strong balance between the basic values of freedom, equality, solidarity and efficiency. Van Dongen et al formulated a number of normative combination models as the basis for the policy debate on the future division of labour. One of these models, the complete combination model, was selected as the most desirable policy model and was further used for the elaboration of a consistent set of policy perspectives.

During 2001-04, the Combination Model was a major inspiration for democratic political parties and societal organisations (trade unions, employers' organisations, gender organisations, family organisations) in Flanders. The model invited stakeholders to reformulate their long-term policy vision and goals more explicitly, resulting in a dynamic political debate. Most policy actors largely subscribed to the general idea of the new policy model as a guideline for future policy debate, but it takes a long time to change policy views. The fairly strong policy changes demanded by the new policy model and the lack of national and international empirical support did not stimulate the use of the policy model for the policy debate.

At the same time, some alternative policy models were developed abroad and also enjoyed some attention in the scientific and policy world, for example the TLM model and the flexicurity model. As a consequence, little attention and energy could go to collaboration between the different research groups and to the comparison and integration of the new policy models.

Unlike these other policy models, the development of the Combination Model could continue. Van Dongen and Danau (2003) gathered additional empirical material to illustrate the actual development of the Combination Model in Flanders, using 1999 time use data and 1997 income data. The Combination Model was explicitly linked to the development of the concept of societal equality in Flanders and Europe, as a basic value in a democratic society. In general, this study also supported the choice of the complete combination model as the most desirable policy model and further elaborated the policy perspectives following from that policy model.

In the same period, some practical applications of the Combination Model were developed. Danau and Van Dongen (2002) reported on the development of the 'Family and Busines Audit' (FBA) resulting from a number of case studies in different Flemish organisations. The FBA project was largely inspired by the complete combination model and the policy perspectives resulting from it, in particular the need for a sufficiently equal division of labour between men and women and for a gender- and family-friendly work policy in companies. The FBA aims at supporting organisations to realise a modern family and business policy that focuses on all relevant aspects of the work organisation.

To place these case studies in a broader context, Van Dongen (2004b) offers an analysis of the availability of different 'family and business' or 'combination' facilities in 760 Flemish companies with more than 50 employees. The data came from the 'Family and Business Policy' module of the 2002 Flemish Survey (Panel Survey of Organisations, or PASO) (Delarue et al, 2003). Unfortunately, since the PASO Survey was suspended a few years ago, this research cannot be extended any further. In general, the study made clear that Flemish companies still have a long way to go in order to realise a more gender- and family-friendly work organisation that is compatible with the basic idea of the complete combination model. More specifically, there is a substantial need for more part-time jobs of 25-35 hours/week, for a four-day working week, for flexible work schedules, for more flexible workplace arrangements and for adequate supportive family and personal services.

Van Dongen (2004c) tries to answer the policy question of how the external daytime education/care for children under three years of age should be further developed in the Flemish Community (and other European countries). The study starts from the pedagogical, social, material and financial meaning of external daytime education/care as formulated by the Combination Model, in the first place for the development of children and for the daily division of professional and family work of the parents, and also for the day-to-day functioning of professional organisations and for the labour market as a whole. Starting from the historical background of childcare during the 20th century, the development of daytime education/care in Flanders during 1990-2002 is presented by means of some indicators: availability, participation, uptake, occupancy, productivity, cost-efficiency and personal financial contribution. The analysis shows that the so-called 'multiple track policy' of the Flemish government has been rather complicated and inefficient. As such, it can no longer be the basis for future policy in a democratic society. Starting from the empirical analysis, a few future scenarios are elaborated which are connected with the normative combination models for the daily division of professional and family labour within families. For each scenario the central policy perspectives are formulated. Following the Complete Combination Model, the need for the transformation of external daycare to full external daytime education is emphasised as a basic provision for the youngest children. This daytime education should be fully streamlined with basic education, pedagogically, organisationally and financially.

Finally, in line with the previous work, Van Dongen (2006d) offers a general analytical model for the efficiency of societal services ('caregiving') that are being subsidised by the (Flemish/Belgian) government to a large extent. The different societal services are placed within a general approach to the division of time of men and women, within families, neighbourhoods, associations, companies, and so on. Starting from an overview of the relevant aspects of the mechanism of demand and supply, some general indicators are elaborated on for the efficiency of societal services: availability, participation, use, occupancy, productivity, cost–efficiency and direct financial contribution. The study aims to develop practical evaluation instruments that can serve as the empirical basis for a policy discussion on micro and macro levels.

1.5   Meaning of the Combination Model for other European countries

Since these studies are largely located within and bounded by the Flemish/Belgian context, most of them have been published in Dutch, without much international coverage. However, the results were placed within an international context, leading to the proposition that the Combination Model is also a useful instrument for the study of the division of labour in other (European) countries.

The development and applications of the Combination Model in Flanders received fairly positive attention at different international conferences. But at the same time, many researchers questioned the relevance of the model for other (European) countries. After all, most comparative studies largely focus on the differences between countries and emphasise the uniqueness of each country. Starting from these observed differences between the European countries, many researchers could/can hardly believe that the Combination Model, originally developed for the small Flemish Community, is also useful for other (European) countries. This aspect is strengthened by the fact that new ideas, models and instruments of Flemish social scientists and policy makers often receive insufficient attention and means for further development at international level.

As a result, the scope of the empirical and policy study was extended to international (European) level from the beginning of 2005. Step by step an internationally comparative picture of the development of the division of professional and family labour has been created. Since the available means for this project were very restricted, two easily accessible data sources for comparative analysis were mainly used: the Labour Force Survey (LFS, Eurostat) and the integrated multinational time use dataset (MTUS, University of Oxford).

The comparative empirical analysis in this study focuses on the daily division of professional and family labour of men and women, with some attention to other basic activities; however, partial activities are not considered here. During the next few years we would like to broaden the international comparison to the division of income (individual professional and social income, total family income). At the same time, it would be useful to compare internationally the management strategies of professional organisations in different countries, looking at both the similarity and diversity of combination facilities that companies offer, allowing their employees to realise a better division of professional and private/family life. Finally, it would be interesting to study the daily division of time of children and young people using time use data.

1.6   Structure of the book

The structure of this book is simple. It begins with an explanation of the conceptual and normative approaches, followed by empirical analysis, resulting in the presentation of normative policy models and policy perspectives. We know that this structure insufficiently expresses the permanent interaction between the conceptual, empirical and normative dimensions during the complex research process. Yet it is the only feasible way to present the results in a comprehensible way to a broader public.

Chapter 2 presents the *integrated conceptual approach* to the daily life of men and women in a complex modern society, with the daily combination of professional and family labour a central part. The theoretical approach is the result of a long integrating process. Special attention is paid to the new conceptual approach to the market, the market system and the place of the public sector (public services, fiscal system, social security).

Chapter 3 starts from the basic normative question of how the division of labour between men and women should evolve in the (near) future, given the actual evolution in past decades. Our starting point is very similar to that of Fraser (1994, 2006), Crompton (1999), Gornick and Meyers (2003) and all other researchers who want to find an answer to the still largely unequal division of labour. They clearly emphasise the need for a new normative vision or model for the future division of labour, as a guide for scientific researchers and policy makers. Broad agreement on the long-term policy model could make that process much more effective.

To answer this basic normative question, an adequate normative approach must be formulated to conceive and express future society, in line with the conceptual approach. We use the term 'democracy' as the overall normative concept for society, which expresses a certain combination of four basic values or principles that have to be realised simultaneously on all levels of society: freedom of choice, equality, solidarity and efficiency. So, one can present a continuum of different 'democracies', from a very weak democracy at one end to a very strong democracy at the other. We formulate the concept of 'strong democracy' as a useful normative basis for future policy in democratic countries, expressing a strong balance of the four basic values in all fields of society. Within this general normative concept for society as a whole, we also propose a new normative concept for the market, the market system and the public sector.

Chapter 4 describes the *actual evolution of the division of professional and family labour* in EU countries and some other OECD countries. First, we summarise the evolution from the 'old combination model' or 'survival model' in the period 1750-1900 to the 'new' breadwinner model in the 20th century. By means of some basic indicators or 'empirical models' that were developed for Flanders/Belgium before, we then show the general development from the *strong male breadwinner model* in the period 1950-70 to a *moderate asymmetric combination model* in the period 1985-2005, albeit with several variants in different (types of) countries. These historical models are briefly compared with the largely similar models presented by Crompton (1999) and by Gornick and Meyers (2003).

Graphical indicators are presented, each showing a specific aspect or side of the division of labour: the labour situation of the male and female population; the general division of the main activities; professional activity rates of men and women (by age group); the number of hours of professional labour, family labour, leisure time and personal care; and some aspects of the temporal quality of the jobs of men and women. In all parts of the empirical analysis, we emphasise the overall similarity of the development in all countries, but at the same time, the differences between the (types of) welfare states (Esping-Andersen, 1990, 1999; Korpi, 2000) are illustrated.

Chapters 5 and 6 deal with the policy discussion, starting from the basic normative question of Chapter 2: what kind of division of labour should be developed in the future and which policy perspectives can and should be formulated? This task is done in two steps.

Chapter 5 presents three normative combination models for the division of professional and family labour in the future: the strong combination model, the complete combination model and the moderate combination model. To a certain extent, these models reflect the main normative views in society (variants of democracy) and the practical link with actual development.

Next we argue that, starting from the normative perspective of a strong democracy and from actual development during the past decades, the *complete combination model* is the most suitable long-term policy model for all democratic welfare states. It is briefly compared with the other normative models: the combination model, the TLM model, the flexicurity model, the dual earner/dual carer model and the universal caregiver model.

Following the complete combination model as the long-term policy orientation, Chapter 6 formulates a consistent set of basic policy perspectives regarding the relevant societal fields:

- promotion of the normative concept of 'strong democracy' and the Complete Combination Model as a policy model for a democratic division of labour;
- an integrated full employment policy for all men and women in the professional population;
- adequate societal provisions for children and young people;
- adequate societal provisions for adults;
- an efficient combination policy in organisations;
- efficient data systems concerning the daily life of men and women, from a life course perspective.

Chapter 7 concludes with an overview of the main empirical results and policy perspectives.

We have recently noticed increasing interest in the societal division of professional and family labour in the EU and elsewhere, in connection with an ageing population. More stakeholders are looking at it from a wider perspective, that is, searching for a new approach to the daily division of labour between men and women, with sufficient attention to basic activities and differentiating factors. A number of Flemish societal organisations (in particular gender organisations) and some political parties have used the Combination Model to evaluate and further develop their policy view and to reformulate their policy programme. They have experienced that an open and consequent application of the model offers a strong basis for an effective policy debate that leads to a new and (more) coherent policy view. We hope that this study is both an invitation and an incentive for all democratic societal and political organisations to use the Combination Model as a policy-oriented instrument to develop a consistent contemporary vision and an effective policy programme for decades to come.

TWO

An integrated conceptual approach to daily life

This chapter deals with the *integrated conceptual approach* of the Combination Model to the daily life of men and women within a complex modern society, the division of professional and family labour being a central part. As a starting point for presenting the new integrated approach, the first section of this chapter provides a short overview of the evolution of the traditional (economic) approach.

2.1 Traditional (economic) approach to daily life

2.1.1 Traditional dual approach to human activities

The general concept of activities within daily life is the result of a long conceptual development in social sciences during past decades, which is most apparent in economics. Since the middle of the 20th century, the microeconomic approach has been dominant, emphasising the dual concept of 'labour versus leisure' (non-labour) or 'production versus consumption', as shown in Figure 2.1 (Malinvaud, 1972; Kirzner, 1976; Gravelle and Rees, 1987, Kreps, 1990). Labour or production is almost completely identified with professional paid labour, referring to all productive, economic, market-oriented, value-creating activities – paid labour is conceived as the only basis for the welfare of society. All other activities are seen as consumptive, non-labour, non-productive, non-economic or non-market, 'consuming' the value or welfare created by productive paid labour. This concept of 'productive labour' is the result of the conceptual widening process of the classical economists (for example, Smith, Ricardo, Malthus, Stuart Mill, Marx) against the background of the Industrial Revolution. This was mainly a reaction against the narrow labour concept of the physiocrats (for example, Quesnay, Turgot, du Pont, de Nemours in the 18th century, who claimed that only agriculture offered real productive labour and was the basis for societal welfare (Baeck, 1984).

This basic dualism is a major inheritance of the long philosophical tradition of the western world, together with many other dualisms such as body versus soul/mind, nature versus nurture, subject versus object, material versus non-material and individual versus collective. This tradition was initiated by Platonic philosophy about 2,000 years ago and formalised to a large extent by Cartesian philosophy in the 18th century (Adam, 1990; Van Dongen, 1990, 1993). This basic dual view of the world is strongly embedded in the basic paradigm of classical mechanics, which in its turn was largely the inspiring conceptual basis for modern theories in economics and sociology during 1900–1980 (Mirowsky, 1984; Neuberg, 1989).

Figure 2.1   Traditional economic classification of human activities

1. *Productive activities: labour of work*
   - paid professional work: official job, paid chores, etc.
2. *Consumptive activities: leisure*
   - sleeping, resting
   - leisure activities: watching television, visiting a bar,
        music education, games, sporting, etc.
   - unpaid household activities
        for own family (members)
        for external persons/organisations

In her revealing study of the changing meaning of the concept of 'time' in natural and social sciences, Adam (1990) argues that most conceptual dualisms go hand in hand with an (implicit) hierarchical evaluation, which strongly influences the overall normative view on society. The above-mentioned dual concept explicitly includes an hierarchical evaluation, which says that productive, economic activities produce (more) value for society and are therefore more important for the development of society.

This classical dual definition had already been challenged by Reid (1934), arguing that a number of so-called non-productive activities in the household are also productive since they produce a tangible product that can be consumed by family members. Reid questions the production border in microeconomic theory and introduces household labour as a separate productive, economic activity. During the 1930s, however, the main scientific focus was on the study of 'leisure' as a valuable good, largely ignoring the fact that leisure is, in the first place, a general term for all kinds of activities. Consequently, Reid's challenging work had only little influence at the time.

From 1965 on, Reid's basic challenge became the main motive for developing the New Home Economics (Becker, 1965, 1975, 1976, 1981; Gronau, 1973a, 1973b, 1977, 1980; Pollak and Wachter, 1975; Hawrylyshyn, 1976, 1977; Ferber and Birnbaum, 1977, 1980). The traditional definition was strongly challenged with an argument that household or family labour is also a productive, economic activity, since it produces a valuable output by combining market goods and household time as inputs. This argument was the basis for the development of a broader definition of 'paid and unpaid labour' (see Figure 2.2).

In this context, Hawrylyshyn (1977) formulated two criteria to support the new definition and classification, largely inspired by Reid (1934). According to the first criterion of 'direct versus indirect utility', family labour is 'productive' or 'economic' because it produces 'indirect utility', which refers to material goods, next to 'direct utility', which consists of immediate satisfaction or immaterial services. On the contrary, non-economic activities produce only 'direct utility' (immediate satisfaction or immaterial services). Additionally, the related 'third man' criterion argues that family labour is also economic because it can be done by another subject (possibly in the market) without an essential difference in material output (indirect utility). The possibility of replacing it by a market activity implies that an economic value can be placed on it.

Figure 2.2   A new economic classification of human activities

The broader definition of productive labour in the New Home Economics implied that for household labour the traditional consumption function (maximising utility or personal satisfaction) was replaced by a production function (maximising commodities as an economic output), combined with a consumption function for the remaining 'final' consumption activities. Creating a production function for household labour resulted, in its turn, in an intense scientific search for the most adequate production function in order to integrate and deal with all possible aspects and problems (for example, human capital, joint production, direct and indirect utility, non-linearity, investments, and so on).

Another major question or challenge following from the new definition was whether and how household production can be expressed in monetary terms. During 1970-1985, this resulted in a huge scientific effort to develop methods for determining the monetary value of household production (for example, Gronau, 1973a, 1973b, 1974; Hawrylyshyn, 1976, 1977; Murphy, 1976, 1978, 1982; Ferber and Birnbaum, 1977, 1980; Hagenaars et al, 1982; Goldschmidt-Clermont, 1982, 1983). These methods were developed for different purposes, for example determining (the changes in) the total income or welfare of society and the total productivity of individuals and families, quantifying and valuing the relative proportion of paid and non-paid labour or comparing the total welfare of individuals and families or of certain subgroups.

In general, two main types of valuation methods can be distinguished: opportunity cost methods and market replacement cost methods. *Opportunity cost methods* determine the value of household labour as the potential wage in the labour market, with a number of variants depending on the characteristics of (groups of) individuals. *Market replacement cost methods* derive a monetary value for a household activity (labour input) or product (output) from the market value of (very) similar activities or products in the market. An interesting variant is the replacement input–output cost method that determines a monetary value for the added value of household activities by deducting the market value of the inputs of similar market activities from the market value of their outputs. (For a more extensive presentation and a thorough evaluation of these methods see Van Dongen et al, 1987a, 1987b and Van Dongen, 1990, 1993.) We have recently observed renewed scientific interest in the development and application of these valuation methods with respect to household labour, care and the education of children, and voluntary work (Gustafsson and Kjulin, 1994; Kooreman and Wunderink,

1996; Souza-Posa et al, 2001; Egerton and Mullen, 2004; Ironmonger, 2004; Folbre and Yoon, 2005; Folbre et al, 2005; Ruuskanen, 2005; Ghysels and Debacker, 2007; Kwon, 2007).

The differences between the results of these valuation methods are substantial and the possible criteria to decide which method is the best are not straightforward. All these methods give a certain measure for part of the total input–output and exchange process, which is by definition not a correct measure for the real exchange value of the non-monetary activities and objects. The validity or relevance of each method depends on the specific context of the non-monetary activity and on the objective of the monetary valuation. The central conclusion is that it is not possible to express correctly the real exchange value of non-market activities and objects in monetary terms. But neither is it possible to determine the real exchange value of the non-monetary parts of market activities. Consequently, the relevance or usefulness of the main objectives of these methods must be fundamentally questioned. Since these methods give a measure for part of the overall valuation process in human activities, they can only be used for specific practical problems in daily life.

Since this descriptive and evaluative research was the starting point for developing an integrated approach to the division of labour in society, we shall deal with this issue again in the next section.

The new formal definition and classification of activities of the New Home Economics evoked an almost endless conceptual discussion on (the definition of) 'productive activities' during 1980-2000 (Hagenaars, 1988; Van Dongen, 1990; Gershuny, 2000, 2005; Gronau and Hamermesh, 2002; Folbre, 2006a, 2006b).

First, the question was raised as to what extent the education of children (within or outside the family) could be seen as a productive activity. Becker (1975) created the basis for 'human capital' theory, emphasising the importance of external education for the future productivity of young people in the market sector. The main output of external education (qualified human capital) is an important input for market activities, implying that external education is a productive activity.

But what can we say about education or care at home? Folbre (2006a, 2006b) provides a good synthesis of this conceptual discussion. On the one hand, the education of children at home is seen as a consumption activity that mainly aims at direct utility or satisfaction for the person(s) involved. On the other hand, education/care at home is a form of production because some output elements are important inputs for productive activities in the market sector. At the same time, education at home can be replaced by an equivalent market activity, meaning that monetary value can be placed on it. Moreover, the activity 'produces something of value for others', implying a sort of exchange process among the family members during which money and time are being exchanged, just as it happens in the market sector.

Related to this discussion, Hagenaars (1988) argues that other 'consumption activities', such as sleeping, eating, personal care and physical exercise, are also 'productive to a certain extent', because they imply an investment in a person's own human capital and offer necessary inputs for (real) productive activities. This can be formulated in a negative way: what would be the (negative) effect on other activities if a person did not perform these activities during a certain period? Hagenaars uses the term 'investment in human capital' to express the 'productive' character of these activities. Folbre (2006) argues that, similar to household activities, these personal activities can be replaced by an equivalent market activity, which means that monetary value can be determined and the economic value becomes visible. She also shows that these activities produce a certain value for other people and are linked to exchange processes with family members or people outside the family.

Furthermore, voluntary work, as part of total leisure, was also being integrated in the broader concept of 'productive unpaid labour' (Wilson and Musick, 1997; Wilson, 2000; Hook, 2004). In line with the new definition of household labour, voluntary work is also seen as a productive economic activity since it produces a specific valuable output by combining market goods and social time as inputs. Again, these activities can be replaced by an equivalent market activity illustrating the economic value. The main question is, then, how these voluntary social activities can be placed against paid professional labour and unpaid household labour. What are the main differences between these activities? How can they be defined in a logically consistent way?

The literature of the past 20 years has shown that the conceptual 'border of production' has been shifted permanently, widening the category of productive activities and narrowing the category of non-productive activities. Nevertheless, the fundamental dual distinction between productive and non-productive activities has survived in most social sciences. This dual concept is apparently deeply rooted in the minds of social scientists and other societal groups and, to a large extent, prevents them from getting beyond it. Even Gershuny (2000) preserves the principal dual distinction between productive labour and unproductive leisure in his conceptual approach, although he stands for a multidisciplinary approach, uses broad time use data to study the division of different human activities and recognises the societal meaning or 'value' of all activities in the daily life of human beings.

This basic conceptual duality is fundamentally and directly related to the teleological and atomistic ontological view of daily life that lies behind the modern (economic) models. The daily life of an individual is then seen as the succession of separate chains of activities that, step by step, realise the ultimate and definite finality of the chain, in terms of utility, satisfaction or happiness (Becker, 1976, 1981; Hawrylyshyn, 1976, 1977; Gershuny, 2000; Gronau and Hamermesh, 2002; Folbre, 2004, 2006a; Sanchis, 2007). In the first stage of each economic chain, productive paid market activities produce market goods and services. In the second stage, productive unpaid activities (in families or other organisations) transform these market outputs into final commodities. The final stage, then, is the 'consumption' of these commodities by the individual, leading to the ultimate personal utility or satisfaction of a basic want or need, being the end of the 'chain of provision' (Gershuny, 2000).

At the same time, and largely contradictory to this teleological view, the overall economy was mostly presented as a (closed) circular system of streams or flows between different actors. Folbre (2006a) gives a clear overview of the evolution of the conceptual models of the economic system. In this circular perspective, the 'economic chain of provision' is an endless process and therefore does not 'start' with market activities nor end with the consumption of commodities that provide the ultimate satisfaction. Instead, all activities are links in the complex system of circular chains. Consequently, all consumption activities are part of the economic system. We then have to clarify which elements are streaming through all these links (activities) of the chains.

This question was partly answered by researchers studying the direct utility of paid labour. Juster and Dow (1985), Hagenaars (1988) and Folbre (2004), for example, emphasise that professional labour also offers direct utility (direct process benefits or human and social benefits) next to indirect utility (material and financial output). Moreover, the different variants of human capital theory illustrate the meaning of human and social aspects, both as input and output elements in education and care activities. In this line of thought it can be argued that all consumption activities have a broader output, that is, a combination of personal, social, material and financial elements, for example drawing a picture, sleeping, eating, personal hygiene, going to the theatre, watching television, reading a book, and so on. The next step, then, is to conceive the output elements of consumption activities as inputs of other (productive) activities in the next period, since they cannot just vanish. This means, however, that all consumption activities are, in principle, 'productive' and 'economic', since they produce a valuable output, inside or outside the market. So the dual basis of the traditional approach to human activities is completely dismantled and the need for a new conceptual approach to human activities becomes obvious.

This discussion clearly illustrates that the description of activities as input–output processes in traditional microeconomics and in the New Home Economics is neither complete nor consistent, because some of the basic elements (resources) of the input and/or output side of activities, as part of a chain of activities in a certain period, are neglected. In this perspective, the New Home Economics defines and uses 'time' as a resource that enters the production function next to the other resources of 'money' and 'market goods'. But recent scientific discussion shows that time is not a resource for (certain) activities. Instead, time is the permanently present 'path' for all different activities during which the personal, social, material and financial resources are being combined and transformed in certain time intervals. This conclusion calls for a new general approach to the meaning of time in (human) activities.

Discussing the productive character of non-market activities as care/education at home and household work automatically brings the problem of joint production or simultaneous activities (Gronau, 1973a, 1973b, 1974; Becker, 1965, 1976, 1981; Hawrylyshyn, 1976, 1977; Gershuny, 2000; Gronau and Hamermesh, 2002, Ironmonger, 2004; Folbre, 2004, 2006a, 2006b). Joint production occurs when a person simultaneously performs two or more activities; for example, during an education activity other activities are also partially being done or during other activities some education activities are also partially being done. It is easy to observe that this is also the case for other activities (paid labour, household labour, leisure activities and personal care) that take place with some other partial activities at the same time (Ironmonger, 2004; Folbre et al, 2005). One can suppose, however, that care/education for children shows a much higher degree of simultaneous activities since parents have a large responsibility for their children during all other activities.

The problem of simultaneous activities automatically leads to the methodological issue of correctly registering these activities, mainly to count the total time parents devote to their children and to avoid double counting within the time boundaries of every subject (24 hours a day, 168 hours/week). Within the tradition of household economics, Ironmonger (2004) has a broad view regarding joint production and tries to offer a practical solution. Joint production mostly hides the combination of a number of smaller, shorter successive activities and of simultaneous partial activities. Since scientists generally use rough time grids, a number of shorter successive activities cannot be distinguished from simultaneous activities. Ironmonger suggests that shorter successive activities should be sorted out first by using a finer time grid in time use surveys. Simultaneous activities would then be seen as a combination of a primary and one or more secondary activities (for example, cooking while providing some childcare and listening to the radio; travelling while reading and talking; paid work while providing some caring and/or carrying out a leisure activity; watching television while carrying out some paid work and caring). These simultaneous activities have to be registered in a sufficiently detailed way by means of time use surveys. When these data are available, a two-dimensional matrix or table combining all activities as primary and secondary activities can be produced. This matrix is proposed as a practical instrument to avoid double counting partial activities of a joint or complex activity and to count time spent on secondary activities in a controllable way.

At first sight, this is an attractive practical approach, but fundamentally the problem has not been solved. In fact, as Ironmonger (2004) correctly states, all activities can be seen as simultaneous, joint activities since they all contain a certain proportion of other (secondary) activities. But we do not and cannot know the exact share of all possible secondary partial activities in the total time of every joint activity. His matrix is neither complete nor symmetric, since paid work is not introduced as a possible secondary, partial activity in other joint activities and many primary activities seem to have no secondary activities at all. Moreover, the matrix misleads us by asking us to double count again time spent on primary and secondary activities in an indirect way. It is strange that after proposing the matrix to avoid double counting, Ironmonger (2004) is actually double counting when applying the matrix to Australian data, saying that in 1997 Australian women performed childcare for 17.9 hours/week, 15.6 hours of which were done while doing something else. On a macro level this would mean that Australian households spent 188 million hours/week on unpaid childcare, compared to 300 million hours/week on market labour. Ironmonger's calculation suggests that we can count the secondary, partial care activities as full or primary activities.

This example shows that double or multiple counting is always possible for all sorts of elementary activities that are part of several joint activities, depending on the perspective of the researcher, for example walking, resting, talking, writing, thinking, looking, eating, drinking, listening, carrying, and so on. Ultimately, this approach leads to a huge over-estimate of time spent on partial activities that are considered primary. In the case of childcare at home, it could even be said that a parent is always carrying out some caring activity given their permanent responsibility for their child, also when the child is not physically present and/or has no direct contact with the parent, for example during professional work, voluntary work, household work or leisure activities (Ironmonger, 2004; Michelle and Folbre, 2004; Folbre et al, 2005). This seems a correct and attractive starting point, expressing the 'never ending' caring responsibility of parents. But then everyone combines several permanent responsibilities in their life for other important people (partner, parents, friends, neighbours, and so on) and for important material provisions (house, durable goods) and financial means. Even if we agree that the responsibility for children is greater and more permanent and demands more time, other permanent responsibilities are also important and imply that, to a certain extent, everyone is always 'taking care of' other important people, social entities, durable material goods and financial means. The question, then, is how we can count the real share of all these permanent responsibilities (and the partial activities linked with it) in the different joint activities. First, it is essential to understand that 'being responsible' for someone or something at a certain moment is not identical to 'directly doing something for or with' someone. The degree of responsibility is a characteristic of every subject in all activities and can express a certain share of partial activities, but it should not be confused with the activity itself. Given the complexity of all activities, the share of partial activities can be roughly estimated, but the real time can never be registered and counted in minutes and hours.

The basic reason for this 'confusion' is that the different content or qualities of the different 'secondary' or partial activities that are being linked with and placed under the label of the primary activity, for example childcare, are ignored. Being responsible or available for children playing in another room while doing mainly professional work is largely different from playing and interacting directly with these children in the same room (and being aware of or responsible for some household and/or market activities). This confusion also becomes clear in the asymmetric and inconsistent classification of activities, with large basic (societal) categories on the first level and different sublevels of partial and elementary activities. This has huge consequences for the registration and counting of activities. In most time use surveys, for example, only a few partial activities of the broad category 'paid labour' are distinguished, while the broad categories of 'leisure' and 'childcare' are subdivided into many partial or elementary activities. But the elementary activities (walking, resting, talking, writing, thinking, eating, drinking, listening, carrying, etc) also occur to a certain extent in the complex activity 'paid labour'. These partial activities of leisure and childcare are often treated as primary activities while the partial activities of paid work are mostly invisible and are hence not treated as separate activities. So, we need a more consistent definition and classification of complex activities.

Finally, there is the observation that education and care activities go hand in hand with a real exchange process between the people or groups involved (for example, between family members), in which personal, social, material and financial elements are being exchanged (Folbre, 2006a, 2006b). Parents carry out many care activities for their children, offering them a number of personal, social, material and financial benefits. But at the same time they receive a number of benefits from their children. So caring is an exchange process in two directions, which means that parents and children have the role of 'giver' and 'taker'. Folbre (2004), Michelle and Folbre (2004) and Ironmonger

(2004) emphasise the importance of 'contact time' during caring activities, meaning that parents and children are offering each other different personal, social, material and financial benefits.

But if an exchange process occurs within families for education and care activities, this is, logically, also the case for all other activities in the family. In fact, to a certain extent, parents carry out all their activities for their children, for other family members and for a number of external people or families, which means that part of the benefits of the activities is 'given' to other family members and external people, in exchange for some of the benefits of their activities.

So if exchange processes permanently occur for all activities in all families, there is always a process of value formation that leads to a real exchange value as a measure for the exchanged elements or benefits. This implies that the conceptual approach to value formation in human activities and to human exchange processes must be fundamentally reformulated.

This discussion has shown that looking at complex activities and exchange processes with a dual and atomistic approach can never lead to a consistent conception and registration of activities at the different levels of complexity. Activities are always complex in nature, which means that a number of elements must always be combined in a certain manner to give a complete and general picture: content, duration, frequency, place, responsibility, input and output, complexity level, combination of personal, social, material and financial elements, social contact or exchange, positive and/or negative elements, collective versus private elements, monetary versus non-monetary elements, and so on. In the next section, therefore, we present a general, integrated approach to complex activities that offers both a conceptual and practical solution to the so-called 'problem' of joint production.

2.1.2 Traditional basic model of society

The dual conceptual approach to human activities is strongly related to the traditional basic model of society, as the foundation of the western welfare state or the socially adjusted free market system during 1950-2000 (see Figure 1.1, Chapter 1). We use it here as a general frame of reference and as a sounding board in order to formulate a new basic model of society. Figure 2.3 shows the most important and common components of the traditional basic model, with the economic or market sector, the public sector, the subsidised sector and the sector of families/households placed next to one another.

In the traditional basic model, society is almost physically subdivided into a number of basic sectors or spheres that function according to different mechanisms and cannot be placed under the same heading. The economy or (largely) the market sector is regarded as a separate sector, as the real productive system that creates the welfare and therefore is the material basis for the other sectors. The non-economic sectors largely refer to the subjective, social, collective elements for which no real production process and exchange process exist and, consequently, neither a real market nor market prices. The government or the public sector is not a real part of the economy but forms a different

Figure 2.3   Traditional basic model of society

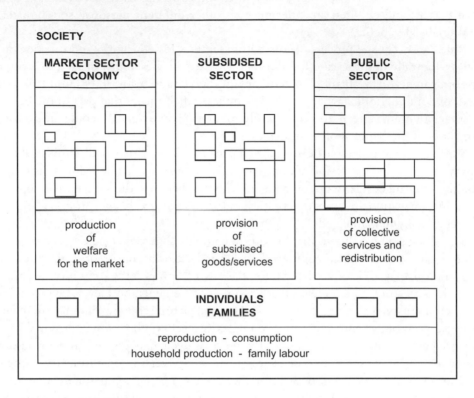

sector. It has a specific relation with and a specific influence on the economy, but in principle is separated from it. The central tasks of the public sector are the provision of collective goods that cannot be provided by the market and the redistribution of wealth according to a certain notion of solidarity and social policy. It is not regarded, however, as a normal production system that operates in a similar manner in the overall market system. So we talk about a mixed economy, with the government 'intervening' in the economic sector as if it is (originally) located outside of it. The major task of redistributing the benefits of the economy or the market sector expresses the basic idea that it does not produce 'real products' by itself.

However, during the past decades the concept of 'economy' or 'economic sector' has been severely stretched by the broadening of the concept of 'productive activities', resulting in several contradictions being cumulated in the conceptual approach. Unlike this broadening process, the basic theoretical and hierarchical duality has been maintained, expressing that some activities are really productive, economic, market-directed, profitable, and so on, and other activities are not, or at least to a smaller extent.

The many subsidised 'social' organisations, which are in fact not included in the economy or the market sector (non-market sector, non-commercial sector, non-profit sector, budget sector, social sector, contribution sector, etc), are indeed valuable or important for society, but their activities are not seen as really productive or profitable.

The family is also regarded as a 'different' entity that functions according to other mechanisms, rules or principles – we can speak of the family or household sector. 'Family life' is seen as being fundamentally different from the daily life of other societal organisations. The family is identified with the location of consumption and/ or reproduction activities, mostly referring to, for example, an immaterial, personal, emotional, sexual, pedagogical finality. The external world is, then, (mainly) identified with the economy, the market, business life, politics, and so on. As previously stated, the New Home Economics introduced the dual distinction between productive and non-productive activities in families or households, which in fact evoked a broad discussion and ultimately resulted in a fundamental attack on the dual approach itself.

The traditional basic model was/is the foundation of most scientific disciplines and theories to describe and explain human (economic and non-economic) behaviour and systems. Moreover, all traditional politico-ideological views with respect to society (the modern welfare state) formulate a certain variant of this basic model, analytically, empirically and normatively. In principle they recognise the need for a certain combination of 'the state and the market'. We call it the model of the socially adjusted free market or the neo-Keynesian model of the welfare state.

Until 1960, the concept of 'economy' or 'economic sector' was almost completely reserved for or identified with the (monetary) market sector in which mainly the private companies produced 'private' (divisible), 'material' (manually tangible) goods. In that context, the situation with regard to other sectors was comprehensible. During the past decades, economic science has paid more attention to the (traditionally spoken) 'non-economic' space: the family sector with family labour and leisure time, the public or government sector and the subsidised sector with a broad diversity of organisations which do not (completely) function as traditional private companies. Although previously economic space could, in principle, be separated from other societal spaces, this has become (more) difficult during the past decades because the economic sector received, and still receives, wider interpretation. The main cause of this is the fact that non-market activities are (again) recognised as productive or economically important activities.

As the economy (and economic science) became more complex, increasingly more objects and activities from other sectors were 'absorbed' within economic theory. They were, in a certain sense of the word, seen as 'part' of the economy. Consequently, new relevant criteria to classify the activities and the organisations had to be found. These activities were also performed by a number of existing organisations that were comparable with but not identical to 'real' private companies. Conceptually, other sectors were slowly converted into 'special partial sectors' of the economy. The concept of 'economy' was systematically broadened so that, in the ultimate version, it would be identical to the concept of 'society'. The question then arises to what extent certain activities still can or must be called 'non-economic'. An unequivocal and consistent answer to that question has been lacking because no criteria could be found to consistently determine this so-called distinction. All more or less new classifications face the same basic conceptual problem, that is, the dual distinction between real economic, productive activities on the one hand, and less or non-economic or non-productive activities on the other (Van Dongen, 1990, 1993).

A central hypothesis here is that the traditional basic model no longer offers a consistent and adequate analysis of society and its subjects, activities, interactions and costs and benefits. Since it was the basic model of society during the past five decades, in theory as well as in reality, it also forms the basis for many large societal problems. As such, most scientific disciplines and political–ideological views were/are confronted with a conceptual crisis. As far as this conclusion is valid, social scientists need to search for a broader and more adequate approach to society.

Due to the different theoretical perspectives of our interdisciplinary education and early professional experience, we were immediately confronted with the main conceptual problems and contradictions of the traditional model of activities and society (Van Dongen et al, 1987a, 1987b; Van Dongen, 1990, 1992a, 1993). Trying to avoid and/or solve these contradictions, this conceptual process resulted at a certain moment in a fundamental conceptual switch and the long search for a new integrated approach (Kuhn, 1962). In the new approach all activities are seen as complex productive labour processes or input–output processes that offer a valuable output and that are regulated by the general mechanism of value formation and social exchange (demand and supply).

However, most social scientists continued to work with and within the traditional basic model and tried to solve the contradictions and ambiguities by means of additionally shifting, broadening or refining existing concepts, classifications and interactions (see, for example, Gershuny, 2000, 2005; Gronau and Hamermesh, 2002; Schmid and Gazier, 2002; Ironmonger, 2004; Schmid and Schomann, 2004; Folbre, 2004, 2006a, 2006b). Basically, the dual conceptual basis of the traditional model remained intact. Folbre (2006a) offers an interesting analytical contribution in this perspective. Starting from her ambition to clarify the societal and economic meaning or value of the 'education of children' within families and society, she restructures and refines the traditional model in Figure 2.3. In fact, she steps out of the traditional basic model and develops a broader approach to the complex production and exchange processes regarding childcare or education. She creates a more complex variant of Figure 2.3 by introducing exchange within families and organisations and with the 'community' as an embracing actor that produces and offers different 'communal' personal, social, material and financial services. Consequently, she has to conceive the activities of the 'community' as productive input–output processes and the exchange processes with the other societal actors as real economic transactions. So, the traditional dual distinction between the societal sectors is further blurred and the need for a new conceptual approach to the societal system is emphasised again. But her differentiated model is still anchored in the traditional basic model since she preserves the fundamental conceptual difference between the activities and exchange processes of the different actors in society. Yet her contribution offers a conceptual bridge to an integrated approach and encourages other researchers to move in that direction. It is not clear, however, whether and how fast such a new integrated conceptual approach will be more broadly accepted in the scientific world.

We notice here that a similar conceptual development occurred in other major social sciences such as sociology and psychology (for example Kruithof, 1968, 1973; Adam, 1990, 1995). The main challenge of this process is to bridge the ontological and conceptual gap between human and social sciences on the one hand, and natural sciences (physics, chemistry, biology, genetics, etc) on the other. The ultimate goal is to develop an overall ontological and conceptual approach to the 'complex world', including both nature and human/social life. A general approach to time, complex activities and development therefore has to be constructed that can be used for all possible actors and time horizons in the complex world, from the smallest entities and time spans in quantum physics, to gradually increasing entities and time spans in chemistry, thermodynamics, biology, human and social sciences, social geography, ecology, and so on, to the most complex entities and extremely large time span in astronomy (Adam, 1990; Van Dongen, 1990).

2.2　An integrated approach to the division of labour

In this section we present an integrated approach to the daily life and life course of men and women within different societal entities or organisations (families, clubs, companies, public organisations, and so on) and within society as a (larger) whole. This is essentially an interdisciplinary approach that reformulates, complements and integrates the useful concepts of traditional disciplines in a new general framework. It can be used for all societal actors and all human activities. Therefore, the approach needs to be consistent with the basic concepts of modern physics, chemistry and biology (evolutionary theory) (Csani, 1989; Rohrlich, 1987; Nicolis and Prigogine, 1989; Prigogine, 1980, 1996a, 1996b; Prigogine and Stengers, 1984; Jones, 1999). We refer again to Adam (1990), who provides a good summary of the ontological and conceptual development of natural sciences towards the overall 'complexity paradigm' and its meaning for the development of social sciences.

2.2.1　The general concept of human activities and daily life

In an integrated approach to daily life, all subjects or actors (individuals, families, enterprises, organisations, public institutions, the state, international systems, etc) and their activities are explained within the same general theoretical model, covering all basic components of the societal system. It is necessary, therefore, to develop a general conceptual frame and vocabulary that is useful for all human and social sciences and that can be integrated within the broad spectrum of scientific fields.

　The *daily life* of human subjects is seen as the daily division or combination of activities or labour processes and of their outputs/results. The activities are the dynamic 'vehicles' of daily life during a certain time span, generally determining the life course of each actor or subject. So, time is the orienting 'medium' or 'path' of all human activities. *All activities of all subjects are seen as productive labour processes*, that is, *material input–output processes* taking place in a certain period that produce a certain valuable output and are regulated by the general mechanism of human valuation and exchange (the mechanism of demand and supply) (see Figure 2.4).

Figure 2.4 A general conceptual model for all human activities

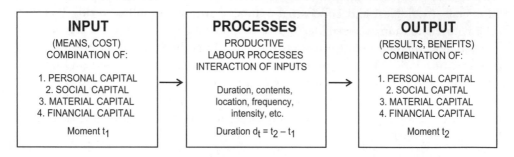

The concept of 'productive' is defined in physical terms: during the labour process, the input elements exchange certain aspects, which result in an output that differs qualitatively from the input. *Labour* is a central part of all activities, that is, the physical energy offered by the inputs during the activity. Labour is then the unity of interactions and exchanged input elements. Interaction is generally seen as an exchange process with other subjects or (non-human) objects, by which the availability of certain objects is changed. The degree of availability is expressed by the character and the number of interactions one can have with an object. Each labour process uses (certain elements of) the overall input and produces an output that differs from it qualitatively, in particular because a number of elements have been altered by interactions during the labour process. Figure 2.4 shows that the different (categories of) input offer different forms of labour or energy that are combined in the activities (labour processes or transformation processes), in order to produce useful output elements. During each activity, the use of inputs (consumption) always goes hand in hand with the production of outputs: while using or consuming the input elements every subject is producing the output.

This basic concept in Figure 2.4 expresses the principle of continuity and the irreversibility of all (human or non-human) activities in time. Life is an ongoing chain of activities or input–output processes. The output of an activity is always the input for a following activity, again leading to a new output, being the input for a new activity, and so on. This means that an activity and its result can never be turned back to the moment of the start. A subject can never go back to exactly the same starting point of a specific activity (Rohrlich, 1987, pp 4-7; Nicolis and Prigogine, 1989; Adam, 1990; Van Dongen, 1993). To a certain extent and in a certain way, this means that everything is always changing in time. Yet every subject can (try to) repeat or copy certain activities as much as possible in order to achieve an almost equal result that is sufficiently satisfying. At the same time, a subject can choose to change the activity in order to get a (largely) different result.

Although every subject (and object) is permanently changing during the activities, a completely continuous time perspective is practically impossible and rather meaningless for human beings. It does not allow them to have a practical perception and use of time (perspectives) within a complex environment. Therefore, every subject determines relevant time perspectives or units ('periods') within which the activities or labour processes can be considered, described, compared, executed, evaluated, and so on. Depending on the content and impact of the human activity, these periods can vary from very small to very large periods. Within each period, the input elements provide labour and are thereby transformed into qualitatively different output elements.

So a correct analytical distinction can be made between the concepts of 'labour' and 'capital': *labour* is the process concept that refers to the transformation or change within certain periods while *capital* is the stock concept referring to the situation before and after the change, to the potential at the beginning and the end of the period, from the subject's perspective. The term 'capital' also expresses that all input and output elements have a certain (subjective) value for the subjects involved. The two concepts are always part of the same process, which implies that all capital forms offer energy or labour during the activities and contribute to their overall output or benefit.

The total available *capital* is a complex system of different means or components that are expressed in terms of quantity and quality, both at the input and output side of each activity. Starting from the long conceptual discussion in social sciences, different components can be classified into four basic categories:

- *Personal capital* consists of the complex organism of a human subject, composed of different dimensions: physical and cognitive abilities, affections and emotions, aesthetic perception, wants or needs and satisfactions, values and valuations and attitudes (Kruithof, 1968, 1973, 1984; Van Dongen, 1990, 1993). These dimensions can be distinguished analytically but they always appear together in all human activities in an interactive way. Let us mention that the distinction between labour and capital can be applied to all these dimensions: for example, knowledge is the stock variable and thinking the process variable of the cognitive dimension; the same holds for the other dimensions.
- *Social capital* expresses the social position of the subject, that is, the subjects, social groups, social structures and networks that are available to a certain degree for (the activities of) the subject, and that offer the subject a number of valuable inputs.
- *Material capital* refers to material objects outside human subjects that are at their disposal to a certain extent, such as durable and non-durable goods, machines, housing facilities, buildings, transport infrastructure and green areas. Here the term 'material' is a societal and not an ontological concept. The scientific (mostly economic) literature extensively shows the different classifications depending on the view on the production process.
- *Financial capital* consists of the different forms of financial resources, from short-term liquidities on the one hand (paper, coin and digital money used for the daily exchange of goods and services), to the long-term assets on the other hand, used to save certain values for later use and/or to invest them in certain societal projects directly.

All activities start from a certain combination of personal, social, material and financial means at the input side. During the labour process, several elements of the input are transformed to a new combination of personal, social, material and financial means at the output side. So, all human activities can be conceived and explained by the same basic model. Depending on the perspective or focus of the analysis and the available data for the different components, sufficient differentiation in the description and explanation of the input–output processes can be introduced. This basic model of human activities is useful for all human and social sciences, allowing them to communicate and collaborate in a correct and constructive way and to preserve the specific useful perspectives and methods in the different disciplines as much as possible. The main condition for horizontal collaboration and integration is that all disciplines start from the same basic model and integrate all basic components of every activity in their approaches.

This basic model implies a fundamentally new approach to the finality of human activities, abandoning the different finality of production and consumption activities in traditional economic theory. The new model says that all activities lead to a certain degree of direct, personal satisfaction, happiness or utility (direct utility) as part of the personal or social benefits at the output side. At the same time, every activity has a certain material and/or financial output (indirect utility). But none of these elements can express the total capital on the output side as the overall and ultimate finality of an activity.

The time perspective of activities in this basic model must be combined with the *complexity principle of activities* saying that *all human activities are complex*: they are always part of larger, more enclosing activities and at the same time they are constituted of a number of smaller partial activities that in turn are also a combination of different smaller activities, and so on. Figure 2.5 introduces the complexity principle, showing the complex combination and interaction between the different partial activities of a certain activity during a specific time interval. In fact, all these partial activities can be formulated by means of the same basic model in Figure 2.4, that they combine different capital elements during a certain period and result in a different combination of capital elements at the output side. So we bring together (again) what has been separated in the traditional (economic) approaches during many decades. At the same time, this integrated approach opens the door to a broad spectrum of new conceptual, empirical and normative perspectives in social sciences, without throwing away the positive, useful baggage of the past and without neglecting the large potential of differentiation and specialisation in social sciences.

Figure 2.5   A general model of complex human activities

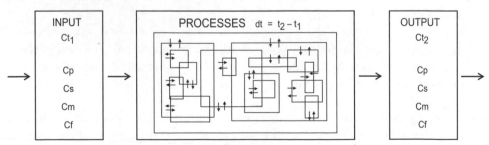

In order to deal with the complex character of activities, it is essential to classify them in an adequate way by means of a number of relevant formal characteristics: complexity level, duration, frequency, relative share of the four capital elements, monetary and non-monetary elements. The starting point is that all activities represent a specific combination of these elements that enables us to create a consistent and meaningful comparison within a multidimensional matrix. In studying daily activities it is essential to treat the different complexity levels in a correct and consistent way, in order to avoid the problems mentioned before, for example the conceptual confusion of different activities with (more or less) the same label, the asymmetric registration and double counting of basic and partial activities, and the application of inadequate methods for the monetary valuation of non-market activities.

2.2.2 Individual division of activities during the life course

In this section we examine the daily life and life course of individual men and women, without reference to the different societal entities (families, neighbourhood, clubs, companies, etc) that they actually live in. This will be dealt with in the next section. All men and women always have a specific individual division or combination of activities during every period of their life course. Time spent on different activities can be expressed in minutes, hours, days, months, years, decades, etc. The concept of 'division of time' implies that the time devoted to one complex activity (for example, professional labour) cannot be devoted to other activities (for example, family work or personal care). During the individual life course and the collective time system everyone has the same amount of time available for all different activities: 24 hours a day, seven days or 168 hours/week, 52 weeks a year, etc. The life course is the 'time path' or 'time road' during which all individuals are performing different activities, in each activity transforming the available personal, social, material and financial capital.

The activities of individual men and women can also be classified in a number of main categories on the basis of their overall societal content or meaning. Starting from different empirical studies, we use six main categories: professional paid labour, family labour, (voluntary) social labour, external education/care, leisure time activities and personal care. We refer to Bianchi et al (2006, pp 142-56) for a similar classification of the activities of children and young people. Of course, other classifications are possible and defensible. These basic activities can be subdivided in a practical way into a number of *partial activities* that still express a specific societal meaning as part of a basic activity. We can give some examples.

Professional paid labour refers in the broadest sense to all paid occupational labour, that is, all the labour that is being done as a profession or occupation on the labour market, with a (normal) monetary payment. It includes the main job and additional paid activities (second job), overtime, breaks during working hours, commuting, travel during working hours and job seeking. The following partial activities can be distinguished: administration, bookkeeping, producing concrete goods, maintenance and repairs, transporting goods and people, general management, financial and human resources management, research and developmental tasks, logistic tasks, commercial tasks, quality control, caring and education tasks.

Family labour refers to all education and caring activities within the family (between the family members) such as bathing the children, playing with children, reading a story, transport to external activities, helping with schoolwork, planning activities, care for a grandparent living in, and to all household tasks such as cooking, cleaning the house, laundry and ironing, shopping and services, household management, gardening and pet care, construction and repairs.

(Voluntary) social labour refers to all kinds of volunteer work for other people, clubs and organisations, without or with only small financial compensation, such as active management of a club, training/teaching/coaching in a club, logistic tasks, organising social activities, bookkeeping, administrative tasks, gathering sponsorship, caring tasks.

External education/care consists of all the caring and education activities of and for children and adults in the household with supervision, caring, teaching, instruction, and so on by people outside their own family/home: school, external childcare, external education activities in other families, clubs and social organisations.

Leisure time includes all kinds of activities carried out in free time for relaxation, for example socialising and entertainment, doing sports, hobbies and games, reading, watching television, walking, going to the theatre, artistic activities, social contact in pubs and restaurants, reading books or magazines, going to parties.

Personal care includes sleep during the night or day, all sorts of resting, having meals, snacks and drinks, washing, dressing, personal hygiene, shaving, intimate and sexual activities and personal healthcare.

These partial activities can be further subdivided into a number of (more) elementary activities that occur in all partial activities in a certain way and to a certain degree: walking, running, jumping, sitting, lying, carrying, knocking, pushing, pulling, scratching, talking, shouting, listening, thinking, feeling, looking, eating, drinking, writing, and so on. These elementary activities are the material components of all activities and can be combined in an infinite number of specific activities.

Following the complexity model in Figure 2.5 all basic, partial and elementary activities occur simultaneously and interact in the complex structure and dynamics of the daily division of activities. Given that complexity, it is impossible to determine the exact share (in terms of complexity and time) of partial activities in the basic activities and the share of elementary activities in the partial activities. Therefore, social sciences have to develop practical, broadly understandable models or pictures of the division of activities, with a consistent treatment of the complexity levels of the activities and the time perspective. In this study, we restrict the analysis to the basic activities because they offer sufficient differentiation for the empirical and normative models of the division of activities that we want to present for western countries. Our starting point is that general government policy in democratic countries regarding the division of time must offer fairly general boundaries and guidelines and should therefore not go (much) further than the level of basic activities. After all, developing policy guidelines on the level of partial activities implies a fairly large direct government intervention in the division of activities within families, what is usually called the 'privacy sphere'.

Contrary to traditional economics, the integrated approach does not suffer from the conceptual problem of joint production and the practical risks of selective and double counting, since all basic activities are complex and contain a number of partial and elementary activities that, to a certain extent, also occur in other basic activities. In fact, the 'complexity approach' offers a simple solution for the old 'joint production' problem of the New Home Economics, just by saying that all activities are complex and that it is both impossible and unnecessary to register or count exactly all partial or elementary activities in order to create a clear and useful picture of the daily division of activities as the basis for policy perspectives. This approach allows us to start from basic activities and then examine to what extent registration and analysis of partial and elementary activities is necessary and desirable. For our analysis, we can leave aside the partial and elementary activities without losing crucial information. When research is more specifically oriented at the meaning and division of partial or elementary activities, one has to start from a consistent classification and registration of these activities. Depending on the concrete purpose of time use research and the complexity level of the activities involved, it is necessary to collect the right time use data in a correct and consistent way. So, it can be useful to study the time people devote to partial and elementary activities across all basic activities, such as doing administrative tasks, being together with the children, going to the bathroom, listening to the radio, working on a computer, using a mobile telephone, riding a horse, talking to people, reading a book, lying down, sitting on a chair, standing up, drinking coffee, having a meal in a restaurant, and so on.

In the same way, the integrated approach is not troubled by the problem of the *responsibilities* of people that are related to their activities. After all, it starts from the basic idea that everyone combines several permanent responsibilities for other people (children, partner, parents, friends, neighbours, and so on), social entities (families, clubs, companies, and so on), material provisions (houses, durable goods, roads, factories, woods, neighbourhoods, and so on) and financial means (liquidities, assets). All these permanent responsibilities are (gradually) important and imply that, to a certain extent, all people are always 'taking care of' or 'caring for' other important people, social entities, durable material goods and financial means. The degree of responsibility is an important characteristic of (every subject in) all activities and influences the overall content and quality, the number of hours, the frequency and timing of activities, but it is not identical to the activity itself. While a child is at school, the parents preserve a certain (overall or final) responsibility for the child while doing their own activities. But a large part of the responsibilities and actual education tasks during that time is delegated or shifted to the school (teachers, management). As long as everything goes well with the child at school, parents' 'overall responsibility' is passive and latent and actually takes only little time and effort from them. As soon as some unexpected (positive or negative) situation occurs at school, parents' responsibility is activated and translated into certain 'caring' or 'education' activities, for example contacting the teacher by telephone during the current activity to inquire after the 'problem' and discussing further steps to be taken, interrupting the ongoing activity and doing something to solve the problem such as driving to school, bringing lunch, calling a doctor, taking the child to the hospital, and so on.

Similar to registering time devoted to different activities, it is impossible to register the exact share of all permanent responsibilities (and the partial activities linked with it) in the different complex activities. Given the complexity of all activities, practical instruments can be developed to register the share or meaning of the different responsibilities during the activities in a simplified way. The basic condition is again that the different responsibilities are treated in a consistent way in terms of magnitude, duration and frequency.

Individual division of time can be illustrated using many different presentations or models. One could give a very detailed presentation of the sequence of different activities during an average day, week or month, for every individual or for certain subgroups. This picture could be attractive to look at, but it would hardly give any useful information for understanding the basic societal problems or challenges regarding the division of activities, that is, how people combine different activities during their life course in order to realise a 'good life'. Figure 2.6 illustrates a simplified conceptual model of the individual division of basic activities of men and women during their life course (Van Dongen et al, 2001). The model is partly based on empirical data for married couples aged between 20 and 75 in Flanders (1992, 1999), and partly on further extrapolation for other age groups. It also shows the (gradual) distinction between the three main stages of the life course.

The picture can be understood in two ways. In the first place, it presents the average number of hours spent on basic activities by every age group at a certain moment in a certain population. At the same time, it can be seen as the division of activities during the life course of an average person of a certain age group in a certain population.

Figure 2.6   Combination of activities (number of hours per week) of men and women

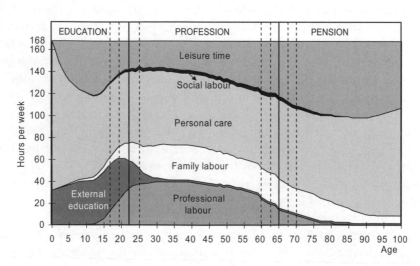

Figure 2.6 shows the basic idea of the Combination Model that all men and women permanently combine basic activities in a certain way during different life stages, from birth until death. The different activities must be combined in time in a suitable way during all stages of the life course. Each activity realises an output (personal, social, material and financial capital) that serves as the input for another activity. This dynamic structure of basic activities (with all the partial activities) deals with the combination of personal, social, material and financial capital. The objectives have been determined by the subject aiming at realisation within a certain period. Every objective itself depends on the realisation of another objective. So sleeping (personal care) is important in order to be fit again for other activities, while paid labour is important in order to purchase the right means to sleep, play sport and so on efficiently. The same holds for family labour, social labour, leisure time and education.

Men and women daily aim at a *well-balanced combination of these basic activities,* which all together must offer the desired *combination of personal, social, material and financial means*, at all stages of their life. Each activity provides a certain output that serves as an input for other activities. The activities are functionally integrated in a complex and dynamic feedback system. All activities are therefore, in principle, equally important in daily life. They (have to) provide each other with the necessary combination of personal, social, material and financial means. The differences refer to the basic functions and specific characteristics of the activities. The combination of professional and family work refers to a central part of the daily life of men and women. As the main subject of our empirical and policy study, this will be dealt with separately in the next section.

As already mentioned, the *life course perspective* is also important. During the various stages of the life course, the division of activities and means changes permanently. An endless number of combinations of activities is possible, according to sex, age, education, family type, and so on. At certain moments during the life course, larger or more drastic changes or transitions occur, due to specific critical events, for example the transition from the school period to the professional period, from the professional period to the pension period, the change from professional activity to unemployment (due to illness, invalidity, closure or restructuring of companies, personal choice for family work, etc).

We can then talk about the basic changes or transitions in the combinations of activities during the life course. Every subject tries to realise the right combination of activities during the different stages of the life course, in order to prevent or solve the different societal risks that occur. The model combines age differentiation and integration into one 'combination perspective' (Muffels et al, 2002; Muffels and Ester, 2004), placed in a life course perspective. The life course perspective is also combined with the perspective of societal development (age groups, generations). (See also Mortimer, 2003; Bovenberg, 2003; Anxo and Boulin, 2006b.)

In the short run, everyone tries to realise a positive result, that is, growth of the total available capital. But from time to time, everyone can/will fail to a certain extent and has to deal with losses. This means that long-term finality is not expressed by the (permanent) growth of total capital but by the ability of persons to change a negative development into a positive one (Van Dongen, 1990, 1993, 1997).

Within the life course perspective, it is clear that the division of time within families strongly depends on the *actual family form*: living alone, living together (married or unmarried), with or without children, with or without other dependent people (older people, people with a disability). In this context, it is very important to use the correct, gradual definition of one-parent families, depending on the new division of tasks and responsibilities between former partners towards their children. So, one can define a gradual concept of parenthood for the single parent. We shall deal with this later.

Figures 2.4–2.6 present in a simplified way the integrated approach that can be the common basis for all social sciences. This approach is not meant to replace or dismantle the traditional 'vertical' disciplines, but to facilitate their mutual understanding and interaction, the renewal and improvement of the models within the disciplines and, at the same time, the consistent integration in a broader scientific context (Juster, 1973; Hues, 1976; Van Dongen, 1993). Many complex problems of individuals, families, organisations, companies and so on can be described and analysed in a broader and more realistic perspective, creating a stronger basis for the formulation of policy perspectives and measures.

2.2.3 Division of activities in organisations and the market system

2.2.3.1 A new basic model for society and the market system

The individual division of activities of men and women is always taking place within one of the different societal entities or organisations. We can place Figure 2.7 alongside the traditional basic model shown in Figure 2.3, as it expresses the principles of the new basic model of a complex society. In this integrated model, the different subjects, labour processes and exchange processes can be located in an adequate way on the different complexity levels of society. A central notion is the gradual distinction between (more) private and (more) collective systems. The mutual functionality and division of

Figure 2.7 A new basic model of a complex society

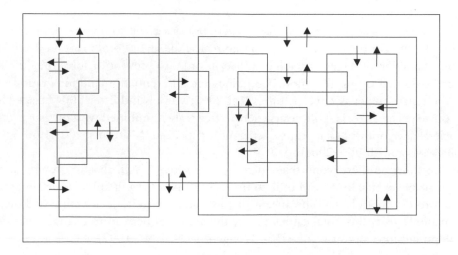

labour is the basic principle, which means that every system provides certain services for and receives certain services from both smaller and larger systems, and the other way around (see the arrows in Figure 2.7).

Similar to all complex activities, all existing subjects are principally complex: they are all part of larger, more enclosing systems and at the same time they are constituted of smaller partial systems. This implies that the traditional distinction between, for example, the economic, social and cultural sector, is no longer recognisable. At first sight, this new model seems to be chaotic, referring to the basic idea of 'chaos theory' (Prigogine, 1996a, 1996b). However, complexity does not imply the absence of structure or order; rather it means that the order has a fundamentally different shape, as shown in Figure 2.7.

Within this general model of a complex society we can arrive at the basic concept and dynamics of the *internal and external division of labour*, the mechanism by means of which the activities and their results are divided among different individuals and organisations, in time and space: families or households, clubs or associations, companies, public institutions, and so on, located in a specific geographical unity (see Figure 2.8). With reference to the time use surveys, one has to decide whether it is desirable, useful and feasible to register the location of the activities (societal organisation and/or physical place) and the social context (with whom one is doing an activity).

The internal division of time and means is called *labour organisation*; the external division of time and means with other subjects is the *market functioning*. The system of market transactions between all societal actors of a certain region is the market system. This means that all subjects participate in the market system to a certain extent and have market transactions that complement their activities and transactions within families, clubs, companies, etc.

Starting from the normative view of society, many different market systems can be conceived, from the strong liberal free market system on the one hand, to the strong collectivist market system on the other, or from a very undemocratic to a very democratic market system. The actual market system of a country or larger region is the complex combination of gradually different partial markets, according to the score on a number of characteristics, such as the proportion of private versus collective ownership and financing, the openness of markets, the degree of product segmentation, the degree of centralisation, competitive pressure, the degree of central planning, and so on.

The division of time of men and women is often analysed in terms of the position within their *family or household*. Each family (member) acquires inputs for the labour and exchange process outside the family through the external division of labour or market transactions. In the same way, the output of the internal division of labour provides inputs for the activities and transactions with subjects outside the family. Also professional and non-professional organisations must be integrated within the analysis of the daily life of men and women.

Division of labour indicates that subjects have more interactions with certain subjects than with others, quantitatively and/or qualitatively. The multiple actual divisions of labour can be formally described in terms of size, frequency, intensity and durability of the interactions of the subjects involved, the kinds of activities and objects, the

Figure 2.8 Components of labour processes, division of labour and market system

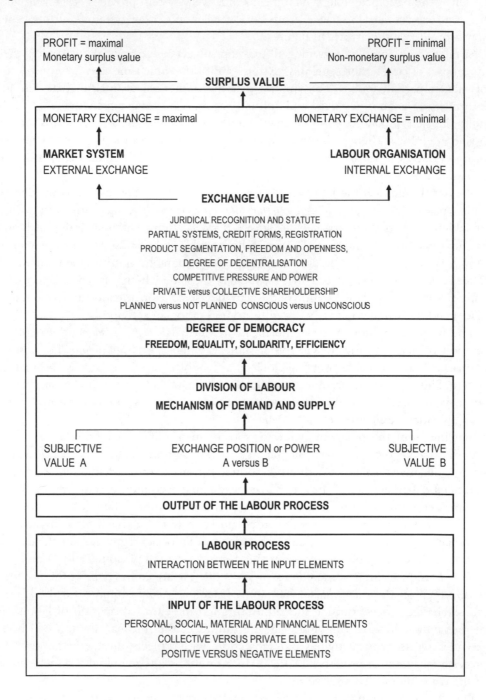

positive or negative character. Division of labour is related to the relative efficiency of the subjects in different activities, expressed in terms of the actual surplus value. One subject is compelled to perform certain activities relatively more often, while the other concentrates more on other activities. Systematic division of labour requires the existence of a certain frequency, regularity and durability in the interactions. The process reinforces itself: a positive division of labour (which offers sufficient benefits) leads to a further expansion of it, until the additional benefits disappear and possibly become negative.

Division of labour has to be described by the same mechanism as the interaction in general, that is, the search of subjects for a relatively higher benefit by way of alternative activities and interactions. *Interaction* is explained by the relatively higher benefit it has by exchange with another subject, rather than by the personal production or labour process. The *division of labour* between subjects is explained by the search for the most advantageous interactions with other subjects. The subjects with which a relatively more beneficial exchange is conducted receive more attention afterwards. As such, we can depart from the idea that division of labour has always existed and will always exist. The societal division of labour as a general term stands for the complex dynamic system of the human labour and interaction processes.

Since division of labour is a never-ending and continuously changing process, the question is: what are the boundaries of labour specialisation between subjects? Whereas in general, division of labour on the micro level is restricted by the *marginal human and non-human benefit* of the interactions, an even stricter boundary is determined by the *marginal personal benefit* of the activity or interaction. The criterion implies that an activity offers personal benefits (aspects of the human capital) that cannot be replaced by output elements of other subjects. To the extent that a subject aims at certain personal benefits of an activity that are directly related to its own organism, another subject cannot perform the activity. The criterion of personal benefits is stricter because the relative proportion of the components of the output is also a basic element of the evaluation. The criterion counts for all activities of all subjects and it is intrinsically connected with the complexity of objects. On all levels of society, the division of labour is limited by the personal benefits because no interaction can be efficient for both subjects involved when this is ignored.

The notion of 'personal benefit' is a generalised version of the old concept of 'direct utility' that was introduced by Reid (1934) and that was used again by Hawrylyshyn (1976, 1977) to formulate the criterion of 'direct versus indirect utility' and the 'third man' criterion. Hagenaars (1988) used the term 'person-related character' of an activity for the classification of human activities. Her formulation was the basis for a general, consistent definition. In our approach the concept is generalised to all activities and expressed in gradual terms, saying that *all activities offer personal benefits to a certain extent*. It can then be used as a general criterion for (the development and the boundaries of) the division of labour, as the degree of substitutability of activities by other people and of possible specialisation between people. The criterion is important for all subjects, since they simultaneously want to develop their personal, social, material and financial capital in a certain way.

2.2.3.2 *Value and value formation as a regulator of human activities and exchange processes*

The different dimensions of personal capital (Figures 2.4-2.8) indicate how the labour process of the subject receives its meaning and is being realised. In the course of each labour process, these dimensions are united in a very complicated and dynamic interaction and they can only be distinguished analytically. The valuation and the value system, as part of overall personal capital, are very closely connected with other dimensions and offer an extra dimension to the activities and the exchange processes between subjects (Kruithof, 1968, 1973). A general, integrated theory of value (formation) can be developed to support the analysis of the division of labour of the different subjects and of the market system as a whole. A general theory tries to bridge the different economic theories of value (classic, Marxist, neo-Ricardian, neoclassic, Austrian) and the value theories in other social sciences (for example, Kruithof, 1968, 1973, 1984).

Figure 2.8 presents the structure and components of the *value formation* within the labour processes and the interactions. The *valuations and values* (as a result of it) are placed within the total structure, together with other dimensions. The cognitive and performance processes indicate the possibilities and limitations of the subject and the preferences; the affective and volitional processes indicate what it wishes, wants, likes or what it does not wish, want or like. The valuation, then, offers an additional dimension and regulation of the behaviour and interactions, indicating what is considered to be more or less *desirable or preferable*. The criterion for the desirability and consequently for the valuation is the 'intersubjective' or societal validity or acceptance of the qualities attributed to the object ('objectification') and the subject's need or wish for a certain availability of the object.

The motives for the exchange are located within personal capital, expressed by the other dimensions: knowledge, emotions, needs, will, dedication, aesthetic experience, and so on incite the subject to search and to use specific objects to a certain degree. Each labour process again creates the basis for the next one, and so too the need for objects one cannot (sufficiently) dispose of. First of all, a subject can produce the object itself if the right personal, social, material and financial input elements are available. If not, it must first obtain these input elements. Alternatively, a certain availability of the object can be obtained by exchange with another subject. This intrinsic dependency on (the objects of) other subjects constitutes the basic ground for societal exchange processes and division of labour.

Every exchange process is a process in two directions between the 'supplier' and the 'receiver', where a certain combination of personal, social, material and financial elements or benefits is being exchanged, starting from their initial needs. The receiver wants the right personal, social, material and financial elements that answer his needs. In return he is willing to give a 'reward' as a specific combination of personal, social, material and financial means. The supplier wants to offer the right personal, social, material and financial elements that sufficiently answer the needs of the receiver. In exchange, he wants to 'receive' the right combination of personal, social, material and financial elements that answer his own needs. Given the complex nature of human exchange processes, all receivers are always suppliers at the same time, and vice versa, permanently demanding and offering a certain mix of personal, social, material and financial elements.

The *central principle* of all exchange processes is *mutuality* or *reciprocity*, which means that nothing is offered for nothing. In positive terms this implies that interaction or exchange always involves the movement of some elements (human and/or non-human, positive and/or negative, monetary and/or non-monetary) in both directions, between two subjects. In order to make exchange possible, the subjects have to determine 'how much is proper for how much'. To do so, the objects are compared to determine the relative proportion of the exchanged elements. The valuation is the medium to express that proportion of (the degree of availability of) the objects.

The value always expresses a physical proportion of quantities (of the availability) of specific objects, which means that the value of one object is expressed in terms of the quantity of another object. The subjective valuation or value (see Figure 2.8) reflects how much someone is prepared to offer for one object in order to dispose of another. The subjective valuation is determined by the components of the available human and non-human capital. Starting from the subjective valuations for the objects, the *demand for and supply of* the objects is being determined. Demand refers to the shortage of the availability of an object, while supply refers to an abundant availability of an object. The mechanism of shortage and abundance therefore works in two directions for each subject.

Given the never ending task of choosing the right objects, each subject is permanently looking for other subjects who can offer or who demand (a certain degree of availability of) objects. This process can vary, from a very spontaneous, unplanned process of demand and supply to a highly planned, organised one.

The subjective valuations of objects (in terms of demand and supply) can easily differ between the subjects, which means that there is no agreement about the relative quantity of the elements to be exchanged. The exchange cannot take place in this case because readiness to exchange is not yet present. In general, a *negotiation process* takes place in the course of each exchange, during which the objects are being compared, weighed or 'evaluated'. This negotiation process can range from very long, intentional and intensive to very short, unintentional and extensive. Moreover, it does not automatically lead to actual exchange.

Given the intention to exchange and given the subjective valuations, the relative exchange position of the subjects involved plays an important role in value formation. It expresses the actual relative power of subjects against one another to realise their own valuation during the interaction. The exchange position is determined by the available human and non-human capital of the subjects at the moment of the interaction. Since subjective valuations are not necessarily identical, each subject will attempt to gain as much benefit from the exchange as possible. This implies that the valuations in principle can always be disputed or questioned. Consequently, the validity of the subjective valuation for other objects must always be justified and established during the negotiation process. This *justification process* can occur in several forms and gradations.

Therefore, each exchange process itself is a labour process that has to be evaluated for its efficiency.

During the exchange, both subjects have their own subjective valuation of the objects. The confrontation between their subjective valuations results in the actual proportion of the exchanged objects, the *exchange value*. The exchange value is the actual socially confirmed proportion of the exchanged elements in the interaction between the two subjects. The existence of an exchange implies that the negotiation process has led to a result. But this does not mean that the result is (equally) good for both. This depends on the extent to which the exchange value (in the positive or negative sense) differs from their subjective valuation. From this point of view, it is the exception rather than the rule that the two subjective valuations are identical from the beginning of the negotiation period.

When the subjective valuations are not equal, at least one of the subjects involved will have to adapt their valuation in order to realise an exchange. One subject will attempt to force an exchange value as close as possible to its subjective valuation. It is important to understand that a subject does not automatically arrive at a positive result. As soon as the exchange has actually taken place, the exchange value becomes effective. Afterwards, a subject can always strive to improve the exchange position and exchange value. The exchange value of an object is therefore always *relative* and is expressed in terms of the quantity (elements available) of another object, depending on the choice of objects it is compared with. The exchange value therefore expresses what the subject is actually willing to offer in order to obtain (a certain degree of availability of) another object.

Some objects have a *negative value* for the subject, which means that they imply a certain degree of damage. Therefore, a subject wants to keep them away or remove them. The negative valuation then expresses what the subject is willing to do/pay in order to remove the object or to keep it removed. Every labour process contains at least a minimum of negatively valued elements that must be deducted from the overall positive output value. In each labour process, the positively and negatively valued elements must therefore be determined (for example, a meal and waste). The distinction between the subjective valuation and the exchange value must, of course, be maintained. The distinction between positive and negative values is the basis for the overall societal discussion on human and non-human damage. The central question is to what extent societal damage can be treated by means of preventive and/or curative action. To the extent that negative value or damage cannot sufficiently be charged for, preventive action cannot be completely successful.

The objects and interactions can also be distinguished according to the *degree of monetary and non-monetary expression*. The objects and interactions in which the non-monetary aspects are negligible, for example most commercial business transactions, are located on the left side of the continuum in Figure 2.8. The monetary transactions of objects are traditionally identified with the 'economy' and mostly form the object of economics. The part of the exchange value of the transactions that is expressed in monetary terms is called the *price*. This means that the price is never exactly equal to the total exchange value. If these transactions are located on the 'market', the exchange value is called the *market price*. In principle, all kinds of objects can be (partly/largely) exchanged for money. Monetary exchanges or transactions are certainly not limited to 'material', manually tangible objects. All aspects of personal capital such as knowledge, skills, emotions, feelings, and so on can be exchanged in monetary terms (for example, the services of a teacher, a sports coach, a psychiatrist, a lawyer, an actor, a prostitute).

On the right side of the continuum in Figure 2.8 one can find the objects and transactions in which monetary elements are negligible and mostly neglected. These objects are nevertheless produced in a normal labour process and are actually exchanged. This exchange also results in an exchange value, as the relative quantity of the objects exchanged.

Between these two extremes, all objects and transactions are located on the continuum according to the relative share of monetary and non-monetary elements. The complex object is exchanged as a whole for another object that is partly expressed in monetary terms. For example, someone performs a certain chore in a friend's house in return for a specific hourly financial reward, some food, temporary housing and some special clothing for the job, an evening out to the theatre and the pub and the general positive social contact. Some exchanges are (partly) calculated in money while no money is actually being used, whereas for other exchanges money is used as a means of calculation and of exchange.

As the gradual concept or dimension expresses, in reality the two extremes do not exist. Purely monetary objects and transactions do not exist because in each transaction at least some personal benefits are not exchanged for money. In the same way, purely non-monetary transactions do not exist, because at least a small part of the exchanged object is or can be exchanged or expressed in monetary terms (for example, the money saved by doing something yourself). Fundamentally, this implies that no strict distinction can be made between monetary and non-monetary objects or transactions. When all objects or transactions contain both components to a certain extent, the traditional distinction between the activities (see Figures 2.1 and 2.2) is no longer meaningful or useful.

Theoretically spoken, the market price (as defined in economic science) in principle never exactly equals the actual total societal exchange value. This has important consequences for (the analysis of) society and the market system. One must therefore always determine the relative share of monetary and non-monetary elements in order to know the total actual exchange value. In practice, it is important to define a number of meaningful and operational intermediate positions or combinations on the continuum, ranging from the minmal to the maximal monetary transactions.

One must also take into account the other dimensions of human activities. It is important, for example, to know to what extent the subject is conscious of the characteristics of the object, of the availability of other objects and of other subjects' valuations. Also important are the intensity and the frequency of the need for a certain object, which expresses the importance of the timing of the exchange. The will of a person has a major influence on the negotiation process and also determines the degree of success. Along with the available personal capital, also the social, material and financial capital is very important. On the abstract level, it is, of course, impossible and moreover pointless to disentangle this completely. At the same time, the costs or the exchange values of the input elements of the labour process are important for the subjective value, in particular with respect to its determination and justification.

As for the registration of time devoted to different activities and the share of different responsibilities in complex activities, it is impossible to register all exchange processes between all subjects, especially within families and societal organisations. However, one can develop practical instruments to register the people with whom one is doing different activities within families and organisations, in order to create a simplified but useful picture of the internal exchange processes. Again, the basic condition is that the different exchange processes are treated in a consistent way in terms of complexity, duration and frequency.

The same applies to the determination of the value of non-market activities and outputs. The different economic methods for determining the monetary value of non-market productive activities, mostly household production and voluntary labour, give a measure for part of the total input or output, but it is by definition not a correct measure for the real exchange value of non-monetary activities and objects. And since one can never exactly measure the real exchange processes within families and organisations, one can never exactly measure the exchange value of these activities and/or products. Given the asymmetry between market and non-market activities in terms of the proportion of personal, social, material and financial input and output elements, and given the fact that one can never unravel these asymmetric complex activities to make them comparable, it is impossible to determine the real exchange value of non-market activities by means of a measure of the monetary value of market activities. Let us emphasise that it is neither possible to determine the real value of non-monetary parts of market activities.

So, once again we come to the basic question with respect to the valuation problem: why should we (want or try to) value non-market activities in monetary terms, knowing that they are complex and that the real value can never be measured in monetary terms? The major motive formulated by protagonists refers to the need to have a 'correct' or 'complete' picture of the total value of all productive activities in society, as 'total welfare'. In that sense, total welfare would be expressed by a broader concept of gross domestic product (GDP), which is supposed to be the expression of the total welfare created by all market activities.

In our integrated approach, however, *all* activities are, in principle, productive. The basic 'economic' motive would then imply that we have to determine the real societal value of all human activities to have a complete picture. But, as shown, this is simply impossible and at the same time senseless and unnecessary. The basic function of human valuation is to orient and guide human activities into a desirable direction and certainly not to have a complete picture of the real societal value of all complex activities of all human beings. Trying to register and count the total exchange value of all human activities goes far beyond the capacity of human sciences and it would actually express the old utopian ambition of positive science in the 19th century to become the almighty actor (to replace God?) that can completely unravel, know and steer society.

Registering and counting must not be a goal in itself but must offer useful instruments for the organisation of daily life. Again, the registered market prices of all goods and services traded in the (official) markets is only part of the total societal exchange value. This means that national monetary accounts of market activities are a practical instrument for society for steering and orienting these activities and exchange processes. The 'total' measurement is also unnecessary since it does not help to solve the major societal problems, for example the search for a fair division of labour, income, social provisions, and so on, within and between different countries in the world.

All economic methods for determining the monetary value of non-market activities measure a certain monetary value, but by definition they only measure what they measure, namely the opportunity cost or the market replacement cost of an activity. These are useful indicators that can be used for a number of practical problems in daily life, namely the search for the right financial compensation in the context of different sorts of conflicts and damage between societal actors. This clearly shows that an integrated approach can answer the practical challenges and problems of everyday life. It is compatible with a large number of practical instruments that have been developed in the past and can also lead to the development of new policy perspectives and instruments. We shall show that this is indeed possible with respect to the daily division of professional and family life in western countries.

2.2.3.3 *Finality of the division of activities in the life course*

Not all labour and exchange processes are equally successful in the eyes of the subjects concerned. The success or efficiency of a labour process is expressed in terms of the value of the input and output elements, called the *costs and benefits* of the labour process. If the output has a higher subjective value than the costs or exchange value of the input, then the process produces a *subjective* surplus value. It therefore expresses the efficiency of the labour process from the subject's point of view, namely the difference between the subjective value of the output and the actual costs (exchange value of the input). However, this subjective surplus value must stand the test of the actual exchange. The *actual surplus value* is realised in the exchange process between two parties and is the difference between the actual exchange value and actual costs. The surplus value indicates that the output is actually more valuable than the input, which offers a higher degree of availability of objects. As a result, it is possible to use more elements in the following activities. Surplus value expresses the overall efficiency of a subject's activity. An activity is overall efficient when a surplus value is created, while the magnitude of the surplus value determines the degree of efficiency, in absolute or relative terms.

The profit is the monetary part of the surplus value, as the difference between monetary costs and benefits of the labour process. Placing the concept of profit within the broader concept of surplus value does not mean that it is unimportant. On the contrary, it is a central concept and condition in the daily division of labour of all subjects.

It is logical that, in the short run, every subject tries to reach a positive result or surplus value in all activities, with or without financial profit, aiming at the growth or positive development of total capital and its major components. Every human activity or labour process, however, is only a part of a long and complex chain of labour processes during a longer period. The *long-term finality* of human activities therefore refers to the development of the subject as a whole. 'Long term' is the succession of several 'short terms', in which the subject attempts 'to make the best of it', without realising or being able to realise the best of it automatically and/or completely. There is always the possibility of failing or losing. If a person suffers loss in a certain period, he will try to realise a positive result in the following period(s). The central criterion for the long-term development of the daily life of men and women therefore is the *capacity to adapt themselves* in time to the demands of the societal context when a negative development occurs and to adjust it in a positive (or a less negative) direction. The *total capital or well-being* of a person is then the overall result of successive positive and negative developments.

2.2.3.4 Conceptual difference between the basic activities

The general application of short-term finality in terms of surplus value and long-term finality in terms of the adaptation capacity of all subjects and of all activities or labour processes does not imply that there are any differences on a more concrete level of analysis. On the contrary, great variety exists, determined by the gradual dimensions of the activities and interactions, as described in Figure 2.8. Here we discuss the distinction between the major activities in Figure 2.6. Following Figures 2.4-2.8, the meaning or value of different activities is determined by the specific combination of personal, social, material and financial benefits, on the input and output sides.

Professional labour is, to a large extent, externally oriented and offers most of the financial benefits necessary to buy different input elements for other activities. Yet direct personal, social and material benefits are also important. In other words, financial reward is very important, but people do not do jobs for money alone.

Social or voluntary labour is also largely oriented towards people or organisations outside their own family, but it offers no or only small financial benefit. The activity aims more at direct personal, social and material benefits. However, in many cases a certain (mostly small) financial compensation or reward is paid for social labour, especially when the task occurs regularly and is essential for the organisation, for example trainers in sports clubs, monitors in playgrounds. At the same time, these non–monetary benefits can be expressed in monetary terms to a certain extent, that is, the amount of money saved by not hiring a fully professional worker.

The basic goal of *family labour* is to directly provide certain personal, social and material services within the family, by means of internal production and exchange between family members. The direct reward for this activity is offered within the family. Indirectly, family labour also offers an output for other activities (outside the family). The benefits here can also be expressed in terms of the amount of money spared. Similar reasoning is possible for external education, leisure time and personal care. Perhaps a few examples of concrete leisure activities will demonstrate that they are also productive. Many children draw or paint beautiful pictures that they give as a 'valuable' present to their parents. These pictures mostly have great personal and social value for the parents (during a certain period), but they also have a financial value, since many parents use the pictures to decorate their houses, and in that way can save on the expense of professional pictures sold in the market. The same applies to all sorts of artistic leisure activities resulting in beautiful pieces that can be used as decoration.

The difference between professional and social/voluntary labour can be clearly illustrated for sporting activities. On the one hand, certain sporting services that are offered by fully professional and commercial firms. The exchange of these services is largely conducted in monetary terms. On the other hand, one can be a member of a sports club that produces or offers certain sporting opportunities for its members. In an extreme case, members do not have to pay any financial contribution at all, but they have to work for/within the organisation in order to produce the service themselves. In order to pay the money cost of all goods and services bought on the market, the club organises a number of social activities to earn the required money. So the monetary commercial transactions of the club concern other (non-sporting) activities, which are now located between the club and all kinds of other subjects (including their own members). In many cases this may look strange, for example when members do not (want to) pay the total professional price of the sporting service but are prepared to organise activities or offer their labour to sell all kinds of other services, often or mostly to themselves.

In many social organisations, labour is not automatically divided equally. Some members devote more time or labour to the system than others, although they do not receive more direct sporting services from it; they may even get less. This does not mean that they do not receive any benefit; it means that their total benefit is composed more of personal and social values, for example the existence and the success of the organisation as a whole and the fact that they are working/leading members of it or their children are active sporting members of the club. As soon as their participation no longer renders sufficient personal and social benefits, participation will diminish and ultimately stop.

So, all activities are located on a dynamic continuum, going from the most professional (commercial) to the most voluntary activity. Starting somewhere on the continuum, every activity has its own development according to success, changing finality, and so on. That development has no fixed order or final goal. All activities are regulated by the general demand–supply mechanism, which means that the position of an activity on the continuum is no indication of its societal efficiency. Some activities are started as personal hobbies that become voluntary labour after time, which may then develop to a commercial activity. Other activities are started and performed as real professional or commercial activities for a while, but become voluntary and/or family labour after some time. It all depends on the composition of the output aimed at, in terms of personal, social, material and financial benefits, in relation to the valuation and the demand of other subjects. This implies that all sorts of activities can be either efficient or inefficient, depending on the total exchange value of the input and output.

2.2.3.5 An integrated approach to the market system

We build further on the analysis of the labour process and the division of labour in Figure 2.8, which offers a number of basic dimensions. Every society has its specific type of division of labour, in which the complexity of the labour and exchange processes, in terms of subjects, objects and activities, is expressed through the combination of the different gradual dimensions. In order to present this complex process in a comprehensible way, it is necessary to choose the relevant levels of complexity on which the valuation is situated. The (gradual) private and collective output elements of the labour processes are distributed between the subjects by means of exchange processes. The (gradual) distinction between the internal and external division of labour, on the basis of the legal recognition of the 'subjects' (individuals, families, companies, institutions, and so on) is also a central aspect here. The internal and external division of labour is interchangeable because the subjects overlap, as an expression of complexity (see Figure 2.7). For practical reasons an analytical distinction is made between the *internal division of labour*, which is called the *labour organisation*, and the *external division of labour*, which is called *market functioning*. In reality, however, they are permanently related and interact. Here we concentrate on the market system as the system of the 'external' division of labour between subjects. The 'market system' of a society is complex and gradual, with different levels of complexity for the objects and subjects. Consequently, all external transactions between *legally acknowledged subjects* are regulated by the market mechanism within a certain market system.

We can introduce some *additional gradual dimensions or characteristics* of the market system (see Figure 2.8). On the one hand, these gradual aspects make it possible to further differentiate the conceptual model of the market system. On the other hand, their general application within the approach to all subjects and activities additionally supports the general and integrated character of the approach. In any case, these formal characteristics are important for the description and comparison of different market systems, without ideological prejudice, since they apply to all subjects and activities.

First, the market system can be described in terms of *production sectors and/or partial markets*, according to some criteria: the type of objects that are being produced and exchanged, the geographical location, the sort of subjects, and so on. Given the principle of complexity, subjects, objects, labour and exchange processes constitute part of several sectors and partial markets at the same time. In practice, any classification of the market system is complicated, with different overlapping subsystems. The actual classification depends on its practical goals and its use, for example in registration, statistics, and so on. The history of economic science shows the evolution of the classification of the different sectors in the market systems.

Second, every transaction can vary in terms of the *credit form* that is used for the payment of the object. The credit form expresses the period of time within which the payment is executed and is related to the complexity and the time dimension of the object, to the size of the value and to the total available capital. All exchange processes are located on a continuum, ranging from payment a very long time in advance (which implies a large credit or loan from the buyer to the seller), to immediate payment in the same period (that is, paying 'cash'), to postponed payment (with an implicit credit to the buyer). The subjects must choose between the many possibilities, knowing that, to a certain extent, the use of credit forms influences the relative exchange value and the availability of the object.

The third factor is the extent to which subjects (can) make use of *product (or market) segmentation* and (can) take advantage of the differential subjective valuation or willingness to pay for the objects. This means that a differential supply (of the availability) of objects can and/or must exist. Product segmentation means that the range (of the availability) of differential objects is increased on account of the differential demand for (the availability of) objects. The concept comes from microeconomic theory but it is generalised here, that is, all subjects, to a certain extent, can apply the gradual instrument of product segmentation. For example, the public railway company can demand differential tariffs for their services depending on their size, regularity, quality, and so on. To attract more passengers, the company can or has to answer the differential needs or preferences of the customers. The success of the product segmentation or 'fine-tuning of demand and supply', therefore, does not depend on the distinction between private and public organisations but on the marketing capabilities of the subjects themselves.

Furthermore, there is the extent to which the market system is *free and open* to the subjects involved and the *degree of competition* between the subjects. This depends on the exchange position or the relative complexity of the subjects and on the legal rules concerning the formation of recognised types of organisations. All (partial) markets are 'to a certain extent' free, open and competitive, just like every transaction or exchange. In that respect, it is pointless to talk about the competitive free market system since the overall market system (of a country) includes many market forms and different gradations of freedom, openness and competition in the (partial) markets. Many people are not aware of the lack of freedom and openness of many partial markets in the so-called western 'free market system'.

The relative proportion of internal and external transactions in societies is also important because it expresses the relative openness and *decentralisation* of society and its subjects. Combined with the gradual distinction of free versus non-free exchange, one can formulate the two-dimensional matrix, with a large variety of market systems. Although the extreme combinations, that is, the maximally 'decentralised free market system' and the maximally 'centralised non-free market system' are often used as expressions of two real systems, they are, in fact, extreme, unreal types of actual and possible combinations.

Finally, we mention the *degree of official registration* of the labour processes and transactions. Within the societal division of labour there is a certain need for registration or bookkeeping of the labour processes and transactions, for internal organisation and for the collective system(s). The nature and degree of registration depends on the need for information about the labour and exchange processes.

The combination of all the above-mentioned factors or dimensions results in an integrated model of the different market systems, at a local, national and/or international level. The core of the model is the gradual proportion of the human and non-human capital, the level of complexity and the degree of damage. The model can be differentiated by introducing the other gradual dimensions or characteristics. Although the multidimensional character can never be completely shown graphically, Figure 2.7 gives a more adequate picture of reality than Figure 2.3. *All* societal subjects or actors (and their activities) have a specific score for each of these dimensions. The combination and integration of the scores determine the actual place in society. The approach makes room for a much more neutral and differentiated analysis and evaluation of the different actors. Consequently, more attention can be paid to the efficiency and the mutual functionality of the subjects within (parts of) the market system.

With the integrated approach one can describe and analyse the market system of all societies (countries, regions) in different historical periods in an adequate way, with sufficient attention to the gradual differences between the maximal liberal free market system on the one hand, and the maximal collective or state market system on the other. This analysis results in new basic questions and perspectives concerning the conditions, efficiency and correctness of existing market systems, as a whole and for subsystems. In the next chapter, we formulate a new overall normative concept for future society and for the future market system.

2.2.3.6 An integrated approach to the collective system of society

Whatever the graphical presentation, it is clear that the divisible outputs of an organisation, which are relatively 'small' in relation to the overall capital of the organisation, can be or are being exchanged with other subjects directly. The (positive and negative) more collective elements at the input and output side are mostly offered and collected by a public authority or 'government'. Which governmental level is responsible depends on the level of complexity on which the activities take place. Theoretically, society is 'infinitely' gradual, which means that one could define an unlimited number of levels of complexity or 'collectiveness'. In practice, people have always created a certain number of practical collective or 'governmental' levels: communal, provincial, regional, national, international, intercontinental, global. Consequently, the actual division of responsibilities is also practical and will never completely match the real complexity levels. So a number of collective objects end up between two levels and mostly come under the larger authority because they are too large for the lower level. The services of the governmental instances are limited to the (geographical) area within which the government is authorised. The national government is responsible for the most general, collective elements that are important to all subjects, as far as a nation is concerned. The national government itself is composed of smaller and larger partial organisations that take part in the market system more or less independently. Along with the national government, the regional, provincial and municipal governments offer a number of collective services on a more local level, in exchange for fiscal contributions (directly or via the higher government). Within a broader, international context, the place and function of the national government is clearly relative. In a complex, internationally growing market system, the lower governments lose certain responsibilities that surpass their boundaries and capacity. At the same time they receive new responsibilities that are more directly related to their level of complexity.

Society therefore always has to search for the most adequate division of 'collective responsibilities' between the different complexity levels. The central question, then, is whether the actual division of responsibilities for the existing levels is efficient. Whatever level we speak about, a collective or governmental system always exists on every level, notwithstanding the concrete size, power, responsibilities, efficiency, and so on. 'Thinking away' the collective system, for whatever ideological reason or to whatever extent, therefore, is useless and even dangerous and will most probably lead to an inadequate and inefficient functioning of the collective system, that is, as a producer of necessary, valuable (more) collective objects for the smaller, more private subjects.

The national collective system (government, community, state, and so on) is the most general instance of the market system of a country. The governmental system does not stand beside the market as is supposed in the traditional basic model (see Figure 2.3) but fully participates in the market (see Figure 2.7). The government itself is a 'normal' subject with its own internal and external division of labour, as all other more private subjects. It produces and provides all kinds of services to other subjects, in exchange for their contributions, on the basis of specific criteria. The daily 'exchange' of individuals, families, organisations ('private' subjects) with national government is also based on the general mechanism of demand and supply, as it functions between individuals, families and organisations. The same qualitative criteria of the value formation and of the market functioning are valid (see Figure 2.8). The government itself is a complex system of relatively autonomous and competitive organisations within the societal system of demand and supply. The government is the producer/supplier and the consumer/user of the most collective elements of the societal activities. Since there are a number of collective elements present in every transaction between subjects, both at the input and output side, the public sector constitutes the basis or foundation of the total societal production and market system (and all its partial markets). The 'national collective' system (fiscal system and public services) settles the collective elements of the daily exchange between the more private subjects. De facto, the basic collective system has a certain share in all more private labour and exchange processes.

Within the complex system, the collective sector, with the fiscal system at the income side and provided services at the expense side, is always the basis or the fabric and, consequently, the most general steering system of the total production and market system. In other words, the (national) government participates in all production processes of all subjects to a certain degree, on all levels of society. Consequently, a change in this system (fiscal tariffs and collective expenses) has an influence, positive or negative, on all subjects of society.

At this point of the analysis it is important to emphasise the *gradation from maximally private to maximally collective payment* of goods and services, related to the degree that the traded objects are separable. (Largely) collective services that are physically divisible can be charged directly to the buyer or user. Examples are the national telephone services, the postal service, electricity, the internet, and so on.

At the other end, we can find collective services that are not offered and charged as separate services. Some collective objects can hardly or impossibly be separated physically, for example 'nature', the coastal area, the army, public roads, social safety, radio programmes. Some objects can be separated relatively easily, but they are actually not separated for specific reasons, for example television programmes, household rubbish, museums, arts centres. The services are offered as a whole and the societal subjects can (almost) freely use them when they want.

These collective services have to be financed by means of fiscal contributions paid by the different legally recognised subjects. Taxes are in fact payment for the daily use of collective objects that are not separately sold to the public. In that sense, taxes are (necessary) credit forms offered by the government to the societal subjects. Different sorts of taxes exist, depending on the factor they are levied on: expenses (input), income (output) or the capital stock of the subject. It is important to mention that any tax on the income of one subject (who has sold something) simultaneously is a tax on the expenses of another subject (who has bought something). So, one can conceive different transaction taxes, with a gradual distinction between very general taxes (on almost all transactions, objects, subjects) and very specific taxes (on very specific transactions, objects or subjects).

Between the two ends of the continuum, one can locate a number of collective services that are based on a gradual combination of private and collective payment. Here we find all organisations that are, to a certain extent, financially subsidised by the government, for many possible reasons. The main reason is the fact that the activities of these organisations are highly valued by the government while, at the same time, they cannot survive on their own in the actual market system. The collective share of these transactions is paid by means of fiscal contributions.

2.2.4 Division of labour within families

2.2.4.1 Micro level

The internal and external division of labour is a complex and dynamic feedback system. On the micro level, this system can be presented as a dynamic multiple communicating vessel (see Figure 2.9).

The division of labour is at any moment determined by the available portfolio of personal, social, material and financial capital (stock variable) and of activities (process variable) within a given time perspective (hour, day, week, month, year, etc). The basic components determine the production capacity and exchange position of the family and its members. Figure 2.9 presents the traditional family with two cohabiting adult partners (mostly man and woman), married or not, with or without children. The figure can easily be modified or extended to represent all family types.

The *starting position* of the partners within the family directly determines the division of labour in the next (first) period and also the boundaries of the division of labour in the longer run. The initial positions are mostly not that equal, since at the start of the household each member has its own history of family and professional life, expressed in a different portfolio of activities and of human and non-human capital. Most men and women, understandably, value their starting position rather highly and they can or will not give it up that easily. Therefore, in most families the margin for conscious

Figure 2.9   Division of labour within families on the micro level

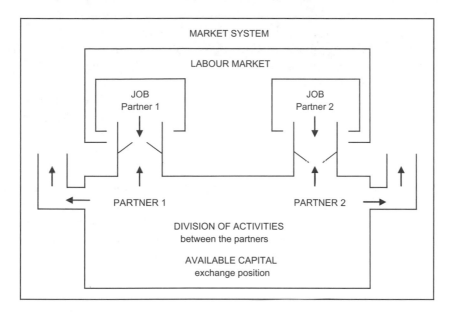

change is not that large. Someone who has been co-habiting or who has been living alone already has some experience with 'managing' his/her own household. From the moment that two people live together, they are part of a new situation that conditions and orients their behaviour opportunities and freedom. They are placed in a new 'communicating vessel', which can be changed, enlarged or improved to a certain extent. In most families the margin for positive deliberate change is rather small.

With the start of a new family or household, a 'new communicating vessel' is constructed and the partners become part of a new system of internal and external division of labour. Because the activities of the partners are bounded by the available time (24 hours/day, seven days/week, etc), there is always a dynamic feedback between the quantitative and qualitative changes in terms of the different activities, the different means and the exchange position. The different components always exercise a mutual pressure. In Figure 2.9, professional labour (paid job) is presented as a major source of pressure on the overall division of activities between the partners. Essentially, one must take into account all activities, including all voluntary and leisure activities, because they are all productive and provide human and non-human benefits to family members.

When the (external) pressure on one or more components is increased, the whole vessel will react, searching for an adequate adjustment of the components. According to the magnitude, intensity and duration of the change, the adaptation process will be more smooth or gradual. Let us suppose a full-time working married woman who – after negotiation with a partner – decides to diminish the number of hours of professional work from 40 to 30 a week. Then, the relative pressure of her job on the total joint system decreases and automatically the pressure of the partner's job increases. The additional available hours must be filled by other activities, the benefit of which will also be evaluated in terms of human and non-human, monetary and non-monetary, positive and negative elements, etc. The temporary 'vacuum' of the woman's time exercises a pull effect, automatically taking over certain activities of the man. When the man cannot instantly adjust his (external) activities, he initiates a push effect, pushing certain tasks to the wife. Of course, the quality of the job is also important in the dynamics of the division of labour.

The flexibility of the adaptation process in the system is largely determined by the personal and social capital of the partners, in particular their attitudes towards the division of labour between men and women. Their actual position is the result of the past division of labour and is related to a number of characteristics, such as age, education level, family background and available material and financial means. These attitudes are presented in Figure 2.9 by means of 'valves' in the channels between the compartments of the system. The existence of these valves refers to the relative durability and independence of the subsystems. Their position and strength then represent the direction and flexibility of the adaptation behaviour of the partners. Some people adjust their division of labour to external changes more easily while others will resist more strongly. Given the historical development of the division of labour between men and women, one can assume that in general men adapt themselves more easily to professional labour (more hours and a higher function), whereas women adapt themselves more easily to family labour.

In the same way, all other components of the integrated approach (see Figure 2.8) can be integrated in the dynamic model: the relative valuations, the exchange processes, the evaluation of the division of labour, the relative power or exchange position of the partners, the degree of democracy in decision making and the proportion of the negative and positive, monetary and non-monetary benefits. In its most elaborated form, the model offers an explanation for the different behaviour and reaction patterns with respect to the division of labour between men and women within the family.

It offers, for example, an explanation for the rigid adaptation behaviour with respect to family labour of full-time working men who, unexpectedly and unwillingly, become unemployed and are actually full-time at home. It also largely explains the 'unequal' division of family tasks within families where both partners officially have a 'full-time' job, recognising that the term 'full-time' hides important differences in the number of hours and in the quality of the jobs. In most families the overall professional position of the man is still stronger: more working hours per week, a higher function, a higher wage, more responsibility, etc. This model has to be placed on a long-term time axis, showing the complex feedback mechanism among all major aspects. During this long-term process, these aspects can alternately be a 'determinant or cause' at a certain moment and a 'consequence or result' at another moment.

As already discussed, Figure 2.9 can be easily adjusted for other family types. For couple families with partners of the same sex, just one of the two partners has to be replaced. The presence of children or other dependent people in the family can also be introduced fairly easily, complicating the internal and external division of labour. For one-parent families, the second partner is to be replaced by one or more children. The single parent then has no internal division of labour with a partner in the strict sense of the word, but only with the children in the family. However, in most cases the former partner is still part of their daily life to a certain extent: there remains a certain division of labour between the former partners, largely related to their responsibilities towards the children. One can see this new 'external' division of labour between the former partners as the remaining 'internal' division of labour of the 'former family'. It is important, then, to look at the gradual division of tasks/responsibilities and means between the former partners, going from, for example, a very unequal 90%/10% division in favour of the father, to a very equal 50%/50% division, to a very unequal 10%/90% division in favour of the mother. Finally, single people can be seen as one-person families, having no internal division of labour with other people and completely depending on the external division of labour with external people.

2.2.4.2 *Division of labour in different family types and life course stages*

The internal and external division of labour is largely related to the family type and/or the family stage in the life course: traditional couple family, family with partners of the same sex, family with one adult partner, families with or without dependent children or other dependent persons, and so on.

Given the complexity of the division of time (Figures 2.5-2.9), it is impossible to give a complete overview of all possible forms of division of time for all family types or all stages during the life course. Therefore, we can only illustrate the immense diversity of combinations by means of some typical examples.

Figure 2.10 illustrates the division of *professional labour* during the different family stages of a 'traditional' couple family (man and woman) with two children, living together for about 50 years, combining two jobs during the whole period of cohabitation. The same picture can be given for the division of family work and other activities. For this type, different variants can be given according to the gradual division of professional (and family) work. The picture shows a fairly *simple family development*, expressing continuity in the combination of professional labour, with a more or less equal division of professional labour during the first years. After the arrival of the children, the working hours of the man increase while those of the woman decrease, increasing consequently the inequality between the partners. At the age of 16, both children start their professional labour (PL child), still living in the parental family. At a certain age, they leave the family, which leads to some changes in the working hours of the parents. In this case, the working hours of the woman decrease step by step. After 45 years of cohabitation, she leaves the labour market, while the man shifts to a part-time job of about 20 hours per week.

Figure 2.11 shows the division of professional labour during the different stages of a *complex family development*, seen from the life course of the woman. The first period of her family life is the same as in Figure 2.10. After 10 years, her partner leaves the household and she lives as a lone parent for about five years, increasing her working hours again to the original level. She does not manage to realise an equal division of tasks/responsibilities and means with the former partner, resulting in an unequal

Figure 2.10 Division of professional labour (hours per week) during the life course of a traditional couple family with two children

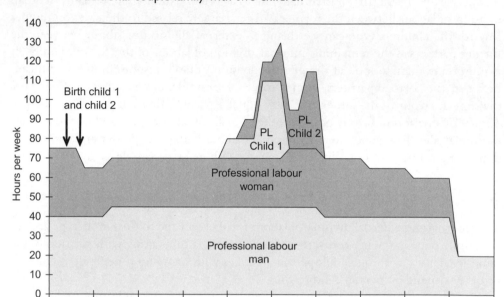

80%/20% division in favour of the father. She has a few very hard years, being almost solely responsible for all the education and household tasks.

After some years, she starts a new family with another man, which lasts for about 18 years. The two children stay in this household most of that time, before they start their own household. During the first period, the partners have an equal division of professional work, but when the children start a small job, she diminishes her working hours. Due to promotion, the man starts working more hours, increasing the inequality in professional and family work between the two partners. After 18 years of cohabitation, the man suddenly dies because of an acute illness. Afterwards, the woman lives alone for five years with a job of about 30 hours a week. Her children have already left home, so the daily household burden is much smaller than before. Now, she can spend more time on her hobbies. Sometimes she takes care of her young grandchildren.

After five years, she starts a new family with a third man, who has a job of about 40 hours per week, together with his 15-year-old child. After a few years, both partners diminish the working hours, resulting in about 20 hours for the woman and 30 hours for the man, while the child starts a small part-time job. The working hours of the man increase again after three years, but he changes back to a lower number fairly quickly. The next year, the adult child of the man leaves the household. After living 13 years together, they both finish their professional career.

This graph shows a fairly complex family development, expressing the discontinuity in the division of professional labour during the life course of the woman. Again, the same picture is possible for the division of other basic activities. Different variants can

Figure 2.11 Division of professional labour (hours per week) during the different stages of a complex family development

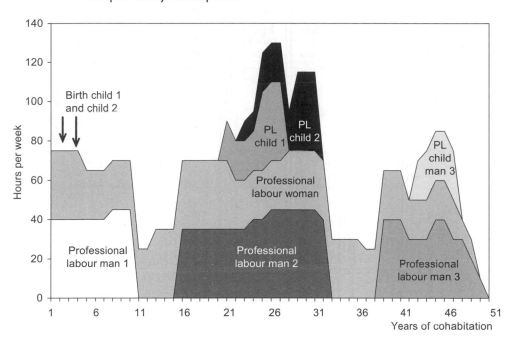

be given according to the gradual division of professional (and family) work. Finally, one can show many variants between the fairly simple development in Figure 2.10 and the complex development in Figure 2.11. It is understood that still more complex variants are possible.

2.2.4.3 *Typology of the division of time*

Starting from the dynamic model in Figure 2.9, one can construct a typology for the individual division of labour of men and women. Figure 2.12 shows a gradual typology of individuals according to the combination of the number of hours of professional labour (PL) and family labour (FL) per week (Van Dongen et al, 2001, pp 27-8). The number of hours of leisure time (LT) and personal care (PC) is kept constant, since most previous studies illustrated that these activities show no significant differences between men and women.

On the left side of Figure 2.12, one can find the maximally profession-oriented (PO) men and women (about 60 hours of professional labour and only a few hours of family work). On the right side one can see the maximally family-oriented (FO) people (no hours of professional labour and about 70 hours of family work). Five more equal types are located between these extreme types, with the equally profession-oriented and family-oriented people (35 hours of professional and family work) in the middle.

Next, Figure 2.13 shows a gradual typology of families with two adult partners, based on the combination of the hours of professional and family labour of both partners

Figure 2.12 Typology for the individual division of time

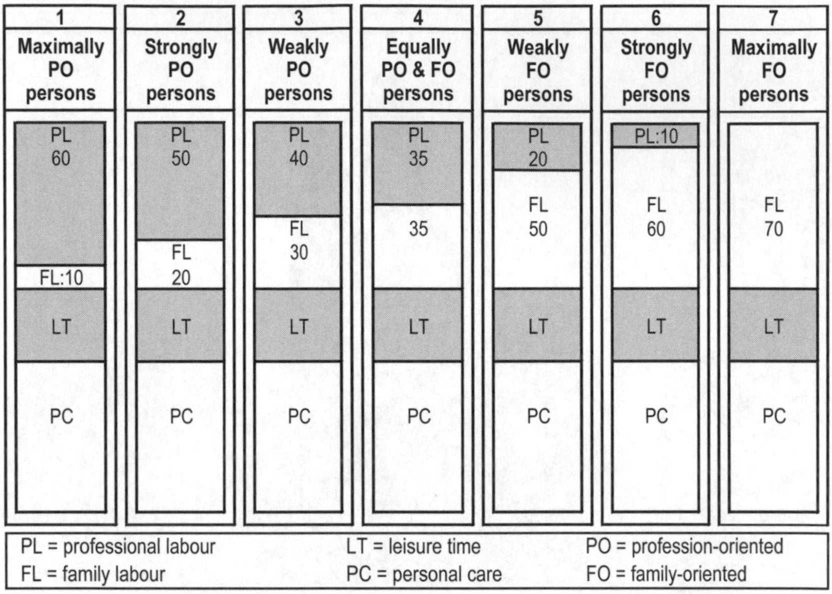

1	2	3	4	5	6	7
Maximally PO persons	Strongly PO persons	Weakly PO persons	Equally PO & FO persons	Weakly FO persons	Strongly FO persons	Maximally FO persons

PL = professional labour   LT = leisure time   PO = profession-oriented
FL = family labour   PC = personal care   FO = family-oriented

(P1 and P2). The typology depends on the absolute and relative division of professional and family labour, on the individual and family level. Again, the number of hours of leisure time and personal care is kept constant. Each family type represents a number of families with more or less the same division of professional and family labour. For families with a male and a female partner, the typology ranges from the strong male breadwinner family on the left side, to the complete combination family in the centre, to the strong female breadwinner family on the right.

While the figure refers to the traditional family, with a man and a woman, with or without children, it can easily be translated to other family types. When there is only one adult, one partner is skipped in the typology, so it becomes a typology for families with one adult, with or without children. As previously said, the typology can also be used for studying the remaining division of labour and means between former partners, in the so-called 'former families'. When both partners are of the same sex, the typology can be reduced to types 1-4, changing the labels. Let us emphasise that the typology is not a goal in itself but a practical instrument to study reality in a useful way.

In families with children or other dependent people, the typology has to be differentiated for the division of time with these people. We shall not deal with this further complication here.

In the strong male breadwinner family (1), the man is responsible for (almost) all professional labour and the woman for (almost) all family labour. Going to the complete combination family in the centre (4), the relative share of the man and the woman in professional and family labour equalises increasingly. From the complete combination family to the strong female breadwinner family (7), the division of labour becomes

Figure 2.13 Typology for the division of time in families

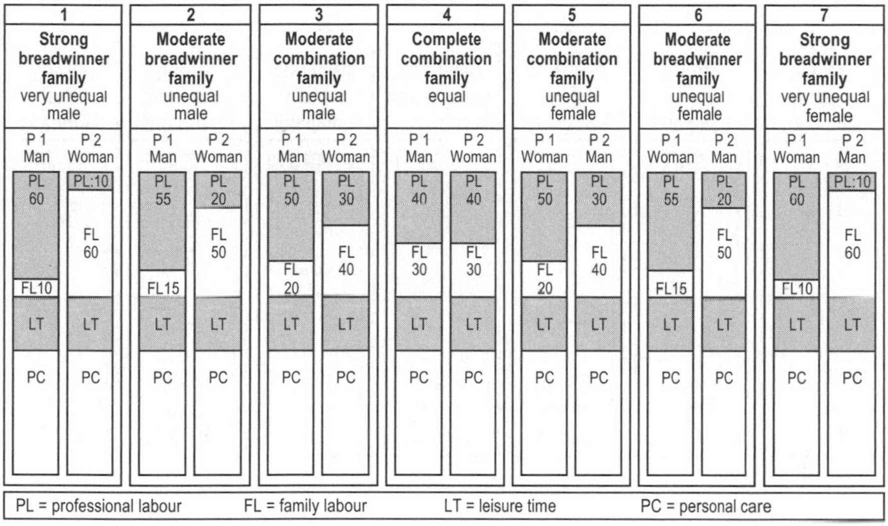

	1		2		3		4		5		6		7	
	Strong breadwinner family — very unequal male		Moderate breadwinner family — unequal male		Moderate combination family — unequal male		Complete combination family — equal		Moderate combination family — unequal female		Moderate breadwinner family — unequal female		Strong breadwinner family — very unequal female	
	P 1 Man	P 2 Woman	P 1 Man	P 2 Woman	P 1 Man	P 2 Woman	P 1 Man	P 2 Woman	P 1 Woman	P 2 Man	P 1 Woman	P 2 Man	P 1 Woman	P 2 Man
	PL 60	PL:10	PL 55	PL 20	PL 50	PL 30	PL 40	PL 40	PL 50	PL 30	PL 55	PL 20	PL 60	PL:10
		FL 60		FL 50	FL 20	FL 40	FL 30	FL 30		FL 40		FL 50		FL 60
	FL10		FL15						FL 20		FL15		FL10	
	LT	LT	LT	LT	LT	LT	LT	LT	LT	LT	LT	LT	LT	LT
	PC	PC	PC	PC	PC	PC	PC	PC	PC	PC	PC	PC	PC	PC

PL = professional labour   FL = family labour   LT = leisure time   PC = personal care

more unequal again but in reverse, that is, the woman doing the larger part of paid labour and the man doing the larger part of family work. Although these family types occur very rarely in reality, they are essential to have a correct and complete typology that is the basis for comparable family models (Van Dongen et al, 1998, 2001).

Finally, Figure 2.14 presents a gradual typology of organisations, with seven types, based on the division of working hours of men and women in the organisations. Each type represents a number of organisations with more or less the same internal division of labour. The typology ranges from the very strong male organisation on the left side, to the complete combination organisation in the centre, to the very strong female organisation on the right.

In the very strong or strong male organisation (1 and 2), the share of the labour of men is (very) dominant. Going to the complete combination family in the centre (4), the relative share of the labour of men and women equalises. From the complete combination family to the very strong female organisation (7), the division of labour becomes more unequal again but in reverse.

This simple typology is an instrument to study the division of labour within organisations from the perspective of the relative position of men and women. The typology can be further differentiated by introducing some other aspects of the work organisation, for example the distinction between basic activities (management, development and logistics, production, maintenance, administration, marketing and communication), the functional levels and wage levels. Although such typologies are more clear-cut, their practical usability is mostly smaller because of the large number of types distinguished.

As for families, a profile of each type of organisation can be constructed, based on empirical data for a number of characteristics of the employees (age, education level, professional seniority and/or experience, functional level, profession, income,

Figure 2.14 Typology for the division of time in organisations

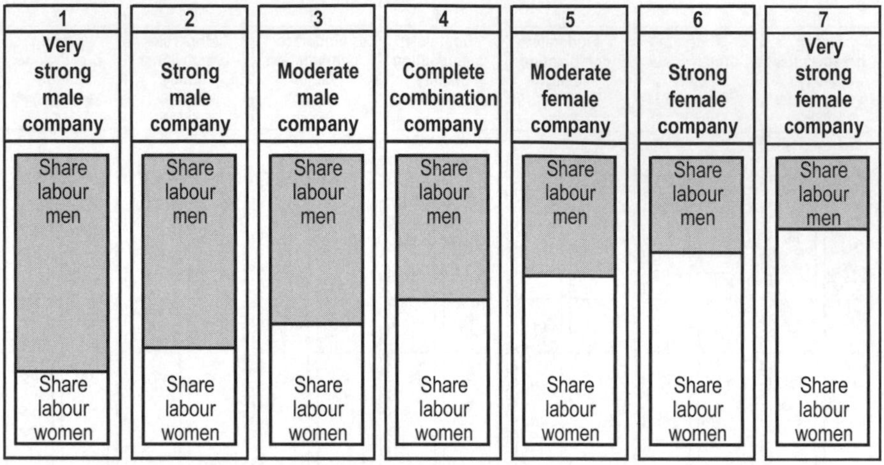

1	2	3	4	5	6	7
Very strong male company	Strong male company	Moderate male company	Complete combination company	Moderate female company	Strong female company	Very strong female company
Share labour men	Share labour men	Share labour men	Share labour men	Share labour men	Share labour men	Share labour men
Share labour women	Share labour women	Share labour women	Share labour women	Share labour women	Share labour women	Share labour women

motivation, family form, work-related attitudes, and so on) and some characteristics of the organisation (sector, number of employees, total turnover, working time schedules, company culture, quality of the work, communication, and so on).

The combination organisations (types 3, 4 and 5) are then characterised by a (more or less) equal share of the labour of men and women, but also by a largely equal share in the basic activities, functional levels and wages. Very strong and strong male and female organisations (types 1, 2, 6 and 7) have a (very) unequal division of labour of men and women, in terms of number of hours, basic activities, functional levels and wages.

For the time being, it is very difficult to find sufficient internationally comparative data on the micro level to produce such profiles for the different countries. Therefore, we shall not deal with this empirical task in this book.

2.2.4.4 Societal models of the division of time

Starting from these typologies, societal models to divide the time of individuals, families and organisations can be developed in the form of quantitative distributions of different types of individuals, families and organisations within society. So a large number of conceptual, empirical and normative models can be constructed. The name of such models is mostly related to the dominant type or to the overall character of the distribution. In the next chapter, some empirical models are used to show and describe the historical development of the division of time. The conceptual model, the normative approach and empirical models are then the basis for some future normative models, to orient and guide (the policy debate on) future development. The central question, then, is which model is the best normative guide for future policy.

For didactical reasons, the models are kept rather general and simple. First, although the models mostly refer to families with two adult partners, sufficient attention should also go to other types of families, for example one-parent families. Second, the societal position of children and older people must receive full attention in the models. Third, it is useful to produce a profile of the family types within the empirical models, picturing the different aspects of daily life, for example the other activities and the personal, social, material and financial means. Fourth, the different stages of the life course of men and women and of their family context must be taken into account. And analogous models must be explained in more detail for the position of men and women within clubs, companies, public institutions, and so on. Finally, to make international comparison possible, the models must be usable for all countries, both conceptually and practically. This is one of the main objectives of this study, as will be presented in Chapter 3.

Figure 2.15 shows two extreme conceptual models: the extreme male breadwinner model with a very unequal division of professional and family labour between men and women (both at the individual and family level) and the extreme combination model with a very equal division of professional and family labour.

The upper part of Figure 2.15 shows the frequency distribution of men and women (Y-axis) for the number of hours per week of professional and family labour (X-axis), following the typology of individuals in Figure 2.12. The lower part shows the frequency distribution (Y-axis) of the family types in Figure 2.13 for the relative share of the

Figure 2.15 Two extreme models for the division of professional and family labour in families

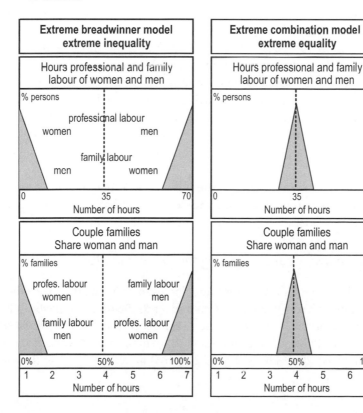

number of hours of the woman in the total number of hours of professional and family labour in the family (sum of man and woman) (X-axis).

The *extreme male breadwinner model* expresses the extreme inequality, implying that only strong male breadwinner families exist. For lone men and women (with or without children), only the upper part is relevant, in that case meaning that all lone women would stay at home and all lone men would work very long hours. Lone women would have to receive their income completely via social transfers.

The *extreme combination model* expresses the extreme equality, saying that only strong or complete combination families exist, with a maximal equal sharing of professional and family labour between men and women, at the individual and family level. The model also says that both lone men and lone women would have equal professional and family tasks.

The two models are extreme and give very little space for diversity between individuals and family types. This also implies a very low level of potential change during the life course and family stages. These extreme models are far from representative for western societies during the past decades, and they cannot be useful guidelines for future policy in democratic societies.

Complementary to the models in Figure 2.15, one can easily illustrate the same extreme models for the division of labour within organisations, replacing the (couple) family as a unity by the organisation. Because of the strong similarity, we do not give the figure for organisations here.

All more realistic models are located between the two extremes, showing much more diversity in the division of labour between men and women, at the individual, family and organisational level. In Chapter 4, we shall show more realistic empirical models for different countries, expressing the actual development of the division of labour during past decades. From the conceptual approach and the actual development, we come to the normative discussion. Starting from a broad normative concept in Chapter 3 and some empirical models of the past development of the division of labour in Chapter 4, some relevant normative models for the future will be presented in Chapter 5, which are then the basis for the formulation of a consistent set of policy perspectives in Chapter 6.

First, however, we want to come back to the other conceptual models in this field and show to what extent these models are compatible with the broad conceptual approach of the Combination Model.

2.2.5 The Combination Model: integrating the existing models

At the conceptual level, the Combination Model aims to integrate the major theoretical perspectives being used in social sciences with respect to the division of labour between men and women during the past decades (for example, Gershuny et al, 1994; Bianchi et al, 2000; Gershuny, 2000; Windebank, 2001; Gornick and Meyers, 2003; Hakim, 2003; Fuwa, 2004; Geist, 2005; Hook, 2005a, 2005b). The research reveals the following major (groups of) models:

- specialisation model, rational choice model, time availability and potential earnings model, human capital theory, life cycle theory;
- underlying preferences model, preference essentialism;
- social exchange model, economic bargaining model, relative resources model, power struggle model;
- gender role model, gender ideology model, socialisation model.

The *specialisation model* is largely based on the economic approach of Becker (1965, 1975, 1976, 1981), arguing that the (unequal) division of labour between partners is mainly determined by the rational choice of the partners to maximise the material and financial output of the household, starting from the comparative advantage and higher earning potential of the male partners in professional work. Therefore, men specialise in professional work while women specialise in family work. During the past decades a number of variants of this basic model have been developed, dealing with the basic elements of specialisation, rational choice, time availability and potential earnings (Bianchi et al, 2000; Hook, 2005b). Another variant of this model is human capital (Becker, 1975). The theory emphasises the importance of investment in human capital (knowledge and competences) by means of education. A rational person invests in additional education to the extent that the expected future benefits are higher than the expected future costs. This is largely generalised in the life cycle theory, placing the rational economic decisions of individuals in the longer perspectives of the life course. A rational person chooses the combination of paid work and other activities that offer the highest benefit over a longer period or the (total) life course. Since everyone is facing many uncertainties in daily life, the expected future benefits are used.

The *underlying preferences model* (Hakim, 2003) says that the unequal division of labour reflects the fundamental difference in the underlying preferences of men and women. These preferences are seen as essential characteristics of human beings, related to their biological and psychological constitution. So, Hakim (2003) elaborates a typology of women and men with respect to the division of labour that is based on their preferences with respect to the division of professional and family work. This typology is then used for the empirical study of the division of labour within families, showing that the actual division of labour largely reflects the preferred division of the labour of men and women.

The *social exchange model* and *economic bargaining model* (Blood and Wolfe, 1960; Manser and Brown, 1980; Lundberg and Pollak, 1996) start from the possible conflicting interests of partners with respect to available resources. The (unequal) division of labour is the result of the permanent negotiation process between partners, based on the relative power or the relative availability of resources. As such, partners do not primarily maximise the joint output but rather their own individual output. Since women have fewer resources available (human capital, earnings potential), they are more dependent on their husbands. Therefore, women have to spend more time on household work and hence can invest less time and other resources in their professional career.

The *gender role model* or *socialisation model* (Ferree, 1990; Brines, 1994; Greenstein, 1996a, 1996b, 2000; Bianchi et al, 2000) says that the (unequal) division of labour between partners is mainly the result of gender role attitudes that are being socialised. Women and men who share a more egalitarian gender role will realise a more equal division of labour in the household. Since the breadwinner role model became dominant in most societies, most men and women realised an unequal division of labour within their household. A more equal division of labour is only possible when an egalitarian gender role becomes dominant in society.

Referring to Figures 2.4–2.9, each of these models combines some of the basic components of the integrated model of the division of labour. They all bring in some elements and relations that play a certain role in the complex process. Consequently, it is not surprising that all four (types of) models have partially been supported and contested by empirical evidence (Hook, 2005a, 2005b). But by fundamentally reducing the complex societal process to some components of it, all four models get stuck in their chain of reasoning, especially with respect to the order and causality in the interaction processes and the consequent application during a longer historical period. The models largely suffer from 'the chicken or the egg dilemma': which element or factor was first; which is the cause and which is the consequence at what moment and on what place? For that reason, these theories have been strongly criticised during past decades.

Applying the *specialisation model* in a consequent way leads to a dead-end street, since one cannot explain the origin of the comparative advantage of men nor the (differences in) preferences and utility functions. Above all, the opposite development has been largely observed during the past four decades. As such, the model cannot explain the major historical turning points of the division of labour: from the 'old combination model' in the 19th century to the breadwinner model in the 20th century, and then to the modern combination model in the second half of the 20th century. Moreover, the model is too focused on the material and financial components of the activities, neglecting to a certain extent the personal and social aspects.

In the same way, the *underlying preferences model* does not give a solid explanation for the origin of the deeply rooted preferences. Again, which was first: the underlying preferences or the actual division of labour? According to the integrated approach, all preferences are the result of previous activities but have an effect on the next activities. To explain the process towards a more equal division of labour in the past few decades, the changing preferences that are the basis for the changing division of labour have to be explained. Moreover, in a normative sense, the existence of preferences does not imply that these preferences and the division of labour based on it are desirable and acceptable for society as a whole. So the model can only partly be the basis for future policy.

The same can be said, more or less, of the *bargaining* or *relative resources models*. Everyone will recognise that negotiations and the relative power of partners play a role in the division of labour. But the model does not explain the process leading to the different resources. Again, one would see that the relative sources and bargaining position is the result of the previous division of labour. One could argue that the specialisation process is one of the reasons for the differences in resources and for the need to bargain. Moreover, empirical evidence shows that in most households, partners (also) try to realise joint household goals to a certain extent, next to their individual goals and the joint goals in other societal organisations.

For the same reason, the *gender role model* or *socialisation model* is only a partial model, not being able to explain the origin and dominance of the traditional gender role in society. This refers to the interaction between attitudes and the visible behaviour or actions in human life. After all, the dominance of the traditional gender role (breadwinner role) during a certain period cannot explain the development toward a more equal division of labour. It could only explain the slowness of the process towards a more equal division of labour.

Applying the separate models to the actual division of labour leads to an 'either/or' attitude and to quite contrasting empirical perspectives (Van Dongen, 1990; Gershuny et al, 1994; Windebank, 2001; Hook, 2005b). On the one hand, there is the 'adaptive' or 'optimistic' perspective, which says that the increasing participation of women in professional labour (in terms of the participation rate and the number of hours) during the past five decades went hand in hand with an almost equal increase in the participation of men in family labour (in terms of the participation rate and the number of hours). On the other hand, we can find the 'non-adaptive' or 'pessimistic' perspective implying the inverse relation, that is, the increasing participation of women in professional labour did not lead to a significant increase in the participation of men in family labour. This non-adaptive process has been called the 'stalled revolution' (Hochschild, 1989; Hook, 2005a, 2005b). Between these two perspectives, several intermediate 'realistic' positions are possible. Gershuny et al (1994) speak about the 'lagged adaptation', referring to the slow reaction within two-earner families to redistribute household tasks in line with the changing division of professional labour. The slow adaptation process is related to a number of impediments on all levels of society.

Since all models are at the same time partially being supported by empirical evidence and partly being criticised on theoretical and empirical grounds (Hook, 2005a, 2005b), it would be more useful to combine or integrate their basic arguments as much as possible in a more general approach. Such an integrated approach avoids the 'either/or' story by dealing with the complex interaction process between the different components in time, at all levels of society. In this study, however, we do not have the ambition or the pretension to give a full empirical analysis of this long, complicated historical process. Using a number of complementary indicators of the daily division of labour, we try to show the overall development in the different countries.

During the past two decades, more attention has been paid to the influence of the different types of welfare regimes (macro level) on the daily division of labour of men and women within households, in combination with the major theoretical models mentioned before. This approach is largely inspired by the classification of western welfare states that was introduced by Esping-Andersen (1990). To answer the many critics on the lack of attention to the issue of gender inequality, more integrated classifications were elaborated later on, combining traditional class or income inequality, gender inequality and family policy (for example, Esping-Andersen, 1999 and Korpi, 2000). We agree with Korpi's standpoint (2000) that (in)equality should be conceptualised in a broader way, linking class inequality (largely expressed by means of household income) to gender inequality. In this study, however, we want to present the gender inequality in a more differentiated and efficient way, as part of an integrated approach to the daily life of individuals and families. We argue that gender inequality has a stronger connection with income inequality (household income) than was mostly supposed in the past.

The studies on the effect of the welfare state regimes show different outcomes. Windebank (2001), for example, gives some support for the idea that the influence of the different welfare state policies is not really significant. Gornick and Meyers (2003), Geist (2005) and Hook (2005a, 2005b) show the other view, stressing the specific, additional influence of the different policies, next to the individual, family and organisational aspects. The empirical analysis of the last studies is more convincing in the light of an integrated approach, emphasising the dynamic feedback among the different aspects of the societal division of labour in time. For that reason, we largely follow their hypotheses and try to show both the similarities and differences between the (types of) welfare states, indirectly illustrating the different policies behind the actual development of the division of labour.

2.2.6 Comparison with other 'integrating' models

In the introduction we mentioned some other 'integrating' policy-oriented models of the daily division of labour in society, that is, the TLM model (Schmid and Gazier 2002; Schmid and Schomann, 2004; Muffels et al, 2004; van den Heuvel et al, 2006), the flexicurity model (Wilthagen and Tros, 2004; Wilthagen et al, 2004; Madsen, 2006; van den Heuvel et al, 2006), the dual earner/dual carer model (Crompton, 1999; Gornick and Meyers, 2003) and the breadwinner caregiver models (Fraser, 1994, 2006). All these models aim to be scientific instruments for the study of the division of labour in the modern welfare states and to develop adequate policy models and perspectives. It is therefore useful to give a brief comparison of the conceptual approach of the Combination Model and the other integrating models.

2.2.6.1 The transitional labour markets model

Schmid and Gazier (2002) and Schmid and Schomann (2004) show that the basic TLM model largely follows the broader but still dual definition of activities as shown in Figure 2.2. We found no strong indications of the new basic idea that all activities are conceived as productive labour processes. Starting from the traditional (mainly economic) labour market research, professional labour is seen as the (major) basis for societal welfare and the professional career as the central axis of the life course. However, the other activities and life stages are also important in the daily life of men and women. This basic idea is expressed by the general presentation of the TLM model emphasising the three main 'stages of life': education, professional work and pensions (see Figure 2.16). Contrary to the traditional approach, Schmid pays more attention to the transitions and/or interactions between the different life stages and the changes within the professional stage, but largely seen from the perspective of professional life and the labour market.

Figure 2.16 The conceptual approach of the TLM model

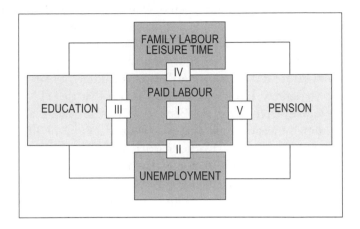

The TLM model was initially launched as a normative policy-oriented concept or model, expressing the search for a better labour market policy in European welfare states. Schippers (2006a, p 23) emphasises that the TLM concept has been developed against the background of high rates of structural unemployment that have characterised Europe during the 1990s. Crucial are the interactions and transitions between the labour market and adjacent fields (education, care or social security). Schmid advocates more fluid boundaries and open relations between the labour market and other sectors or social systems. These fluid boundaries should allow for easy transitions between paid work and non-market activities that preserve and enhance future employability.

Nevertheless, many authors argue that the TLM model can also serve as an analytical instrument to better describe and understand the dynamics of the labour market, in relation to other societal fields. In the first place, it is positive that more attention is paid to the life course perspective, more specifically to the major transitions that all people experience in one way or another during their life course. So it is acceptable that a simplified model is used to study complex daily life from a life course perspective. However, the problem is that in the TLM model the life course is almost completely analysed from and reduced to the perspective of the professional career. The model treats the major transitions (critical events) from one to the other stage and some shifts within the professional stage, but always seen from the perspective of the professional stage and the functioning of the labour market. But is this really such a new perspective? In our opinion, this has been the basic perspective of traditional (economic) labour market research during many decades. New is that the TLM model pays more attention to the empirical study of certain transitions or interactions that were more or less 'forgotten' in the past. Especially new is the search for new normative objectives, that is, the development of better transitions for (socially weaker) people, to realise a better position within the modern labour market and a better combination of family and social life.

Together with Muffels and Ester (2004) and Schippers (2006a, 2006b), we support the positive new aspects of the transitional labour markets approach. From an analytical perspective, they do not see the TLM model as a new general model of the labour market, but rather as a useful heuristic scheme to study the flows within, from and to the labour market, that is, the different transitions and combinations and their mutual interactions. All different economic, sociological and other theories about different aspects of the labour market can be linked to or placed within this heuristic frame. We refer to Muffels and Ester (2004) for an overview of the different (partial) theories. But at the same time, we largely agree with their criticism that the TLM model focuses too much on the 'age differentiation perspective', that is, the fact that most attention goes to the (traditional) transitions between the main stages in the life course, largely seen from the perspective of labour market participation. The TLM model pays little attention to the overall 'combination challenge' during the whole life course. In fact, the model conceives the combination challenge as part of the labour market challenge. This contradicts the basic normative objective of the model to create (new) bridges between the different fields or basic activities during the life course. To do so, the perspective of professional labour and the labour market should be combined with the perspective of the other fields or activities. The authors therefore suggest that more attention should go to an 'age integration perspective' or a 'combination perspective', which looks more to the different actual and desirable combinations of the basic activities (paid labour, education, family work, leisure time) during the different stages of the life course. This perspective broadens the scope of the life course research and can enrich existing labour market research. Unfortunately, they do not further elaborate this integration or combination perspective.

The Combination Model offers a more general and more gradual approach to daily life and the life course in a complex society, as shown in Figures 2.4–2.11. It is more in line with the 'broader' life course approach of Mortimer (2003) and Anxo and Boulin (2006a, 2006b). The main reason is that the model found its origin in a broader research domain, dealing with the daily combination of different basic activities during the life course. In particular, Figure 2.6 shows that, starting from a general life course approach, the Combination Model fully combines the age differentiation and age integration perspectives. The model conceives the labour market challenge as part of the broader 'combination challenge' during the whole life course. Conceptually, it deals with all possible (changes or transitions in the) combinations of activities for men and women, placed within the life course stages and within the complex structure of the market system. Therefore, the life course stages can only be determined in a gradual way: all men and women are combining all basic activities in a certain way at all stages, in quantity and quality. The specific combination of activities in each stage determines the available personal, social, material and financial means, both as an expression of and a (partial) solution to the permanently changing opportunities and risks during the life course. As said before, not all changes or transitions in the daily combination of activities are equally effective or important for the subjects involved and for society as a whole. Therefore, all policy-oriented research is and has to be selective, paying more attention to the changes that have a greater relevance for societal policy.

Furthermore, the historical view of the TLM model on the development of the labour market largely expresses the fairly traditional conceptual approach to the division of labour in the modern welfare states. In the first place, the TLM model mainly starts from the traditional concept of the welfare state that is presented in Figure 2.3. Muffels and Ester (2004) present almost the same frame for the analysis of the welfare states. In line with this, the TLM model starts from the traditional concept of (structural) unemployment and from the deeply rooted perception that structural unemployment (in the period 1980-2000) is a rather recent problem and hardly existed in the period 1950-70. In this traditional labour market view, the large group of housewives was not considered as part of the professional population and, consequently, neither as part of the structurally unemployed group. They were simply seen as 'inactive' people, almost completely placed outside the scope of labour market research and policy. The implicit broadly accepted view was that this large group of 'inactive' housewives had always existed during previous centuries. We shall show in Chapter 3 that this view is no longer valid or useful when we start from a broader conceptual approach and place the unemployment problem in a longer historical perspective. This perception also feeds the basic idea in the TLM model that the modern welfare states are confronted with some new social risks, the major one generally being called the 'combination risk or dilemma'. This means that in modern 'two-earner societies', in fact all families (with children) stand for the trade-off between professional and family work or responsibility. On the one hand, a large group of families not having (enough) paid work have sufficient time for family responsibilities and personal activities, but they run the risk of having insufficient income for buying the necessary goods and services to realise a decent welfare level. On the other hand, a large group of families having (abundant) paid work have enough income for buying the necessary and desired goods and services, but they run the risk of not having sufficient time for family responsibilities and personal activities. The TLM model then leads to the conclusion that modern societies have to develop 'new' instruments of risk management that can deal with this 'new' risk, for example the provision of (more or less paid) long leave arrangements for mothers and fathers (with young children) to stay at home for a certain period during their professional career, the provision of 'sufficient' external childcare for parents that want to continue the combination of professional and family labour and the provision of some family-friendly facilities by companies.

The Combination Model offers a new and broader conceptual frame for the market system and the division of labour within and between families, leading to a more general approach to the employment (and unemployment) challenge and to the different risks in society. More specifically, housewives are seen as part of the professional population, who for certain societal and/or personal reasons are not or are no longer active in the labour market. In that way, they become a (large) part of the overall (un)employment problem in society. This definition implies a different empirical and policy approach, trying to present this group correctly in the empirical studies of the division of labour and formulating new policy perspectives for their future division of labour. During the past few years, traditional labour market research has paid more attention to the labour market position of this fairly large group and to the societal costs and benefits of their actual division of labour.

Moreover, the combination risk is certainly not restricted to the period after 1980. On the contrary, it is a general societal risk for all families in all sorts of societies in all times (past, present and future). Becoming or being a housewife has always been a real major risk for almost all women, at the individual and family level. Again, the broader concept leads to different empirical research, showing to what extent and how the different family types are actually confronted with the societal risks and how different (types of) welfare states (try to) cope with these risks. The policy challenge is therefore not new as such, but can be broadened to the general question of how democratic welfare states can and should cope with these risks in the future. The question is not whether a modern welfare state should invest in (new) risk management, but rather which sort of risk management is the best to cope with the actual (combinations of) risks and to support the development of a democratic division of labour.

2.2.6.2 The flexicurity model

During the past 15 years, yet another model has been developed, also starting from the main challenges of the European welfare states and the labour market as a central part. The flexicurity model has it roots in the scientific and policy discussion of the early 1990s, but it was formulated as a new integrating model by the end of the century. Since 2000, it has become fairly attractive to a number of research and policy groups in Europe, in particular in the Netherlands and Denmark. The concept of 'flexicurity' is the contraction of two important societal concepts or objectives: 'flexibility' and 'security'. It expresses the basic search for a solid and acceptable combination of these two objectives in European welfare states. The model has a fairly strong connection with the TLM model.

According to Wilthagen and Tros (2004, p 169), the flexicurity model was originally formulated as 'a policy strategy that attempts, synchronically and in a deliberate way, to enhance the flexibility of labour markets, work organisation and labour relations on the one hand, and to enhance security – employment security and social security – notably for weaker groups in and outside the labour market, on the other hand'. The normative flexicurity concept, as seen by Wilthagen and Tros (2004), does not imply different possible policy strategies (different combinations of flexibility and security). It refers to one specific policy strategy, combining a (more or less) unique combination of a certain level of flexibility and a certain level of security. The meaning of this normative policy perspective is discussed in Section 5.5. In this section we look at the conceptual or analytical approach of the flexicurity model.

Wilthagen and Tros (2004) and Madsen (2006) argue that the flexicurity model offers an analytical frame or matrix that can be used to study the actual development of the different combinations of flexibility and security in different countries (see Figure 2.17). This analytical frame is closely related to the analytical model of the TLM model. It combines four types of flexibility with four types of security. The analytical multidimensional matrix can then be applied to the dynamic and complex labour markets and welfare states, seen from the side of the employers, the employees (and their families) and the government. In that way, it can lead to the empirical study of the actual combinations in different countries, offering an empirical basis for the evaluation of these combinations from a normative point of view. In one way or another, these studies show the permanent interaction between the conceptual, normative and empirical perspective.

Figure 2.17 The conceptual approach of the flexicurity model

Flexibility	Security			
	Job	Employment	Income	Combination
Numerical				
Working time				
Functional				
Wage				

Wilthagen and Tros (2004) show the actual development of the flexicurity debate in the Netherlands in the period 1990-2000, stressing the fact that it was very difficult to reach a good balance between flexibility and security. Madsen (2006, pp 6-10) discusses the 'successful' Danish flexicurity model, emphasising that it 'is not the result of a well-defined grand scheme, but the outcome of a long historical development with strong elements of path-dependency'. Wilthagen et al (2004) use the matrix to show the actual flexicurity combinations and the concrete policy strategies in a number of European countries, illustrating both the similarities and differences between these countries. They conclude that every country or group of countries emphasises different aspects of the flexicurity matrix in Figure 2.17. In Germany and Belgium, the Fordist or industrial form of flexibility is still dominant, stressing the internal numerical flexibility (part-time work, career breaks, temporary technical unemployment), combined with income and job security. The Netherlands and Denmark focus more on the external numerical flexibility (more changing jobs), combined with work and income security. Kerkhofs et al (2006) present a comparative analysis of the actual strategies of working time flexibility in European companies, starting from a typology based on a number of working time variables concerning part-time work, irregular and flexible working hours, overtime, parental leave, long-term leave, early retirement, flexible contracts and childcare. The study shows, to a certain extent, the gradual differences between the different (types of) welfare states in Europe.

The 'new' flexicurity model enjoys much interest in the European scientific and policy world, as was shown during the international conference in Amsterdam in 2007, 'Innovating labour market policies: transitional labour markets and flexicurity'. As previously stated, the title illustrates a strong link between the TLM model and the flexicurity model. The Dutch Institute for Labour Studies (OSA) has scrutinised, both empirically and theoretically, the two approaches over the past few years. The conference was organised to present the main findings and to discuss them with academic colleagues and policy makers in the field. The organisers formulated the hypothesis that the TLM model and the flexicurity model were the best candidates for innovating and reinventing labour market policies.

Together with the different authors already mentioned, we support the positive contribution of the flexicurity model to labour market research and policy. It deals with a major challenge in European societies, expressed by the combined concepts of flexibility and security. But again, we notice that this broad challenge is mainly seen from the perspective of the labour market (participation), paying insufficient attention to the other main activities or fields in society. The flexicurity model largely follows the conceptual approach of the TLM model and also conceives the 'combination challenge' in a narrow sense as part of the labour market challenge, in that way largely narrowing the scope of it. The model uses the flexicurity matrix as the starting point or entrance to look at the complex welfare state and labour market, with only little attention to the overall division of time in all parts of society.

The Combination Model looks at the same complex welfare state and division of labour from the perspective of the broad combination challenge, starting from the overall division of activities in families, companies and organisations in society as a whole. Consequently, the model treats labour market participation and (all aspects of) the flexicurity matrix as a major part of the overall combination challenge. The Combination Model offers a more general and more gradual approach to daily life and the life course in a complex society, as shown in Figures 2.4-2.11. The elements of the flexicurity matrix are placed within this overall model of the division of labour to create a differentiated empirical picture of the division of labour in the different (types of) welfare states.

The flexicurity model also starts from the traditional concept of the labour market and the welfare state (see Figure 2.3), suggesting that modern European welfare states are now facing (fundamentally) new (combinations of) 'flexibility' and 'security' risks. The normative model, then, is seen as a unique answer to cope with these new risks. However, the problem is that a new normative policy model for the future division of labour in society also needs a new conceptual approach that can offer the basis for such new solutions. The Combination Model offers a new conceptual frame for the market system and the division of labour within and between families, leading to a general approach to the overall division of labour, to the employment challenge in particular and to all possible combinations of flexibility and security risks in society.

2.2.6.3 The dual earner/dual carer model

In their study of the development from the traditional male breadwinner model to the modern dual earner models and to the future dual earner/dual carer model, both Crompton (1999) and Gornick and Meyers (2003) pay little attention to (the development of) the conceptual approach to the division of labour (between men and women). Their work firstly focuses on the actual development of the (unequal) division of labour between men and women, searching for the major determinants of this inequality. Furthermore, they analyse the actual policy models in western countries during the past few decades, mainly starting from an enlarged version of the Esping-

Andersen classification of welfare states, as presented, for example, in Korpi (2000). Finally, they formulate a new normative model or end view for the future division of labour and explore the main policy perspectives following from that policy model.

Implicitly, however, one notices the shift to a broader concept of 'labour' and 'division of labour' in society, with a clear focus on the gender dimension, implying that both paid professional labour and unpaid family labour are (or should be) equally important in the concept of daily life and the life course, more or less as described in Figure 2.2. The implicit conceptual approach behind the societal problem of the unequal division of labour, the empirical analysis and the normative approach is clearly a sort of combination model of the daily division of professional and family labour, in families, organisations and society as a whole. Both the empirical analysis and the normative policy model are largely based on some basic indicators for the division of professional and family work. Starting from these indicators, other aspects of the daily division of labour are being looked at, for example non-standard and flexible working hours, childcare, evening, night and weekend work, income, poverty and the well-being of children. In fact, this implicit combination model covers the use of some of the partial theories we mentioned in Section 1.3, albeit with a stronger focus on the gender role theories and a revised version of the welfare state approach. Last, but not least, the labels used for the historical models and the future policy model also clearly express the idea of the daily combination or division of professional and family work.

2.2.6.4 *The universal caregiver model*

With respect to Fraser's conceptual approach to the universal caregiver model (1994, 2006), almost the same comments can be formulated as for the dual earner/dual carer model. By far, the presentation is very normative and policy-oriented, paying little attention to the conceptual approach to the division of labour between men and women. But again, an implicit 'combination model' is detectable covering some theories mentioned in the previous section, albeit from a strong feminist perspective.

2.2.6.5 *Conclusion*

All the integrating models of the division of labour have been developed more or less separately from one another, determined by the societal background or context, the specific societal problems that are recognised, the scientific disciplines involved, the societal domains dealt with, the conceptual and normative approach to the division of labour, the time perspective and the geographical horizon. Every model is based on a few central structuring factors, leading to an analytical matrix or typology, which, then, is the basis for the societal models, conceptually, empirically and normatively. Around these central factors, other important factors or variables can be introduced to create a differentiated profile of the different types within the model.

These scientific models do not pretend to tell the one and only all-embracing truth about the division of labour in society. All (scientific) knowledge is based on the interpretation of different empirical models, largely inspired by conceptual and normative models. These models (only) have the healthy ambition of offering a useful instrument to study the division of (professional and family) labour of men and women in society in a productive and comprehensible way. The aim is to develop useful conceptual, empirical and normative or policy-oriented models, recognising the permanent interaction between these three basic dimensions, and to formulate adequate policy perspectives that can be the basis for efficient policy programmes. Therefore, it is important to create a permanent international exchange and collaboration to encourage the further development and improvement of the conceptual approaches.

The Combination Model has the same healthy ambition but the future will show to what extent this ambition can be realised. We can only emphasise that the Combination Model is the result of integrating the scientific work of many other researchers and/or research groups who developed different sorts of conceptual, empirical and normative models or approaches in this field. Starting from the integrated approach of the Combination Model and the different partial models, a broad empirical picture of the actual development of the division of professional and family labour can be created, as the basis for future policy perspectives. In the next chapter, therefore, we present the normative view of the Combination Model.

THREE

A new normative approach to the division of labour in society

3.1 Democracy as the overall normative concept for society

All democratic countries or societies stand for the basic normative question of how the division of labour between men and women should develop in the (near) future. To answer this, an adequate normative approach has to be formulated for the new model of future society. Figure 3.1 presents a new general normative approach, for which different variants can be formulated, according to the ideological views in society. It is an instrument for the reformulation of the normative basis of society, in line with the development of a new conceptual approach. So, the instrument can always be discussed and adjusted.

The new normative approach differs from the traditional approach, not regarding the choice of basic values as such, but in particular regarding the concrete meaning and relative weight of these values in the overall normative concept. Democracy was a basic value in the traditional model, standing at the same level as other values such as freedom, equality and economic efficiency. As such, democracy strongly referred to the

Figure 3.1 The basic normative view of the Combination Model

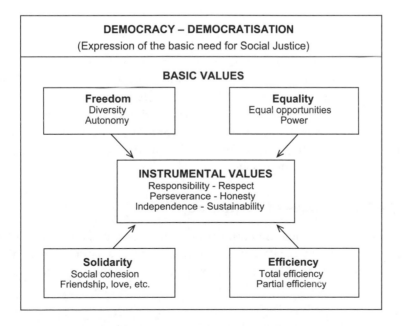

western parliamentary system in politics. During the past few decades, the concept of democracy has been systematically broadened, especially by the increasing application to the daily life of men and women within families, clubs, companies and institutions.

Together with the conceptual approach, the basic normative view has also been changing during the past few decades. To the extent that the conceptual distinction of the activities and the societal sectors became less explicit, the hierarchy of the values has also been questioned. The concept of 'democracy' (and 'democratisation') has been broadened and has been increasingly used for the daily life of men and women in the different social organisations.

In the new basic model, democracy is seen as the overall normative concept for (the daily life or division of labour within) society, from the micro to the macro level (Kruithof, 1980; Van Dongen, 1993, 1997, 2004a, 2005c; Van Dongen et al, 2001; Van Dongen and Danau, 2003; Gratton, 2004). Democracy is defined as the basic multidimensional normative concept for society that combines a number of basic values to be applied at all levels of society: 'democracy of daily life'. Democratisation, then, is the realisation of a higher level of democracy in society, that is, a higher level of at least one of the basic values, without diminishing the level of the other basic values.

One can argue that democracy is neither the only nor the most useful concept to be used as an overall normative concept, and that other concepts can serve that goal in a better way, for example the concept of 'social justice'. Social justice has also been used as a general normative concept covering a number of basic values (for example, Van Parijs, 1992, 1995; Vandenbroucke, 1999, 2001). However, the concept of social justice only expresses the general need of people to apply certain values in order to structure and guide societal life. It does not itself formulate a concrete normative choice or direction for society. In fact, all ideological groups, from extreme right to extreme left, claim the concept to a certain extent and define it according to their normative view. It has no normative distinctive power and the practical use of the concept is strongly restricted.

The concept of democracy, however, has always had an explicit normative direction during its long development. Therefore, it cannot be defined in two opposite directions. In fact, democracy is a concrete expression of the general need for social justice. One can formulate a gradual normative spectrum for society, from a very weak democracy at one end to a very strong democracy at the other. So the concept of 'strong democracy' can be used as a new overall normative concept for future society and all its subsystems (see Figure 1.1), expressing that society needs a further democratisation process to increase the overall level of democracy.

3.2 The basic values of democracy

As said, democracy is a multidimensional normative concept, covering a number of basic values that have to regulate daily life in society as a whole and in all societal entities (families, clubs, neighbourhoods, companies and public institutions on different levels).

A first basic value of democracy is that all actors have *sufficient freedom* to determine their activities: choosing the goals and the means, deciding on the procedure and timing, executing the actual process and determining the destination and use of the output. The concept of freedom is equivalent with the concept of diversity between the actors regarding the division of activities and means. Diversity is an important condition and incentive for a successful adaptation process of all actors within society.

A democratic society also demands *sufficient equality* within and between the different actors with respect to the division of time and means, at the input and the output side. Equality in particular refers to the relative situation or position of the different actors (activities and means) according to gender, age, education, family type, (dis)abilities, origin, and so on.

Freedom and equality are equally important and should not be seen as antipodes but as mutual levers and restrictions. Given the complex nature of society, certain differences or inequalities will always exist and equality will always occur in a gradual way. Society therefore has to determine which differences or inequalities are seen as *unacceptable societal inequalities*. Consequently, these inequalities need to be visualised clearly in order to find an adequate policy to deal with them.

Third, *sufficient solidarity* between the actors of society must be developed. Solidarity implies that, due to specific disabilities or dependencies, certain groups or actors of society have to be supported by other groups, in monetary and/or non-monetary terms. Most solidarity mechanisms are related to the disability of people to have a (full) paid job, due to age (too young or too old), long-term physical or mental disability, illness and forced unemployment. But solidarity between different organisations is also important, in order to support weaker organisations to a certain extent. An effective and efficient solidarity system, therefore, needs an adequate collective system with enough financial means for social investment programmes. It also needs a high level of responsibility from the people and organisations that are able to contribute to the collective system by means of their professional labour.

Finally, a democratic society has to be sufficiently *efficient*, in the broad sense of the word, integrating the personal, social, material and financial elements. Referring to Figure 2.8, total efficiency means that within a certain time perspective the total exchange value of the output of the activities (both in monetary and non-monetary terms) is higher than the total exchange value of the input. In other words, efficiency requires that a certain surplus value is realised, including all the components of the output and taking into account the goals that follow from the other basic values. According to the actual choice with respect to the other basic values, different efficiency measures are possible.

In the complex daily division of time, it is impossible to determine overall efficiency (total surplus value). Therefore, a number of partial efficiency measures have to be used, for example the financial efficiency measure that takes into account the financial input and output elements. Partial measures are necessary and useful for many practical goals, but they can also be misleading when certain elements of the process are largely ignored. So financial efficiency (profit) is a necessary condition for total efficiency, but it is certainly not a sufficient condition.

The selection of the basic values means that other important values can be placed under one of the basic values, as a more instrumental value. Some other important values have an instrumental character with respect to the four basic values. Figure 3.1 shows a few values that are important for the daily combination of professional and family life. *Responsibility*, *respect*, *perseverance* and *honesty* are major instrumental values for the effective realisation of basic values in the daily life of all societal actors, for example to realise the different combinations of professional and family work within a certain normative model. *Independence* can be seen as the combined expression of the basic values with respect to the mutual social relations of people and organisations. *Sustainability* has increasingly been formulated as an important value during past decades, especially in the context of the environmental problems in society. The value refers to the efficiency of activities and their results, in the short and long run, that can be expressed in terms of personal, social, material and financial capital. The concept emphasises the importance of the quality of the means and the need to maximally avoid and/or correct the different sorts of damage in daily life. Therefore, the realisation of the value demands sufficient freedom, equality and solidarity.

3.3 Strong democracy as the maximal balance of basic values

The main normative ambition of the Combination Model is to realise a new balance between the basic values of society, under the general normative concept of 'democracy' or 'democratisation' for all entities of society: freedom, equality, solidarity and efficiency. Within this framework we can speak of a 'democratic market system' as a strong alternative to the 'free market system' (Van Dongen, 2004a). Since perfect democracy cannot be established, the main goal is to feed a permanent process of democratisation in the daily life of all subjects, relative to their actual situation.

In that sense, a gradual distinction can be made between a very weak democracy on the one hand, and a very strong democracy on the other, expressed by the degree of the joint realisation of the basic values on all levels of society. Without ignoring the possible tension between these values, we want to emphasise that each basic value is both a positive lever and a restriction for the other values. In other words, one basic value cannot be (partially) realised without (partially) realising the other and the partial realisation of one basic value prevents the dominance by another. Referring to Figure 1.1 in Chapter 1, the basic empirical question is to what extent society actually can and will move towards a (fully) democratic division of labour.

3.3.1 Democratic division of labour between men and women, within families and organisations

The key question here is how the concept of a strong democracy can be translated to the daily life of men and women, within families and all sorts of organisations, starting from the conceptual approach. And, how can this concept be made operational? This 'translation' firstly refers to the actual development from the traditional breadwinner model in the period 1950-1960 to the moderate combination model during the past few decades. This will be dealt with in the following chapters. Following the conceptual approach, the basic normative concept and the empirical analysis, the second part of this translation concerns the development of some relevant normative future models. The last part, then, consists of determining the most useful 'normative combination model' that can serve as the basis for a coherent set of efficient policy perspectives.

In general, a fully democratic division of labour between men and women implies a sufficiently high score for and a real balance between the basic values of freedom, equality, solidarity and efficiency. All values must be realised in a sufficient way simultaneously, both stimulating and restricting each other.

On the micro level, individuals and families must have sufficient *freedom* to choose the division of labour according to their own historic background, within the societal boundaries. A democratic society needs a diversity of family types with respect to the division of labour. We are looking for a model that explicitly combines sufficient equality and free choice for employees and their families and for employers.

Equality between men and women and within families is very important but it must be achieved in a gradual way, leaving choice for all possible options to a certain extent. The logical basic objective, then, is that on average men and women have an equal division of professional labour, family tasks and other activities, in terms of the number of hours and the quality of the activity, but with sufficient diversity within the two groups. This basic value also demands that in most couple families the main activities are more or less equally divided, in a gradual way, in order to give enough room for personal choices.

The model must also meet the *solidarity* principle, implying that the share of professionally active men and women is large enough (working enough hours and days per week and enough years in their career) to realise a collective (financial) basis that can finance all social investments, including those for financially dependent people or families. The solidarity system must in itself sufficiently encourage unemployed and financially dependent people to become less dependent in the future, largely by participating in the labour market.

Finally, the *efficiency* principle must also be met, in particular by using the human capital of all men and women in a sufficiently efficient way, for professional labour, family labour and other activities. It means that all activities must reach a certain level of efficiency, in terms of the combination of personal, social, material and financial means at the input and output side (see Figures 2.5 and 2.8 in Chapter 2). For professional labour, this efficiency condition seems to be widely accepted. Yet until now a quite narrow version has been used, focusing too much on the financial and material output of the professional activities. The Combination Model emphasises that a broad efficiency concept is necessary to evaluate the different sorts of professional activities, as a basic condition for a democratic division of labour. Professional work has to offer a good balance of personal, social, material and financial results for both employees and the organisations.

Since all activities are productive labour processes, the output of which is again the input for other activities, the broad efficiency condition is also essential for family labour, social labour, education/care, personal care and leisure activities. If these activities are not (sufficiently) efficient, they offer an output/input of lower quality for other activities of the subject (again in terms of the combination of personal, social, material and financial means), with a negative effect on the efficiency of these activities. They can also have a negative effect on the activities of other subjects (individuals, family, organisation). The more activities with a lower efficiency over a longer time, the lower the overall quality of the division of labour and of the total welfare or well-being. So, if a person sleeps in an inefficient way over a longer period of time (due to inadequate inputs, for example an unhealthy sleeping room, a bad mattress, troubles with a partner, chronic back pain), this activity will have a negative influence on other activities, which in turn will lead to less adequate results for these activities, and so on. The same counts for all other activities.

Applying these basic values to the daily life of families, the normative model must be able to meet the demands or rights of all family forms or family stages during the life course: traditional couple families, families with one adult partner, families with partners of the same sex, with or without dependent children or other dependent people, and so on. At the same time, the normative model must be able to articulate and effectuate their internal and external duties or responsibilities with respect to the division of labour. Following the conceptual approach of the Combination Model, one-person and one-parent families run a higher risk of having a less efficient division of labour, mainly because of the absence of an internal division of labour between adult partners. In this perspective, it is important to examine to what extent these families actually have a less efficient division of labour. The policy model then has to provide adequate support for these families in order to realise a sufficiently efficient division of labour. Finally, the model has to deal with the needs/rights and the duties/responsibilities of socially weak and vulnerable people and families in an adequate way, enabling and encouraging them to realise an adequate combination of professional and family labour, in order to achieve a decent level of well-being.

3.3.2 Basic norms for the collective system in a strong democracy

To keep the argument simple, we concentrate on the significance of the national government for the national market system. By producing the (more) collective objects, bringing them to the market and charging for them by way of the tax system, the government strongly determines the allocation of means, activities, investments and consequently the development of more private subjects (families, clubs, companies, etc). The relative tax rates for the collective components used during the activities of the more private actors determine the cost–benefit structure of these activities and therefore also the expenses of all subjects, including that of the government itself. The central question in connection with this is whether the tax system is correct and whether it efficiently attributes the collective elements to the different factors of each activity. In this section we formulate some basic norms for a democratic market system in general, stressing the place and role of the collective basic system. In the next section we concentrate on the fiscal system, including the social security system.

Following the integrated analysis, a *first general norm* says that the national and supranational government or collective system can and must elaborate and play its 'societal' role in an active and efficient way, leaving behind the traditional theoretical and ideological thresholds. Departing from the degree of complexity of existing and possibly new activities, the relationship between the different societal levels, going from the smallest, most private to the largest, most collective organisational form, must be determined and as such be legally described. The dualist choice between the private and public sector has already largely been superseded. One must realise that when the collective system of a society is insufficiently developed, the more private organisations cannot develop their initiatives or activities efficiently. At the same time they need a correctly defined space within which they are able to produce and offer their objects in a purposeful, efficient and correct way.

Following this line, the *second norm* implies that the national and supranational government – for its own benefit and that of all other subjects – must use as much as possible the different qualitative market instruments, according to the physical divisibility of the objects produced and the possibility to charge them separately. To realise this, the collective services must be developed, produced and sold as much as possible by sufficiently autonomous organisations. These organisations are of course (to a large extent) the property of the government, as the representative public entity of the population. As a major shareholder, next to more private shareholders and the representatives of personnel, the government largely determines the basic frame and direction of the production process of these organisations. To work efficiently, daily management must be appointed to a relatively autonomous organisation. Consequently, these (gradually) collective organisations generally function in the same way in the overall market system as the more 'private' organisations, whatever their concrete legal statute, and they can/must also be evaluated in the same way. They are equally submitted to the different qualitative aspects or mechanisms of the market system. In terms of the concrete contents, of course, their activities and outputs differ to a large extent.

A *third general principle*, related to the former, is that of a basic democratic organisation at all levels of the market system. It says that the *gradual actual share* of the collective system in the production processes of the different organisations should be translated in a *gradual legal participation* of the government. So the government can codetermine the basic production policy of the very large organisations according to their complexity and, consequently, according to their impact on the total market system. With such a gradual division of the collective and private shares, according to the level of complexity (see Figure 2.7, Chapter 2), the dualist ideological gap between the private and collective system and between the economy and the political system can be bridged. It can serve as a new basis for a gradual participation of the government in the production system, permanently combining the movement in both directions, that is, gradually privatising and collectivising certain parts, according to the actual degree of complexity and efficiency. In practice, the legal share of the government in the capital of the organisations could be based on a combination of criteria expressing the actual share and impact of (the production of) the organisations in the total market system, for example the share of their total turnover in the total GDP and/or in the total turnover of the collective system, the number of branches and the physical geographic concentration of the production infrastructure.

Logically, this norm should also be applied to the actual share of employees in the production process of professional organisations. A strong democracy recognises employees as real owners of the human capital of the organisation and consequently as joint owners of the total capital of the organisation. Therefore, they should have a proportional representation in the different management organs of the organisation. In that way, the interests of the human capital (employees) can be fully defended, next to the interests of the owners of the material and financial capital. As a consequence, employees can also enjoy a proportional share of the net profit of the organisation, as compensation for the contribution of the human capital to the financial result. The other side of the democratic principle is that the representatives of employees in the management organs are also jointly responsible for major decisions in the organisation, including decisions with a negative impact on the division of labour, number of jobs, quality of the work, wages, working time schedules, and so on.

3.3.3 Basic norms for a democratic fiscal system

Due to the limited physical or organisational divisibility towards the customers, the government always has to produce and distribute a number of highly collective goods/ services that largely need to be financed by way of fiscal contributions (taxes or social security contributions). Since the government or collective system is a productive system acting in the market next to all other systems, it is important that its services are being charged for efficiently and correctly. The basis for the payment therefore is the *actual use* of government services by the different subjects in their activities. The taxation system must therefore approach this actual use as correctly as possible. The *fourth basic norm* then states that the payment of collective services must be carried out as close as possible to the transactions between the different subjects. The most adequate instrument for this is a general transaction tax, whatever concrete form this might have. It has the fundamental advantage that all subjects and services are being taxed in an equal way, according to the basic criteria or components of the production structure (see Figure 2.8). At the same time, the subjects (can) effectively take into consideration the real costs of the collective services that they actually used and/or can use. The *general transaction tax* is an alternative for the complicated fiscal systems in all countries with many tax forms: direct income tax, company tax, indirect tax (mainly value-added tax and excises), different forms of 'eco-taxes' and all other specific levies.

In the traditional economic approach, the public sector is not seen as a normal productive actor and taxes (mainly income taxes) are often associated with 'skimming' the results or benefits of private companies (the so-called 'real' economic actors). Consequently, the government should only be active in the societal domains the private companies are not interested in.

In the integrated approach, the government or the collective system is a normal productive actor. Moreover, it constitutes the basis or foundation of society and the market system, without determining its relative 'share' or 'weight' in an absolute and definite way. It can and must likewise take productive initiatives and fully charge its goods/services, including the (possible) surplus value. The general transaction tax is the adequate expression of the principal theoretical equality of the different subjects and their activities and of the complexity principle, saying that all labour processes of all 'lower' or more private organisations use a specific amount and quality of collective objects. It is the government's main instrument to produce and distribute its (largely) collective objects in an efficient way. It is clear that the public companies that autonomously act in the market as other more private organisations (according to the second norm) are also submitted to the general transaction tax.

Departing from the analysis of the basic components of the labour and exchange process of the subjects and from the former basic norms for the collective system, it is possible to formulate some basic *norms or criteria for a democratic tax system*, to realise a good balance of basic values in the market system. The following fundamental argument applies here: if specific components of the labour process are not being taxed sufficiently in proportion to the government services used for their production and the resulting (negative) outputs, the private costs being charged are too low for the organisation with regard to actual societal costs. The consequence is that the organisation systematically uses that factor more often, which in turn results in a systematic distortion of the total societal division of labour. The relative tax burden refers to the basic components of the labour processes.

The first norm says that only the *monetary part of the external transactions between legally recognised subjects* is submitted to a fiscal charge. This means that the tax burden relatively decreases as the monetary part becomes smaller. The norm contains two elements. First, taxes can only be levied on external transactions between legally recognised subjects. Internal transactions within families and organisations, therefore, are not submitted to the tax system. This distinction is gradual and depends on the legal definition of the subjects. If the national government also charges the internal transactions, the legal definition, demarcation and protection itself would become meaningless. Every organisation is in fact an 'internal market' that also has an internal 'tax system' to charge for the collective elements of the internal transactions. All forms of collective charging ('fiscal systems') are thus integrated on the different levels of the overall market system (see Figure 2.7).

Second, the monetary character of a transaction is the combined expression of the external character or the market orientation, legal recognition, frequency, regularity, origin and development of the object, degree of labour specialisation, complexity and input of collective services. The higher the combined score of a transaction on these elements, the larger the monetary part. This has to be linked to the degree of reciprocity, in terms of direct human benefits for both parties involved. So a friendship can frequently and regularly bring along transactions, but both subjects largely focus on the direct human output. A lawyer also provides human services but the direct human benefit is only a small share of the output they have in view. Individuals and families are legally recognised subjects that are consequently submitted to the tax system.

The norm is also necessary for practical reasons because the collective system is not able to deal with all non-monetary personal elements of the transactions of all subjects.

The financial cost of registering them all would greatly supersede the possible fiscal revenues.

The second norm refers to the *proportion of human and non-human labour or capital* in the input–output processes and says that the total average tax rate must be the same for human and non-human labour/capital. After all, there are no reasons to assume that, on average, more collective goods/services are used for the production of one of both forms of labour/capital.

The central point here is the choice of society with respect to the overall development of human and non-human capital. If, for example, non-human capital is in general submitted to relatively lower taxes than human capital, in proportion to the actual societal costs needed for its production, the subjects will systematically spend relatively more means on objects with a higher share of non-human labour/capital. After all, the demand for and supply of human and non-human capital is determined on the micro level by (the management of) the different organisations, which depart from the particular relative costs and benefits of the two factors. This means that they will invest relatively faster and more in new and better forms of non-human or material capital. When this mechanism is imbedded in society, it results in the qualitative and quantitative neglect or postponement of (some major parts of) the human capital. Furthermore, this process has major differential consequences for the subjects in society, since they strongly differ in the proportion of human and non-human labour/capital. If higher taxes are levied on human capital in general, the subjects with a relatively higher intensity of human labour must carry part of the collective burden of the other subjects. In the long run, such a process implies a systematic distortion and a transfer of means from human-intensive activities to non-human-intensive activities and organisations.

A third aspect is the *complexity level of the subjects*. In general, a more complex subject makes more use of collective services, both in absolute and relative terms. The main reason is that along with the separate use by the partial subjects, some additional use is made by the more complex entity. For more complex organisations, the government must provide more complex services that cost more. A more complex system is automatically more collective, which means that the 'share' of collective services is relatively bigger. In order to take into account the different complexity of subjects (human and non-human capital), it is necessary to use *progressive transaction taxes*. It is then necessary to agree on the criteria needed to determine the degree of complexity. So it is possible to reach a (more) correct tuning of the actual collective level of an organisation and the legal title or the distribution of the shares between the more private and more collective actors.

The fourth norm states that the tax system must charge for the *negative collective elements (human and material damage)* of the production system in a correct way. If no extra taxes are levied on the labour processes with a relatively higher share of damage in the (human and/or non-human) output, regardless of the actual reason, too much of that output is systematically being produced in proportion to the actual societal costs. As long as this relative tax advantage exists, distortion or inefficiency will continue to exist because individual subjects react to the particular costs that are being charged, which results in the fact that they systematically pay insufficiently. This basic problem can only be solved by the general evaluation of all labour processes in terms of the quality of the human and non-human inputs and outputs. Since every labour process produces human and/or non-human damage to a certain extent, this damage must be charged in all transactions. This can be achieved by means of a variable transaction tax, according to the degree of damage caused by the activities.

Furthermore, with a general transaction tax the profit (monetary surplus value of the labour processes and transactions) is automatically being charged. The tax can be seen as payment for the share of the collective system in (the result of) the different production processes at lower levels.

Finally, we should not forget the other side of the tax coin. In addition to the use of collective means at the input side, one has to determine to what extent the different more private subjects produce positive collective benefits for society. In a democratic collective system, these collective benefits should be 'paid' to the more private organisations producing them, by means of a correct, transparent and gradual 'subsidy' system.

3.4   Comparison with other models

Generally speaking, the normative view of the combination scenario (Commissie Dagindeling, 1998; Plantenga and Schippers, 2000), the TLM model (Schmid and Gazier, 2002; Schmid and Schomann, 2004), the flexicuritymodel, the dual earner/dual carer model (Gornick and Meyers, 2003) and the breadwinner-caregiver models (Fraser, 1994, 2006) can be placed under this broad normative approach. All these models are developed from the basic challenge of going beyond the traditional welfare state and finding new perspectives for the future welfare state, largely aiming at a stronger democracy on all levels of society. Yet we notice that all these models still largely use the concept of democracy in the traditional sense and not so much as a general normative concept for daily life in (all parts of) society.

Schmid and Gazier (2002) implicitly express the normative view of the TLM model when they evaluate the European social model, proposing a 'new employment compact' for Europe. The same counts for Muffels and Ester (2004). Four basic normative criteria or values are used to evaluate the employment models for Europe and the more specific policy perspectives: individual freedom (or autonomy), solidarity between different societal groups, effectiveness and efficiency. The most striking thing is the absence of the basic value of (gender) equality in the formal evaluative approach. However, further explanation and practical applications of the TLM model illustrate that (gender) equality is also an important principle or objective.

More or less the same can be said about the normative flexicurity model, which is fairly easy to understand given the strong link with the TLM model. The basic normative view behind the practical normative matrix is not explicitly clarified, but further explanation of the policy strategy illustrates that largely the same values are actually taken as a normative starting point.

Gornick and Meyers (2003) do not give an explicit formulation and explanation of the basic normative concept underlying the dual earner/dual carer model, but the presentation of the normative future model clarifies the importance of the values of 'free choice' and 'equality' with respect to the daily life of men and women. Placed within the larger context of the welfare state, they also emphasise the solidarity principle as a basis for the development of (more) adequate societal provisions for families and organisations. Evaluating (the effect of) the different policy packages and perspectives in different countries, a fairly broad efficiency principle is also being used, relative to the other basic values.

On the contrary, Fraser (1994, 2006) explicitly formulates the normative approach of the three future policy models that she presents. Similar to our normative challenge, she also starts from the unsatisfying development of the division of labour between men and women in the period 1970-90 in terms of (gender) equity and the different (normative) reactions of the separate feminist groups. Although she finds the still largely unequal division of labour unsatisfactory, she is strongly convinced that normative theorising remains an indispensable enterprise for feminism and for all social movements. Society needs a vision of the future division of labour and a set of standards for evaluating various policy proposals. She argues that the equality/difference impasse is real and cannot be simply sidestepped or embraced.

Fraser fully recognises the need and value of developing a new future ideal model or view for the division of labour that can orient and guide scientists and policy makers on their long and difficult journey. She also thinks that a (sufficiently) broad agreement on the future normative model could make that long journey much easier and effective.

From that standpoint, she conceptualises the broad concept of gender equity, in the broad sense of 'fairness or justice', as a complex normative principle, consisting of five distinct norms for different aspects of the daily life of men and women in society. These central norms must be realised jointly and sufficiently in order to be able to speak of real gender equity. First, the anti-poverty principle must be met, implying a minimum income for all (adult) men and women. In addition, the anti-exploitation principle demands that all men and women should become sufficiently independent in their division of labour. Third, she proposes three equality principles, each referring to a major aspect of daily life: income equality, leisure time equality and equality of respect. The latter means that a new attitude with respect to the division of labour must be realised, respecting all groups in an equal way. The anti-marginalisation principle expresses the need for the full participation of all men and women in all basic activities. Finally, the anti-androcentrism principle implies that men also will change their view, attitudes and actual behaviour during the next decades.

As previously said, the five norms must be realised together to have real gender equity. Moreover, equity must also be applied to other societal issues, implying the need for ethnic equity, generational equity, class equity, and so on. Finally, (gender) equity must be placed next to some other basic values in society, in particular liberty/freedom and efficiency, in order to have an integrated normative approach to the division of labour within the modern welfare state.

Fraser uses this normative approach to evaluate the actual division of labour and some ideal models of the future division of labour and the welfare state. The key question here is also how society should allocate (the responsibility for) care work between families, civil society, professional organisations and the state. Fraser then presents the universal caregiver model as the model that maximally satisfies all the normative principles.

Although her vocabulary is largely different from ours, Fraser's set of normative principles is fairly similar to the basic values we have formulated, without, however, using the general concept of democracy. These values have to be translated to all basic aspects of daily life: the division of basic activities, the division of personal, social, material and financial capital and the decision making processes.

As for the conceptual approach, therefore, it is useful to develop more international collaboration to compare and improve the normative view of the different models of the division of labour. Starting from these experiences, one can look at how to streamline the basic normative concepts.

FOUR

Actual evolution of the division of professional and family labour

This chapter explores the *actual division of professional and family labour* in EU countries and some other OECD countries. By means of some basic indicators that were formerly developed for Flanders/Belgium, we show the general development in different (types of) countries from the *strong male breadwinner model* in the period 1950-70 to a *moderate combination model* in the period 1985-2005. These models can be compared with similar models presented by other researchers, for example Crompton (1999) and Gornick and Meyers (2003).

In the first section we start with a wider historical perspective, illustrating the general development since 1850. In fact, this can be seen as the long development from the 'old combination model' or 'survival model' in the 18th and 19th century to the traditional breadwinner model in the 20th century, as shown in Figure 1.1 (Vanhaute, 1997a, 1997b, 2002; Van Dongen, 1993; Van Dongen et al, 2001, Van Dongen and Danau, 2003).

The second section explores a general historical model for the period 1950-2005, covering three historical periods or partial models. This analysis is based on two general indicators presented in a graphical way: total activity rate and average number of hours of professional and family labour of men and women, both for the total groups and for the different age groups. These data show that the empirical model is applicable in all countries of the western world. At the same time, the gradual differences between the (types of) welfare states will be shown.

In the third section, the actual development in the period 1985-2005 is illustrated by means of some complementary indicators: general labour situation of the male and female population, general division of the main activities, professional activity rates of men and women by age group, division of the number of hours of professional labour, family labour, leisure time and personal care, average number of hours by age group of professional labour, family labour, leisure time and personal care and some other aspects of the working time of men and women (temporary work, shift work, night work, Sunday work and working at home). The combination of the indicators gives a differentiated picture of the evolution of the division of professional and family labour in western countries, which is compatible with the longer-term picture in the first sections.

4.1 Historical evolution of the division of labour between 1850 and 2000

Together with many other researchers (for example, Sullerot, 1979; Lis, 1984; Segalen, 1986; Folbre, 1991; Smith and Wallerstein, 1992; Seccombe, 1992, 1993; Vanhaute, 1992, 1997a, 1997b, 2002; de Vries, 1994; Horell and Humphries, 1995, 1997; Creighton, 1996, 1999; Janssens, 1997; Goldscheider, 2002; Gornick and Meyers, 2003; Schmidt, 2005; Goldin, 2006; van Poppel et al, 2006) we have always placed the development of the division of labour in the period 1950-2000 in a broader historical perspective, for example the period 1750-2000 as shown in Figure 1.1 (Van Dongen, 1990, 1993; Van Dongen et al, 1998, 2001; Van Dongen and Danau, 2003).

During the past few decades, many contemporary economic and sociological researchers or research groups have tried to explain the increasing labour market participation of women since 1950, often starting from the basic idea that the labour market participation of women was always very low during previous centuries. In fact, they paid little attention to the long-term development during previous centuries.

The basic idea of the (fairly recent) broader historical research is that the dominance of the 'breadwinner model' in the 20th century cannot be observed in previous centuries. According to many modern historians, most women have always been economically active within the context of the household economy and small-scale local enterprises, in that way directly contributing to both the household and the market production process. A certain part of the production of men and women in the local economy was used within the household and the other part was offered/sold on the local markets, with a relatively high level of non-monetary trading. This 'market-oriented part' of production must be seen as the professional labour or 'paid job' of men and women. Productive activities of women were generally located in or around the home, while productive activities of men were generally located outside and away from the house(hold). Therefore, it was more difficult to distinguish between the 'market' and 'household' work of women than of men.

Mainly based on a diversity of micro data, these historical studies show that in previous centuries most families had to pool two or more 'jobs' (market activities) and incomes to make ends meet, according to the average welfare level of most (poor) people. So at that time, most families were 'multi-earner families' or 'combination families'. By their active participation in the local economy, women had a relatively strong position in the daily division of labour, albeit within generally poor living conditions. All ordinary men and women had to work hard to realise a minimum welfare level, both within and outside the household. This period could therefore be described in terms of a real 'combination model', essentially being a 'survival model' (Figure 1.1), within a strongly patriarchal society.

Between 1850 and 1940, women were increasingly forced out of the labour market in all western countries, step by step, consciously or not, by means of several mechanisms or instruments such as restrictive laws, rules of conduct, wage discrimination and subsidies, working conditions, dismissal of women who became pregnant or pregnancy leave without pay, stereotyping, special taxes, and so on. In all countries, the male breadwinner family, with its very unequal division of professional and family labour between men and women, increasingly became the new ideal family type. The underlying idea was that the main job of the husband should result in a 'family wage' that was sufficient to support the whole family. This new family model first found support in the higher social circles and then spread to the different layers of the working population.

Decade after decade, the professional position of women systematically weakened, both in quantitative and qualitative terms, albeit with a different intensity and timing in the different countries and regions within countries. By the end of the 19th century or the beginning of the 20th century, the broad labour movement, including the socialist unions, strongly promoted the new male breadwinner model, largely neglecting the basic gender-related problems that would follow from it (Seccombe, 1986, 1993). In fact, by introducing the male breadwinner model and the male 'family wage', the effective basis for a stable family income resulting from the paid work of both partners was undermined for many decades.

It is interesting to note that during past decades many historical researchers have tried to explain the origin and rise of the male breadwinner family and the housewife from the first half of the 19th century to the middle of the 20th century. This research is important for better understanding the increasing (re-)entry of women in the labour market since 1950. After all, the transformation process from the old combination model to the breadwinner model is as complex as the recent process from the breadwinner model to the modern combination model. This research reveals the same interactive process between the major components of daily life (basic activities and different means) of men and women in a complex society (see Figures 2.7 and 2.8). Both long-term transformation processes can be presented and explained with the conceptual approach of the Combination Model, albeit in the opposite direction and under different societal circumstances.

Unfortunately, it is very difficult to find internationally comparative macro data for this period. After all, the distinction between the family-oriented and market-oriented part of the production process was not so clear in practice at that time, especially for women. Consequently, one cannot expect a decent registration of the daily division of professional and family labour during that period. Even for the total activity rate, as the most general indicator, strong and consistent macro data can hardly be found in the different countries for the period 1800-1940.

It is useful to mention that the actual expulsion of women from the official labour market in the period 1800-1900 went hand in hand with the expulsion of 'new' housewives from official labour market statistics, mostly national censuses that became common since the middle of the 19th century. Folbre (1991) clearly describes that process of statistical devaluation of domestic work for England, Wales, Australia and the US. In the period 1800-1850, the domestic work of women was still largely seen as productive, market-oriented work and integrated in the national census. The rise of the male breadwinner model encouraged the conceptual distinction between 'productive market work' and 'non-productive housework'. Consequently, the 'new' housewives (and their housework) were increasingly removed from labour market statistics. In the first stage, they were still placed in a separate category, such as 'without occupation', 'keeping the house' or 'non-productive', implying that their housework was not seen as economically relevant. The devaluation process was completed around 1900 when housewives were mostly categorised as 'dependents' and their work was seen as economically non-productive. Until now, labour market statistics have excluded housewives from the 'professional population'. The productive work in the household and the structural unemployment of these women have been hidden for many decades (Van Dongen, 1993, 1998; Van Dongen et al, 2001).

During past decades we collected data to connect different parts of the long period 1845-2004 to give an overall view of the development of the division of labour of men and women in Belgium. Figure 4.1 illustrates this historical view by means of the officially registered total activity rate of Belgian men and women, that is, the percentage of all men and women registered as having a paid job. It is the most general labour market indicator and as such, the indicator also gives a general idea of the economic basis of the country. As we can see, the lowest participation rate of women is clearly observed in the period 1950-1960, after a long period with a systematically decreasing activity rate. Yet we strongly suppose that for the period 1800-1940, the official activity rate of (lower-class) women is an under-estimation of their real activity rate. After all, many women working in the local household economy were not registered as being professionally active. To a lesser extent, the same holds for the period after 1920, during which a certain number of officially registered 'housewives' were working in the (black) market.

Figure 4.2 gives the same picture for the Netherlands, based on Pott–Buter's research (1993) and completed with Labour Force Survey (LFS) data for the period 1990-2004.

The Dutch picture emphasises two major differences compared to the Belgian picture. In the first place, the total activity rate of women was already low in 1850 and remained low until 1970. A possible explanation is that the decline in the total activity rate of

Figure 4.1   The total activity rate of Belgian men and women in the period 1845-2003

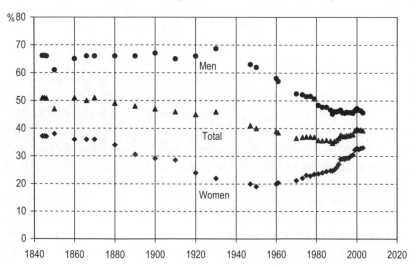

Figure 4.2   The total activity rate of Dutch men and women in the period 1845-2003

women started some decades earlier than in Belgium, due to the specific economic and cultural situation in the Netherlands at that time. However, due to the lack of data about the earlier periods, it is difficult to verify this argument. In this context, van Poppel et al (2006) offer interesting data about the occupational participation of women at the moment of marriage in the period 1812-1915, based on the marriage certificates of women in five provinces of the Dutch Republic. In their approach, marriage is seen as a major life event that largely determines the future division of labour within families. The bold curve for all married women in Figure 4.4 shows that in the period 1845-55 about 50% of married women had an occupation at the time of marriage. However, these data cannot tell us to what extent and how fast married women left the labour market after their marriage, for example *after* the birth of the first child. The second difference with Belgium is that the re-entry of women since 1970 occurred at a higher speed in the Netherlands, in particular as a result of the much stronger increase in number of (small) part-time jobs. This aspect will be discussed again at a later stage.

Figure 4.3 shows the same development in the UK until 1990, again suggesting that the larger decline in the participation rate of women had started some decades earlier than in Belgium. Given the empirical support from different historical micro-studies, we can hold this strong hypothesis for the other countries. Against the basic idea of many people, this process also occurred in the Nordic countries to a large extent, as is illustrated by recent historical research (Christiansen et al, 2006; Borchorst, 2008; Lundqvist, 2008; Melby et al, 2008; Ravn, 2008). Yet, the societal forces for a more equal division of labour were relatively stronger in these countries, leading to a less dominant or powerful breadwinner policy.

The rise of the breadwinner model during the 19th century is a story of substantial differences between professional or social classes at the beginning of the process and a story of convergence during the long process. Van Poppel et al (2006) clearly show this process for married women in five provinces of the Dutch Republic in the period

Figure 4.3   The total activity rate of British men and women in the period 1850-1990

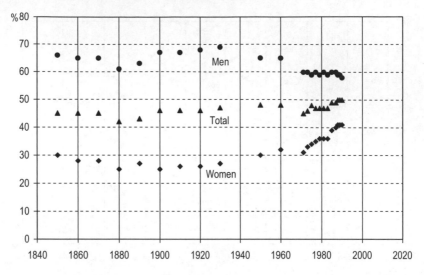

1812-1915 (see Figure 4.4). The idea of the male breadwinner family was introduced by the upper classes and then systematically spread to the lower classes over the course of many decades. In the Dutch Republic, at the start of the 19th century, the housewife was already a common phenomenon in the higher and middle classes. Less than 10% of the wives of men in the highest professional groups had an occupation at the time of marriage. At the other end, 60%-80% of the wives of men in the low professional groups had an occupation at the time of marriage. The development of the activity rate

Figure 4.4   Percentage of Dutch women with an occupation at the time of marriage, by professional class of the husband and period of marriage (1812-1922)

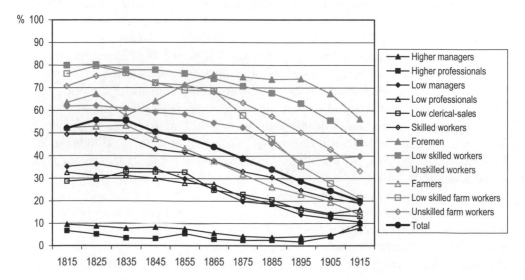

at the time of marriage for all married women is given by the bold black curve, starting from an activity rate of about 56% in 1825 to an activity rate of 20% in 1915-20.

Decade after decade, the new normative model of the housewife and male breadwinner found its way into the lower classes that systematically decreased their (official) female labour force participation, in particular in the period 1860-1920. This process was different in the five provinces, according to the degree of urbanisation and socioeconomic context. By 1920, the choice for women to enter marriage without an occupation was dominant among all classes. Yet about 20%-50% of lower-class wives were professionally active at the time of their marriage. Van Poppel et al (2006) illustrate the strong influence of societal norms on the daily division of labour, in interaction with the other main components of societal life. Due to a lack of data about the earlier periods, they cannot show when and how the breadwinner model was spread among the higher classes.

4.2   Historical evolution of the division of professional and family labour between 1950 and 2000

Following the conceptual approach and the empirical data for the period 1850-1950, one can formulate empirical models for the period 1950-2000, using some complementary indicators:

- total activity rate of men and women as a general labour market indicator, as part of the long-term development in Figures 4.1-4.4;
- average number of hours spent on professional, family and total labour (sum of both activities) of men and women;
- average number of hours spent on professional, family and total labour of men and women, for the different age groups.

4.2.1 Total activity rate of men and women

Figure 4.5 shows the total activity rate of men and women in the period 1960-2003 in a number of countries and regions. It is part of the long-term development in Figures 4.1-4.4, also giving a general idea of the economic basis of these countries/regions during this period.

This indicator can be compared with the share of the traditional professional population (percentage of people having or looking for a job) and with the traditional activity rate (percentage of professionally active men and women within the professional population or within the age group 18-64 years).

It shows the general development in most countries, with a systematic decline in the total activity rate of men and a systematic increase in the total activity rate of women. Yet in 2003, all countries still show a significant difference between men and women, with the smallest difference (highest activity rate of women) in the Nordic and English-speaking countries and the most substantial difference (lowest activity rate of women) in the southern European countries of Italy, Spain and Greece. The Netherlands and

Figure 4.5 Total activity rate of men and women in some countries, 1961-2003

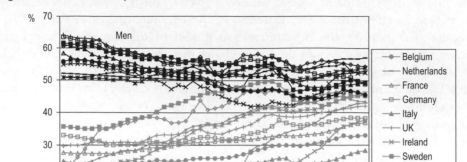

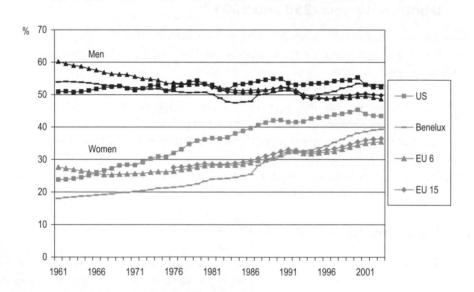

Ireland also showed a very low activity rate for women until 1980, but it increased strongly afterwards. In the continental countries of France, Germany and Belgium, the activity rate increased in a more constant way but at a slower rate.

As expected, the differences between the countries/regions are much more significant for women than for men. Therefore, the differences between women largely determine the gradual distinction between the types of welfare states.

We do not give the figure for the development of the traditional professional population since it is largely similar, albeit that all curves are somewhat higher, depending on the official unemployment rate in the different countries/regions during this period. The same counts for the evolution of the traditional activity rate (percentage of professionally active men and women within the age group 18-64 years). The shape of the curves is largely similar, but all percentages are higher (between 80% and 90% for men and between 30% and 50% for women), since this reference group (denominator) is much smaller.

4.2.2 Average number of hours of professional and family labour

4.2.2.1 Presentation of the general model

Figure 4.5 does not tell us anything about the number of hours of professional or family work. Therefore, Figure 4.6 shows a general hypothetical model of the development of professional labour (PL) and family labour (FL) between men and women in the period 1950-2005. It also gives the development of the total labour (TL) of men and women, being the sum of professional and family labour. The curves show the average number of hours spent on these activities in the different years. The model is complementary to the previous one, illustrating the historical development in a simple but clear way. The bold black lines of *professional labour* (PL) express the hypothesis that the average number of hours of men declined systematically, from almost 50 hours/week in 1950 to 37 hours/week in 2005, while the average number of hours of women increased systematically from about 15 hours/week in 1950 to 25 hours/week in 2005. The grey lines give the inverse evolution of total *family work*: the average number of hours of women declined systematically, from about 42 hours/week in 1950 to 30 hours/week in 2005, while the average number of hours of men increased systematically from about 8 hours/week in 1950 to about 17 hours/week in 2005.

Figure 4.6 A general hypothetical model of the division of labour between men and women in the period 1950-2005: the average number of hours of professional labour (PL), family labour (FL) and total labour (TL)

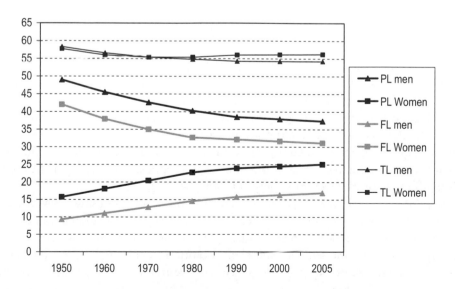

The upper thin black lines show the almost equal evolution of the total labour of men and women. In general, this means that the total workload of men and women has been largely equal during this long period. Moreover, the figure suggests that it almost remained at the same level, around 55 hours/week. Yet it says that from 1980 on, the average number of hours of women became somewhat larger than that of men. The reason is that the number of hours of professional labour of women increased somewhat more than the number of hours of family work of men. This refers to the 'lagged adaptation process' of men, as formulated by Gershuny et al (1994) and Gershuny (2000).

This hypothetical model is largely in line with the long-term view in Figures 4.1-4.5. The advantage of the general model in Figure 4.6 is the clear and simple presentation of the general historical development, making abstraction of the differences according to age, education, family type, etc. However, before 2000, systematic comparative data for sufficient countries and sufficient years were not available.

The model has been derived from some recent empirical analyses of the division of professional and household work, showing the development during this longer period. These studies are largely based on the broad MTUS database that has been collected piece by piece during the past 20 years (Gershuny, 2000).

If we only look at the period 1980-2005 (which is the case in many studies), the picture suggests a rather 'pessimistic' perspective on the historical division of labour (a 'stalled revolution'), implying that the increasing participation of women in professional labour did not lead to a significant increase in the participation of men in family labour. By bringing data together for a longer period, the more 'optimistic' perspective becomes visible, saying that the increasing participation of women in professional labour (expressed by the participation rate and number of hours) during the past five decades went hand in hand with an increase in the participation of men in family labour (participation rate and average number of hours).

Bianchi et al (2000) show that this model largely expresses the actual development of the division of household work in the US. More recently, Aguiar and Hurst (2006) and Bianchi et al (2006) give more evidence for the development of professional labour, family labour and leisure time in the US, based on the time use data of the period 1965-2003. The figure resulting from these data is very similar to Figure 4.6.

Gershuny (2000) presents a broader comparative analysis, with data for separate countries and with pooled data, showing that the model comes out rather well. He emphasises the notion of the 'lagged adaptation', that is, the slow reaction of two-earner families to redistribute household tasks, in particular the slow adaptation of men to increase their engagement in family work. This is mainly related to the complexity of the long-term interactive process, containing some opposite aspects, partial processes or impediments on all levels of society (Figures 2.7-2.9).

Hook (2005a, 2005b) presents a sophisticated multilevel analysis using the MTUS data of about 20 countries. She shows to a certain degree the complex interaction between different aspects of the long process in the period 1965-2000. She also corroborates to a large extent the model, with sufficient attention to the differences between the (types of) welfare states. She concludes that one cannot speak of a stalled revolution but of a clear and systematic movement towards a more equal division of professional and family work, both in absolute and relative terms. Yet the gap between men and women is still fairly large in all countries, illustrating that it was not easy to further decrease that gap since 1980. Therefore, more attention should go to both the positive and negative feedback processes during this long period, avoiding the either/or story and the chicken or the egg dilemma of the different partial models.

Unfortunately, we were not able to use the original MTUS datasets that contained data for some countries for the period 1960-80. Therefore, we are very grateful to Jennifer Hook, who provided us with the necessary tables, based on the MTUS datasets (Hook, 2005a, 2005b) for men and women of age 20-59 years. We selected eight western countries with at least two useable observation years (covering a sufficiently long period): the US (1965, 1975, 1985, 1998, 2003), the UK (1975, 1987, 2000), Norway (1981, 1990, 2000), the Netherlands (1975, 1985, 2000), Canada (1971, 1986, 1998), France (1965, 1974, 1998), Germany (1965, 1992) and Belgium (1965, 1999, 2004). The Belgian data for 1999 and 2004 are in fact data for Flanders coming from the TOR research group of the University of Brussels (Glorieux and Moens, 2001; Glorieux and Vandeweyer, 2001; Glorieux et al, 2003, 2006). Starting from the available observation years, a simple estimate was made of the average number of hours of men and women for the missing years. In that way, a trend line was created for each country for the period 1965-2000 with an observed or estimated value every five years. Next, a general trend line was calculated for all these countries together, based on the relative share of the population of each country in the reference group. We assume that these countries sufficiently represent the western world.

Because many European countries are not included, we have given the US a weight of 50% in the general trend line, more or less the share of the US population in the total population of the western world. Gradual changes in the relative weight of the US population hardly influence the average trend line. Consequently, introducing additional countries would not change the general trend line significantly.

4.2.2.2 Average number of hours of professional labour

Figure 4.7 shows the development of the average number of hours per week of professional labour (excluding commuting time) in the eight countries. The upper curves for men are presented in black, the lower curves for women are in grey.

The actual evolution of the number of hours of professional labour largely follows the basic (moderately optimistic) model, at the same time showing the gradual differences between the countries. Only the Netherlands is an outlier, with a much lower average number of hours for women and for men (until 1980). After 1980 the number of hours of men increased again, largely maintaining the gap with women. Almost the same process can be observed in the UK, where 1985 is a turning point.

During the past two decades, the decrease in the gap between men and women continues at a lower speed, confirming the idea that policy in the period 1980-2000 did not manage to further decrease that gap. The meaning of the general model and

Figure 4.7   Average number of hours of professional labour of men and women (20-59
years) in some countries (1965-2000)

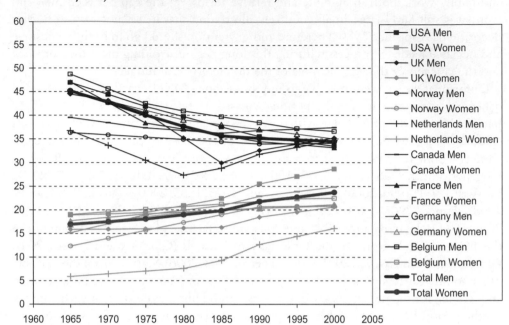

this last observation is very important for the policy debate on the desirable future
development of the division of labour.

4.2.2.3   *Average number of hours of family labour*

Complementary to this, Figure 4.8 presents the development of the average number
of hours per week spent on family labour in these countries. The black curves for men
are now at the bottom and the grey curves of women at the top.

The development of the hours of family labour follows the basic model in Figure
4.6 very neatly, again with the gradual differences between the countries, albeit smaller
than for professional labour. In fact, there are no outliers for family labour. Also for
family labour, the difference between men and women has been decreasing at a lower
rate during the past two decades. The basic policy question is then how to deal with
this process in the future.

In most countries, lower-educated women had fewer hours of professional labour
than higher-educated women during the whole period and the differences remained
more or less stable. Lower-educated men had more hours of professional labour than
higher-educated men until approximately 1985 in most countries, but it turned around
afterwards and the gap increased during the past decades.

In all countries, lower-educated women had more hours of family labour than higher-
educated women during the whole period, but the differences decreased to a certain
extent. The difference between lower and higher-educated men was very small during
the whole period, but followed the development of professional labour in a reversed

Figure 4.8   Average number of hours of family labour of men and women (20-59 years) in some countries (1965-2000)

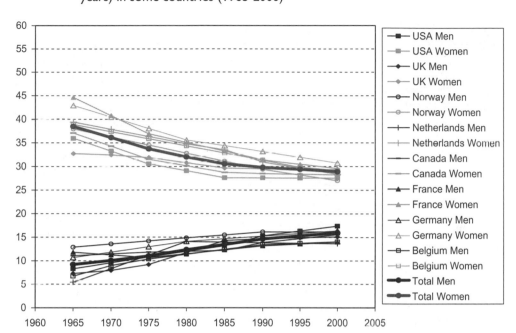

way: lower-educated men had fewer hours of family labour than higher-educated men until approximately 1985 in most countries and it turned around afterwards.

4.2.2.4 Evolution of the number of hours of total labour

Finally, Figure 4.9 gives the evolution of the hours of total labour in these countries, that is, the sum of the hours of professional and family labour. Here, a completely different picture emerges, as was expected from the conceptual and the historical model. While professional and family labour separately show significant (gradual) differences between men and women in all countries, the total labour of men and women is on average largely equally divided in all countries. This 'on average equality' for total labour, however, hides a still large inequality for both professional and family labour and a possible large inequality in a number of couple families.

The average trend lines for all countries show that the average number of hours of total labour for women is somewhat larger than that for men during the whole period. The increase of this difference since 1985 is completely related to the development in the US (see Figure 4.10). When we calculate trend lines for the European countries, the line of women is higher than that of men during the whole period, but the evolution is the other way around. The gap is then higher in the period 1965-80 and decreases systematically in the period 1980-2000.

The differences according to education level are not that clear since they are the result of the differences in professional and family labour. In all countries, total labour

Figure 4.9   Average number of hours of total labour of men and women (20-59 years) in some countries (1965-2000)

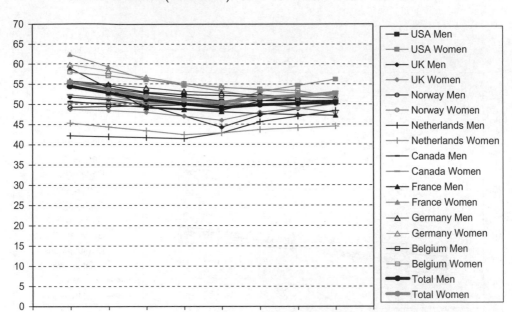

of lower- and higher-educated women is largely equal until about 1985. In the UK and Canada, this remains so until 2000. In the US, the total labour of lower-educated women becomes larger than that of higher-educated women, while the total labour of lower-educated men becomes smaller than that of higher-educated men. In Norway, the Netherlands and Belgium, total labour of lower-educated men and women becomes smaller than that of higher-educated men and women, while in France and Germany it is the other way around.

Figure 4.10 presents for each country separately the development of the average number of hours of professional, family and total labour of men and women in the same period. We can observe some interesting differences in that evolution.

In France, Germany and Belgium, the number of hours of total labour of women has been larger during the whole period, but the difference has decreased systematically, to become small to very small in 2000. The Netherlands shows the same process until 1985, but afterwards men had more hours and the gap increased. Canada and the UK had a very slow evolution to an equal number of hours in 2000, but with two more turning points in the UK. In the US, men had more hours of total labour until 1985, but from that year on it turned around and the difference increased. In Norway, the hours of total labour of men and women were very equal during the whole period, but since 1990, the hours of total labour of women decreased while those of men remained the same.

Figure 4.10 Average number of hours of professional, family and total labour of men and women (20-59 years) in some countries (1965-2000)

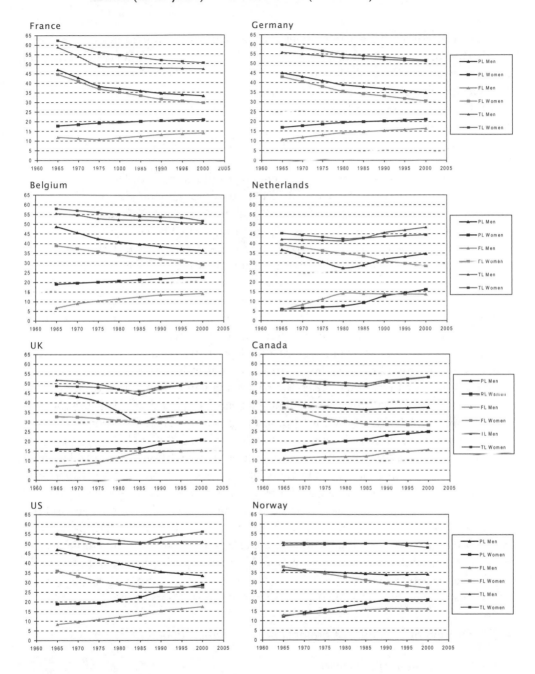

4.2.3 Average number of hours of professional and family labour for different age groups

In this section we show the development of the average number of hours of professional, family and total labour for different age groups (from 20-59 years), between 1965 and 2000. According to the available data, different years are given for the different countries. Notwithstanding the limited available data, the figures give additional support for the general historical model in Figure 4.6. Figure 4.11 illustrates the development of the average number of hours of professional labour of men and women for different age groups, Figure 4.12 shows the development of family labour and Figure 4.13 that of total labour.

According to Figure 4.11, the most recent curves of professional labour of men and women are closer to one another than earlier curves. In general, this is related to an increase in the number of hours of women in almost all age groups and a decrease in the number of hours of men in almost all age groups. For France, Germany, Belgium and the US, the gap between the 1965 curves is much larger than that between the most recent curves. Although we lack the earlier data for the other countries, we can strongly suppose the same idea. At the same time, one can see that after 1970-80, the process slows down. In some countries, the number of hours of men increased again (for some age groups), for example the Netherlands, Canada and the UK. We shall look at the period 1980-2004 more closely later on, using annual LFS data.

Figure 4.12 shows the same process for family labour: in all countries, the gap between the most recent curves of men and women is significantly smaller than that between the earliest curves. In most countries, the narrowing gap is related to a large decrease in the number of hours of women in almost all age groups and to a (smaller) increase in the number of hours of men in almost all age groups. Again, we notice that the process slows down after 1970-80.

Finally, Figure 4.13 presents the development of the total labour of men and women during this period. In general, all the curves lie very close to one another, supporting the general model in Figure 4.6. Yet some gradual differences are visible. In France, Germany and Belgium, the curves for 1965 are higher than the later curves and the curves for women are a little higher than those for men. In the UK, the US, Canada and Norway, the curves for the total workload are almost the same over the whole period, with almost no differences between men and women. The Netherlands show a fairly large difference between men and women in 1975, but this gap almost disappeared afterwards, largely due to the increase in the professional hours of men.

4.2.4 Division of the hours of professional and family labour

4.2.4.1 *Presentation of the model*

This section deals with the gradual division of the number of hours of professional and family work. The main purpose is to give a better picture of the gradual equality or inequality in the division of labour, both between men and women as two groups and within the group of men and of women. An additional historical model can be constructed which is complementary to the models presented before.

Figure 4.11 Average number of hours of professional labour of men and women of different age groups in some countries (1965-2000)

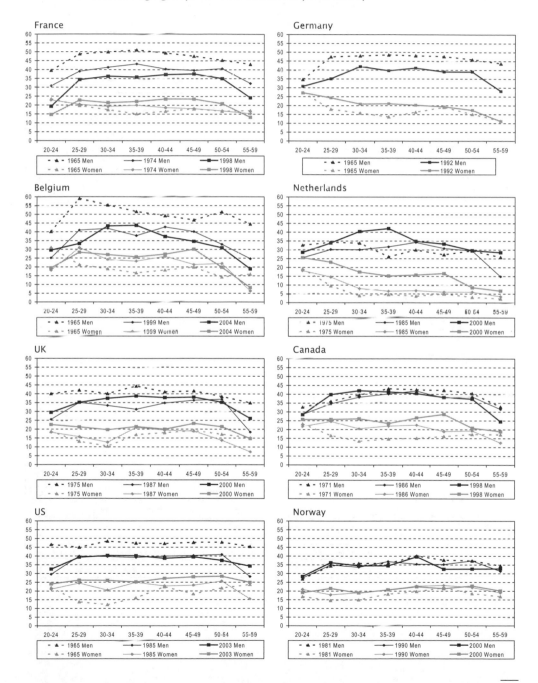

Figure 4.12 Average number of hours of family labour of men and women of different age groups in some countries (1965-2000)

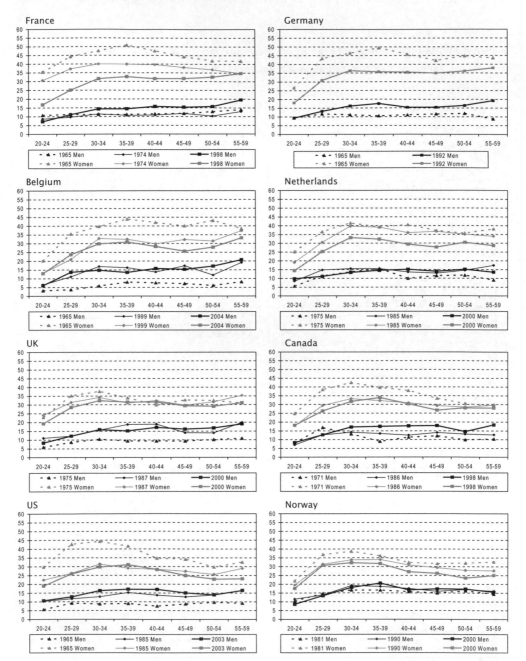

Figure 4.13 Average number of hours of total labour of men and women of different age groups in some countries (1965-2000)

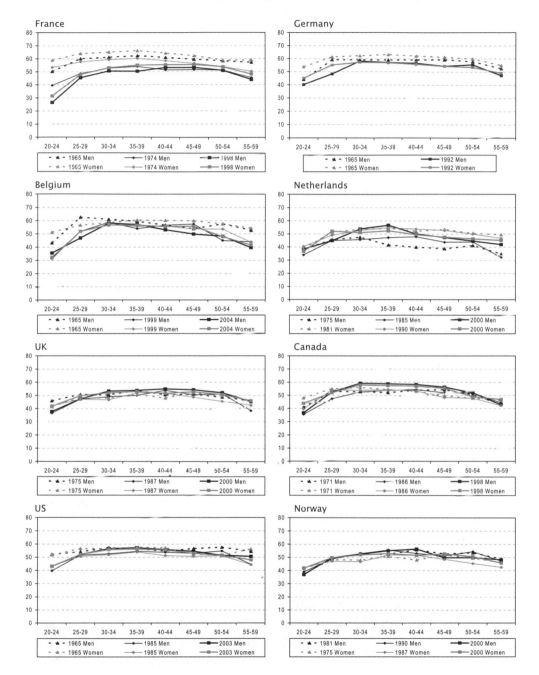

Figure 4.14 shows the historical model for the period 1950-2005 for the division of professional labour (upper part 1) and family labour (part 2) between men and women, based on the *distribution of the number of hours*. It contains three partial models covering three successive periods: the strong breadwinner model in the period 1950-70, the moderate breadwinner model in the period 1970-90 and the moderate combination model in the period 1990-2005 (Van Dongen et al, 2001; Van Dongen and Danau, 2003. Mainly for didactical reasons, we have chosen to present only three partial models, emphasising the gradual differentiation and development within and between the three periods. If necessary, one can construct more partial models for shorter periods, in particular to show more clearly that gradual development in time.

The models show the *quantitative distribution or division of professional and family labour of individual men and women* (upper part) and the *relative division of labour between partners within families with two adult partners* (lower part).

The division of labour of individual men and women in the upper part of each figure is expressed by the relative share of the different jobs of men and women, in terms of the actual number of working hours per week.

The lower part of each figure gives the division of labour within families with two partners. It shows the relative distribution of the seven family types presented in Figure 2.13, based on the relative share of women in the total professional and total household labour in their family. For professional labour, it ranges from the strong male breadwinner family on the left side (type 1: the man is responsible for almost all professional labour and the woman for almost all family labour), to the complete combination family in the centre (type 4: the relative share of the man and the woman in professional and family labour equalises), to the strong female breadwinner family on the right side (type 7: the woman is responsible for almost all professional labour and the man for almost all family labour). Evidently, the family types are ordered the other way around in the figure of family labour.

The name of the historical models is related to the dominant family type in the actual distribution during that period. While the lower part of the models refers to the traditional families (man and woman), with or without children, this part can easily be translated to other family forms. Furthermore, the societal position of children can be integrated in the models without much difficulty.

The models are the result of historical reconstruction, largely based on empirical data of past decades and supported by empirical data of the period before (Figures 4.1-4.9). Of course, the demarcation of the periods can be discussed, especially when applied to different countries. In fact, the models give an empirically supported but still hypothetical expression of the real development in different countries. In the first place, they can be used for the comparative analysis of the historical development of the division of labour in different (types of) countries, for example according to the classification of Esping-Andersen (1990, 1999) or Korpi (2000). Secondly, the models are the expression of the actual combination of the basic values in the daily division of labour: freedom, equality, solidarity and efficiency. In that way, they reflect the actual policy models in these (types of) countries to a high degree. Finally, the models are the empirical basis for the development of future policy models, in line with the normative views in society.

The objective of this chapter is to present additional supportive empirical data for the development of the division of labour in European (western) countries. Unfortunately, these curves cannot be constructed for the period 1950–85 since comparative labour

Figure 4.14 Three historical models for the division of professional and family labour between men and women and within families (1950-2005)

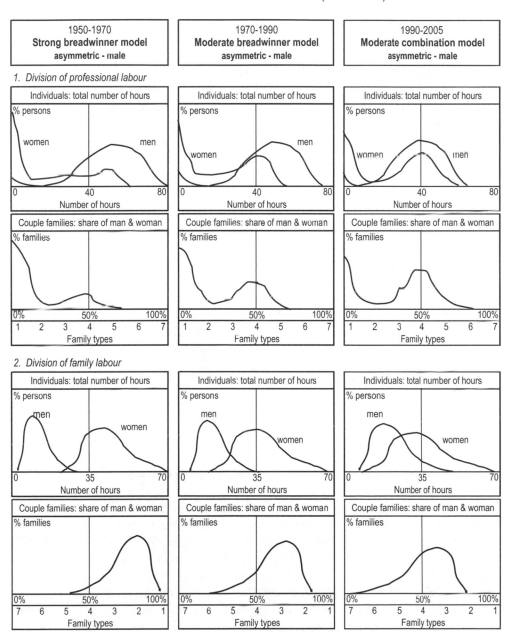

market data are not available and the MTUS samples (time use data) for that period were mostly too small to create reliable curves. Therefore, starting from the general historical model in Figures 4.7-4.12 (based on the average number of hours) we present these curves for the period 1985-2004, together with some other indicators. So, we can preserve the hypothesis that Figure 4.14 presents the overall development between 1950 and 2000 in most European (western) countries fairly well, albeit with gradual differences between these countries.

4.2.4.2 *The period of the strong breadwinner model (1950-70)*

In the period of the strong breadwinner model, the strong breadwinner family was dominant in quantitative terms. The majority of (married) women had no or only a very small share in the total professional labour of the family. Yet an important number of the women remained professionally active, mostly unmarried women having a full-time job, since part-time work was not yet very common.

Around 1950, most western European countries took the strong breadwinner family as a reference for the development of the welfare state and introduced a number of policy instruments to support it. Following the long period of expulsion of women from the labour market in the period 1800-1950 (Figures 4.1-4.4), the societal context of the 1950s formed a good feeding ground for this family type. Likewise, this family type was largely legitimised by the principle duty (often expressed in terms of the free choice) of families to raise young children almost completely within the family. In reality, the breadwinner family was strongly promoted and supported by the government (and social partners) in most countries, by means of discriminative legislation and strong financial support within the fiscal and social security system and public provisions. The strong breadwinner model goes hand in hand with a very unequal division of professional and family labour between men and women, both on the macro and micro level. At the same time, the financial basis for the solidarity system was relatively weak (unlike the high economic growth in that period), that is, the financial capacity of the government to invest in children, older people and people with a disability and people with inadequate education. Finally, the efficiency principle was largely sacrificed by the inadequate use of human resources provided by women in business life and human resources provided by men in family life.

4.2.4.3 *The period of the moderate breadwinner model (1970-90)*

Since 1960, more women (re-)entered the labour market in most western countries (Figures 4.1-4.12). Moreover, (married) women increasingly remained professionally active after the arrival of children. The strong breadwinner model was systematically losing impact. There were more part-time jobs, so the number of moderate breadwinner and combination families increased. At the same time, the average number of hours of paid work of men systematically decreased. Consequently, we can speak of the period of the moderate breadwinner model. In this model, families have somewhat less free choice with respect to the division of labour and the education of children in order to realise a more equal division of labour between men and women, a stronger solidarity system supporting financially dependent people and a more adequate use of female resources in business life. With some delay, the division of household work also changed step by step, with a decrease in the share of women and an increase in the share of men.

4.2.4.4 The period of the moderate combination model (1990–2005)

Since the beginning of the 1990s we can talk about a moderate combination model in most western countries, albeit with some variants. After all, the combination families with a more equal division of professional and family labour became the majority in most countries. This model was largely supported/stimulated by the emancipation movement working for a more equal division of time and means between men and women, both on the micro and macro level. This process included the increasing awareness of the importance of high(er) professional participation to achieve a sufficiently high family income, a strong collective financial basis (solidarity system) and a more efficient use of women's resources in market activities. In the period 1990–2005, the total activity rate of women (the share of professionally active women in the whole female population) further increased. At this point in time, most countries can be placed under the umbrella of the moderate combination model. It is therefore useful to give a differentiated picture of the period 1985–2000, starting from Figure 4.15 which shows some stages or types of the moderate combination model for professional labour. The same picture can be shown for family labour.

Figure 4.15 Stages or types of the moderate combination model (professional labour)

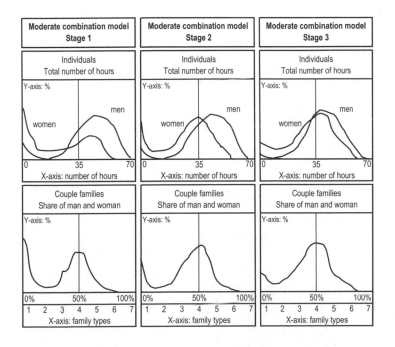

The main question, then, is: what stages are the different (types of) countries at now? In the next section, we give empirical evidence for the period 1985–2005 by means of some basic indicators for the division of labour between men and women.

4.2.4.5 Comparison with other models

Following Crompton (1999), Gornick and Meyers (2003) present three similar models for the period 1950–2000, illustrating the evolution from the traditional male breadwinner model to the recent dual earner models (see Figure 4.16). The *traditional male breadwinner/female carer model* was dominant in most western countries in the period 1930–70 and is still fairly dominant in most southern European countries. The *dual earner/female part-time carer model* emerged from the traditional model and became dominant in the continental European countries. In this model, most men work full time and women experience a gradual division of labour that differs for the varying countries: having no job, working part time or working full time. The partial professional work of women is combined with partial family and partial external care (provided by the private sector and/or by the state). The *dual earner/substitute carer model* is the next step in this development, with two variants. The dual earner/state carer model was dominant in the Eastern European countries and to a lesser extent in the Nordic countries, while the dual earner/market carer model was typical for the US and, to a lesser extent, for Canada and the UK. Both models leave a large share of the care for young children to external caregivers. In the dual earner/state carer model the state provides or finances public childcare, while in the dual earner/market carer model external childcare is mainly provided by private suppliers, with little financial support from the state.

In general, we fully share the basic scientific goal of these models, that is, to develop a flexible framework to conceptualise change and to compare, across countries, current resolutions to the schism between employment and care (Gornick and Meyers, 2003, pp 90–1). These models serve as the stepping stone towards an idealised normative model for future society: the dual earner/dual carer model. In the next chapter, which deals with normative future models, we compare this normative model with the future 'Combination Models' that we have developed during the past ten years.

In our opinion, these models are largely compatible with or similar to the models in Figure 4.14. The strong breadwinner model (1950–1970) refers to the male breadwinner/female carer model. The moderate breadwinner model (1970–1990) is similar to their dual earner/female part-time carer model. The moderate combination model refers to their dual earner/substitute carer model, with some variants, as presented in Figures 4.15 and 4.16.

Unfortunately, Gornick and Meyers did not develop a clear graphical presentation of their models as we do in Figures 4.14 and 4.15. Consequently, a complete comparison or matching of the two sets of models has so far not been possible. It would therefore be useful to set up more international collaboration in this field, to have a more complete comparison and mutual translation of the models.

Figure 4.16 Historical models for the division of professional and family labour between men and women

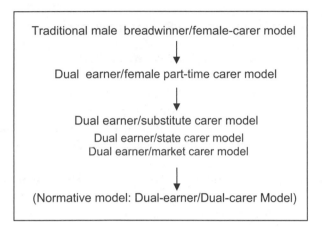

4.3 **Evaluation of the division of professional and family labour between 1985 and 2005**

To provide further comparative analysis of the development of the division of professional and family labour between men and women during the past two decades in western countries, we use a number of basic indicators, showing both the similarities and differences between the (types of) countries. During the past 10 years, (most of) these indicators were first created for Flanders/Belgium. Since the beginning of 2004, an international comparative database with basic indicators has been developed for EU countries and for some other OECD countries. We shall also give some indicators for Eastern European countries, as far as possible. The following indicators are presented and discussed:

- Labour situation of the total male and female population, with six categories: professionally active, looking for a job, staying at home, on a pension, studying and other.
- General division of time of men and women in different age groups: professional labour, family labour, social labour, external education, personal care and leisure time.
- Professional activity rate of men and women by age group.
- Hours of professional labour: division of the number of hours and average number of hours by age group.
- Hours of household or family work: division of the number of hours and average number of hours by age group.
- Hours of leisure time: division of the number of hours and average number of hours by age group.
- Hours of personal care: division of the number hours and average number of hours by age group.

- Some other characteristics of professional work: temporary work, shift work, night work, Sunday work and home work.

4.3.1 Labour situation of the total male and female population

4.3.1.1 Labour situation in Belgium and the Netherlands

Figure 4.17 shows the general labour situation of the total male and female population in Belgium and the Netherlands in the period 1947-2003, with six categories: professionally active, looking for a job, staying at home, on a pension, study (pupils/students) and 'other', consisting mainly of people who cannot work due to complete disability.

The figure shows the large similarity and the gradual differences in the development of the relative share of the different categories of the population. More information is therefore given about the relative position and evolution of the different groups. This figure can also be drawn with the absolute numbers (Van Dongen and Danau, 2003). It was presented for the first time in Van Dongen et al (1998) as a useful complementary labour market indicator.

Within our broad conceptual approach, the *professional population* is a broader category than in the traditional approach and consists of the three lower categories, that is, people actually having a job, people looking for a job and people staying at home (mostly housewives). After all, these three groups are basically able to search for and to have a job. The other groups are (officially) exempted from paid labour. We can see that since 1990 the share of the professional population has been very stable, with a small increase in Belgium and a small decrease in the Netherlands during the past years.

The *total activity rate*, then, is the share of people actually having a job in the total population, which is a useful indicator for the economic basis of the whole population, since this group earns the total monetary income of the country, supporting the other categories financially. The figures clearly show the positive development of the total activity rate during the past few decades, except from 2003-04.

The *effective employment rate* or *professional participation rate*, then, is the share of people actually having a job in the professional population. It expresses to what extent the professional population is really active in the labour market. Consequently, the total unemployment rate (new definition) is the share of all people having no job (people looking for a job and people staying at home) in the professional population.

Although pupils/students, people on a pension and completely disabled people are officially exempted from professional labour, they can and do participate in the labour market to a certain extent, mostly in the form of (temporary) small part-time jobs. So, the 'total potential professional population' is somewhat larger than the 'official professional population'.

The development of the share of professionally active people is largely similar in both countries. The most important difference concerns the share of people on a pension and of women staying at home. For women, until recently, this was largely related to the difference in official age for pensions: 65 years for Dutch women against 60 years for

Figure 4.17 Labour situation of the Belgian and Dutch population (1947-2004)

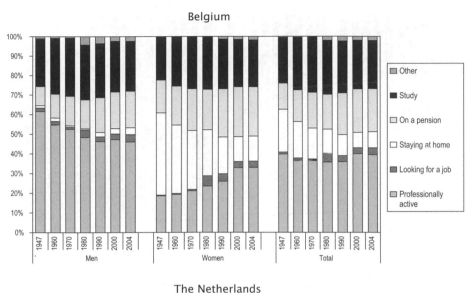

Belgium

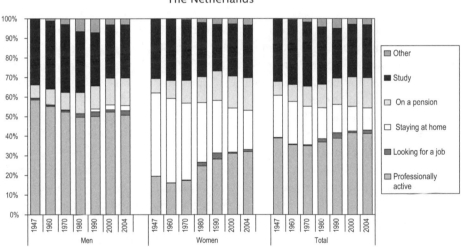

The Netherlands

Belgian women. The share of people looking for a job was smaller in the Netherlands, whereas the share of the group 'other' (mostly people declared fully disabled for the labour market) has been larger.

Figure 4.18 gives a more detailed picture of the evolution in Belgium in the period 1989-2004, emphasising the slowly changing composition of the male population and the more rapidly changing composition of the female professional population. The total professional population according to the new definition (including people staying at home) has been very stable since 1989, with a very small increase during the past decade. The total activity rate (men and women together) increased permanently, strengthening the economic basis.

Figure 4.18 Labour situation of the Belgian population (1989-2004)

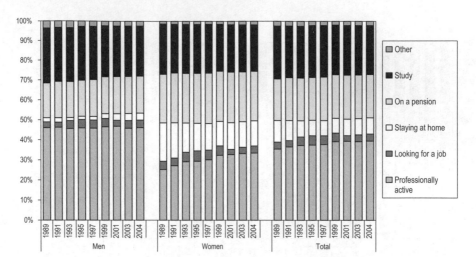

4.3.1.2 *Labour situation in some EU-15 countries (1998-2004)*

This indicator can also be constructed for the other EU-15 countries with LFS data (Eurostat), but only for the period after 1998. Figure 4.19 gives the results for some countries to show the major similarities and differences in the development of the general labour situation between the southern European countries at one end and the Nordic countries at the other.

In the southern countries of Italy, Greece, Spain and Malta, the relative share of women staying at home (housewives) is still fairly large. Portugal is the exception, with a much lower share of housewives. At the same time, the share of officially unemployed men and women is relatively large. In Ireland, the share of housewives is also still large, but the share of unemployed men and especially women is smaller. The Irish population is much younger, illustrated by the high percentage of pupils and students and the low percentage of people on a pension.

The labour situation in the continental countries (Belgium, France, Germany, Austria), the UK and Portugal is more or less the same, with a larger share of professionally active women, a smaller share of housewives and a fairly similar share of unemployed people, people on a pension and pupils/students. In Portugal and the UK, men have a higher employment rate than in Belgium, France and Germany.

The Nordic countries have a significantly higher female employment rate and a much lower share of housewives. But also within this region there are some differences, from Finland showing the lowest employment rate for men and women and the largest share of housewives and unemployed women on the one hand, to Iceland having the highest employment rate and the lowest share of people on a pension on the other. Iceland also has a relatively younger population than the other Nordic countries. Finally, these countries have a higher percentage of 'other', that is, mostly people completely unavailable for the labour market.

Figure 4.19 Labour situation of the total population in some European countries (1998-2004)

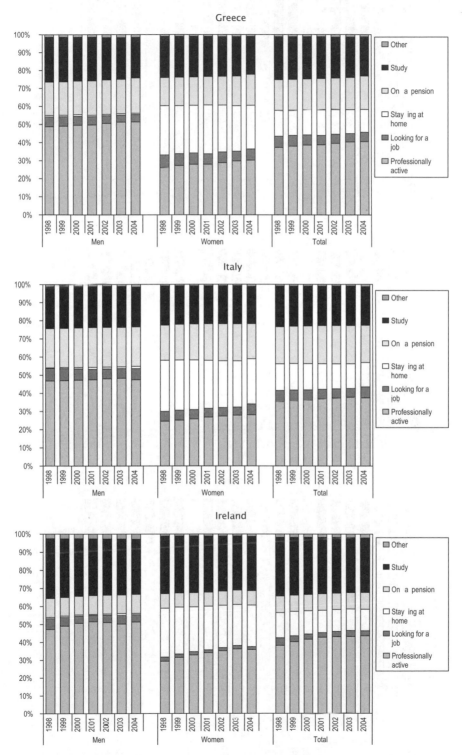

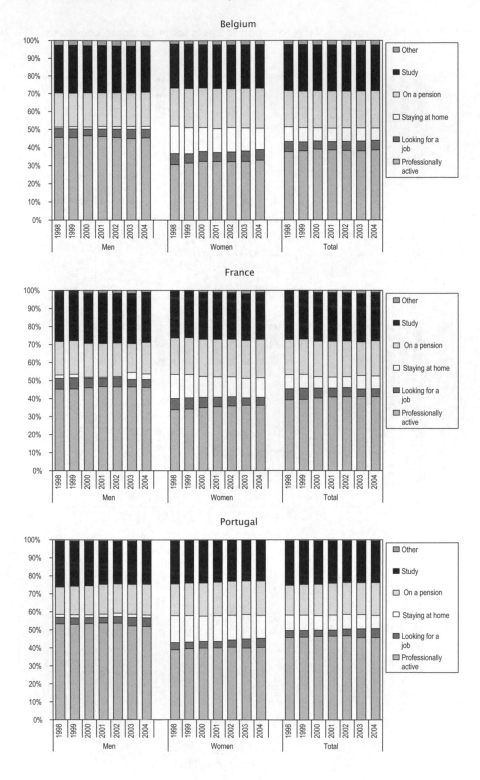

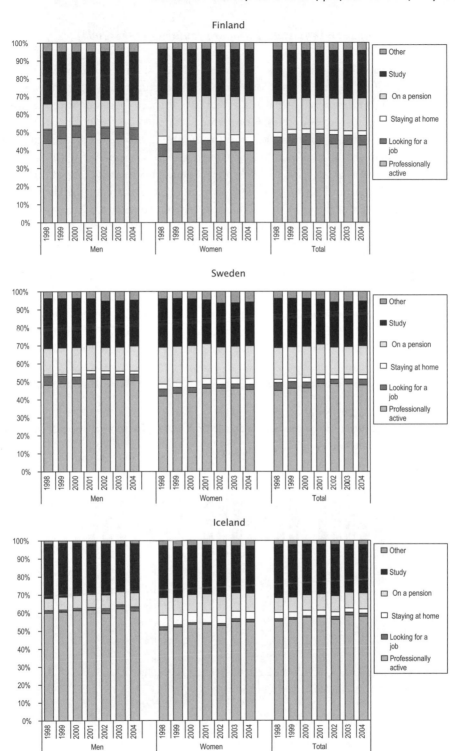

4.3.1.3 Labour situation in Eastern European countries (1998-2004)

Data regarding the labour situation is also available for most Eastern European countries, so we can present the same graph for some of these countries (see Figure 4.20). In general, for this indicator all these countries are located between the continental countries and the Nordic countries. Compared with the continental countries, these countries have a fairly equal share of working women, a lower share of housewives, but a higher share of unemployed and retired women. Compared with the Nordic countries, they have a lower share of working women, but a higher share of housewives, unemployed women and retired women. In general, the share of pupils/students is largely similar to that in the continental and the Nordic countries. Moreover, the share of the people looking for a job is relatively high in these countries. It should be noted that the average welfare level in these countries is much lower than in the continental and Nordic countries.

Again, the similarities and gradual differences between these countries has come to the forefront, with the more 'Nordic'-like countries such as Estonia, Lithuania, Latvia, Slovenia and Slovakia on one side, and the more 'continental' countries such as Poland, Hungary, Romania, the Czech Republic and Bulgaria on the other. In Estonia, Slovenia, Hungary and Latvia, the employment rate increased in the period 2001-2004, while in Poland, Romania, Lithuania and the Czech Republic, it decreased. Finally, we notice that the share of people on a pension differs quite a lot between these countries.

Figure 4.20 Labour situation of the total population in some Eastern European countries (1998-2004)

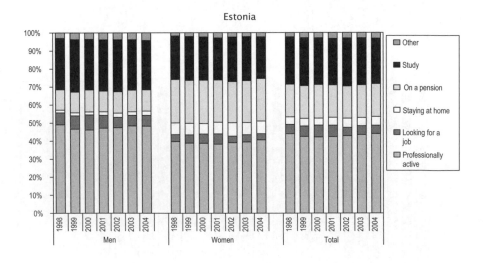

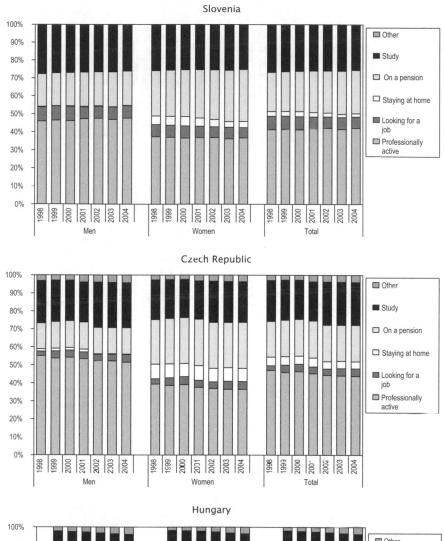

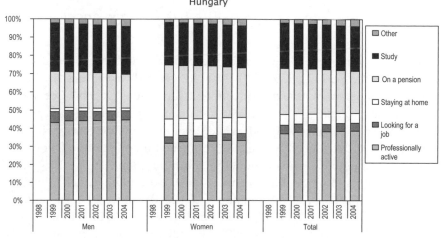

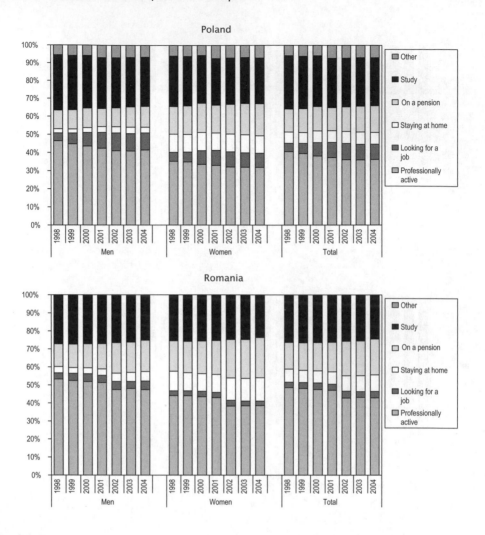

4.3.2 General division of time in different age groups (1989-2000)

Figure 4.21 shows the general division of the basic activities of men and women in 10 countries in the period 1989-2000 (MTUS, Oxford), by means of the average number of hours per week (Y-axis) for different age groups (X-axis) (see also Figure 2.6). Largely the same differences between men and women emerge for professional and family labour, as observed in Flanders and Belgium (Van Dongen, 2004e). Yet there are some significant differences between the countries for both men and women, going from a still moderate breadwinner model in southern countries like Italy (1989), to a moderate combination model in Germany (1992), the Netherlands (1995), France (1998), Belgium (Flanders, 1999) and the UK (2000), and to a further developed combination model in the US (1992) and Canada (2000) and in the Nordic countries such as Norway (1990) and Finland (1999). The difference between men and women is not significant for the other basic activities.

Figure 4.21 Combination of activities (hours per week) in 10 European countries between 1989 and 2000 (MTUS, Oxford)

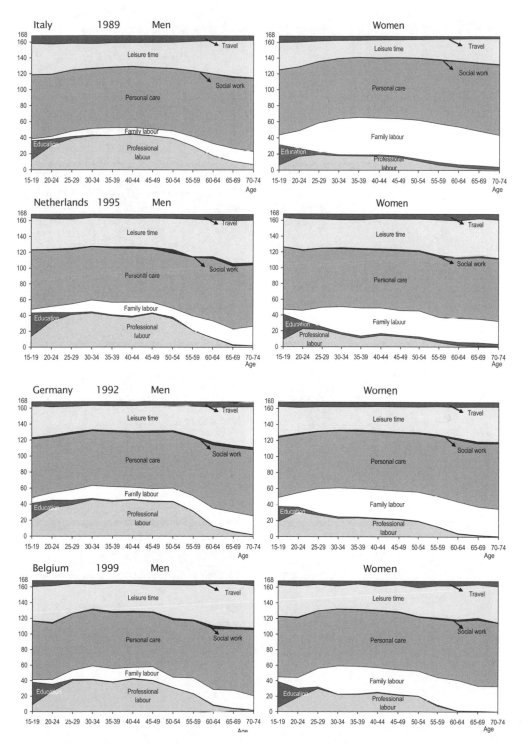

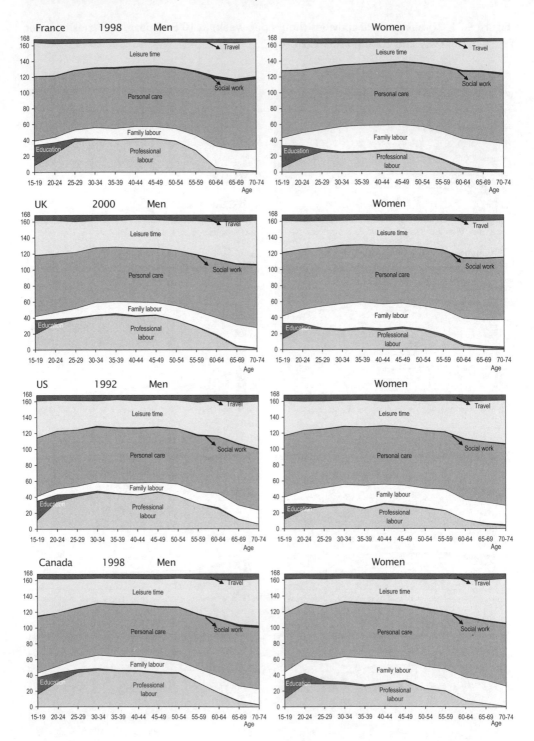

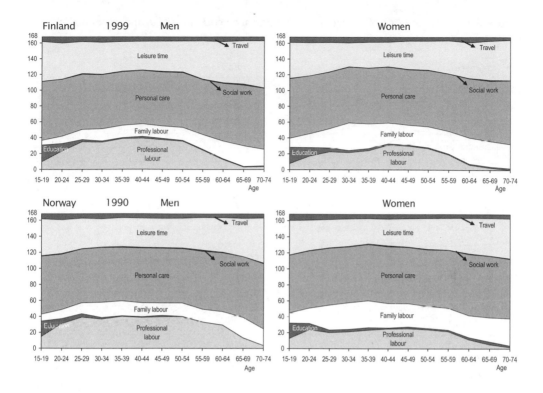

In addition, the difference with respect to education level and family type is fairly evident: a smaller number of working hours for lower-educated or qualified women, especially those with (more) children.

We can see some remarkable differences in the division of labour according to age between the continental countries such as Belgium, the Netherlands and Germany and the Nordic country Finland. In the continental countries the average number of professional working hours of women is the highest around the age of 20-30, which decreases after the arrival of children and remains (very) low for older age groups. In Finland, however, the average number of working hours of younger women is lower than that for older women, with the highest number for the age group 40-50. The difference in working hours for different age groups reflects to a large extent the main difference in the policies of these countries. The Nordic countries support a combination of professional and family life in early years in a more efficient way, resulting in more continuous professional participation and a higher number of working hours for older women.

4.3.3 Professional activity rate of men and women by age group

4.3.3.1 *EU-15 countries*

Figure 4.22 shows the activity rates of men and women by age group during the past few decades in 12 EU-15 countries in the period 1985-2004.

125

Figure 4.22 Activity rates of men and women per age group in 12 European countries (1985-2004)

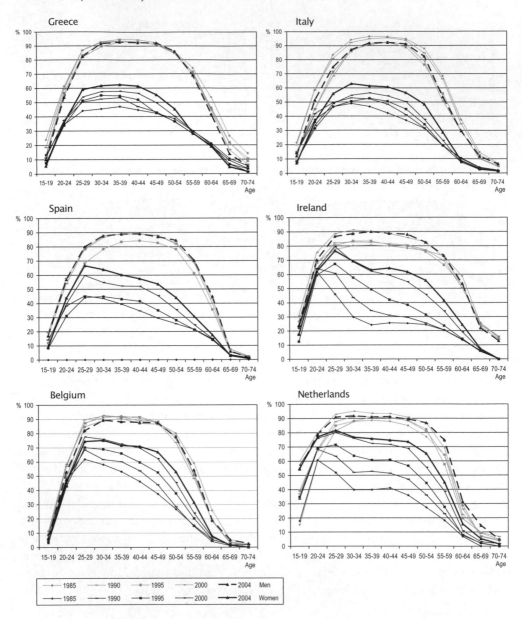

Although this indicator has been used in traditional labour market research for a long time, it remains important in the total set of complementary indicators. The activity rate of men is presented by the dotted curves above, that of women by the full curves below.

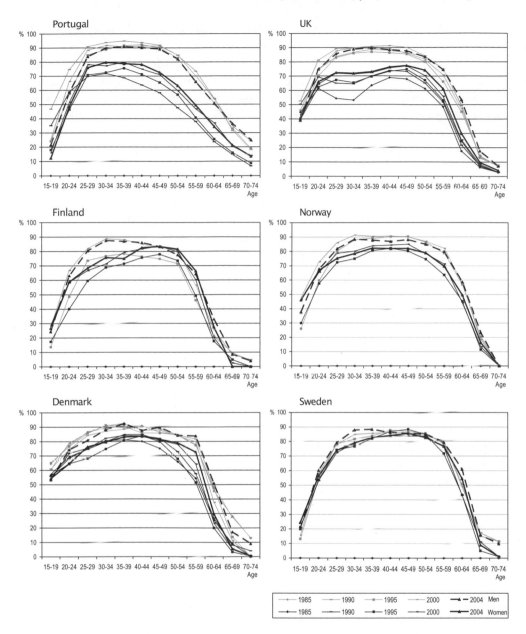

The figure immediately shows the gradual differences between the countries, from the more traditional countries in the south (except Portugal, which is more similar to the UK) to the Nordic countries. This empirical picture is clearly in line with the three stages or types of the moderate combination model presented in Figure 4.15.

In general, the activity rate of men has changed only to a small extent during the past two decades. In most countries the activity rate of older men still increased, while it diminished in Belgium and Ireland. As expected, the picture of the labour market participation of women is different. Almost all countries show a strong increase in the female participation rate in all age groups, in particular in countries where the participation rate used to be smaller (Greece, Italy, Spain, Ireland, the Netherlands and Belgium). In Portugal and the UK, the increase is also significant but relatively smaller. In the Nordic countries, the participation rate of women was already high in 1985; it remained more or less the same for the age group 20-50, but it increased for older women. Again, some slight differences between the Nordic countries can be observed (see also Borchorst, 2008; Lundqvist, 2008; Melby et al, 2008). Denmark shows a higher participation rate for men and women in the age group 15-19 and a more substantial difference between men and women in the older age groups.

Furthermore we can tell that the figures for Germany and France are between that of Belgium and the Netherlands, and that the figure for Iceland is very similar to that of Denmark, albeit the participation rate of women is somewhat higher than in Denmark.

We can also see substantial differences in the participation rate of the 15-19 age group, largely reflecting different culture and policy with respect to education and paid work of young people. In some countries (Belgium, Italy, Greece, Spain, Ireland and Sweden), this age group has a low labour market participation rate during the whole period. In Denmark and the UK, their participation rate is very high, during the whole period. In Portugal, the participation rate of this age group has fallen to a large extent, while in the Netherlands it has grown considerably.

Again, one could easily show the main differences with respect to education level and family type: a lower activity rate for men and women with a lower education level and for women with (young) children.

Finally, since it is impossible to gather data for the whole life course, these figures also express the employment rate during the life course, using the age groups as an indicator of the life course of men and women.

4.3.3.2 *Eastern European countries*

This indicator can also be constructed for Eastern European countries, for the period 2000-2004. Figure 4.23 presents the activity rates of men and women by age group in 2000 and 2004 for Hungary, the Czech Republic, Poland, Bulgaria, Lithuania and Slovenia.

The figures are, to a large extent, similar to the figures for the Nordic countries, with relatively high activity rates for women. Yet the activity rate of people in the age group 25-54 and the age group 55-74 seems to be somewhat lower, which shows the higher unemployment in these countries. In Hungary, the Czech Republic, Poland, Slovakia and Estonia the participation rate of younger women is clearly lower than that of men, hence resembling more the situation in Finland. As for the Nordic countries, the slight differences between the Eastern European countries are also very clear. Finally we can see the positive evolution in most of these countries, that is, the (small) increase in the activity rate of men and women since 2000, except for Poland and Romania.

Figure 4.23 Activity rates of men and women per age group in some Eastern European countries (2000-04)

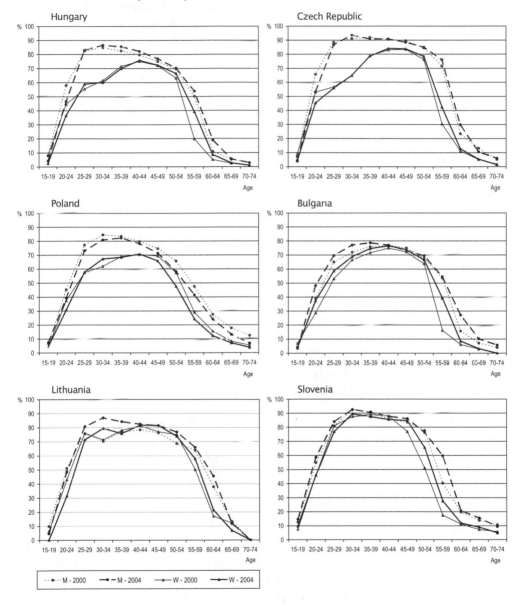

4.3.4 Hours of professional work: division of the number of hours and average number of hours by age group

In this section we look at the number of hours of professional work, by means of three partial indicators. Although time use surveys offer the best data, they were not available for all the countries in a systematic way for a sufficiently long period. We therefore use LFS data (Eurostat) for 1985-2004, in order to show the evolution during the past 20 years.

4.3.4.1 Division of hours of professional work in EU-15 countries

Figure 4.24 shows for the period 1985-2003 the division of the number of hours of professional work (in short, 'working hours') of men and women in a number of European countries, for the age group 25-64, mainly to exclude (the influence of) students. The figures for Greece and Italy are not included since the data were not complete. However, we can tell that these figures are very similar to those for Spain.

In our previous research, this basic indicator was used for constructing and presenting the historical models in Figures 4.14 and 4.15, and also for the normative future models that will be presented in the next chapter (see Figure 5.2) (Van Dongen et al, 2001; Van Dongen, 2004e, 2005c). The indicator clearly expresses (the change in) the gradual equality and/or inequality (or diversity) with respect to the division of working hours of men and women. Above all, we should look at the specific form of the diversity expressed by the curves.

Again, both the general similarity and the gradual differences between the more traditional countries and the more modern countries are clear. Even more clearly, the figures are in line with the stages of the moderate combination model in the upper part of Figure 4.15. Unfortunately, data for the distribution of family types concerning the relative division of hours between partners (the lower part of Figure 4.15) are not available.

The division of working hours of men has changed to a small extent during the past few decades. In Spain, Ireland and the Netherlands, the share of men without a job decreased. In Belgium, the UK and Sweden, this share increased somewhat while in Portugal and Denmark it remained unchanged. In most countries, the share of men with a job of more than 40 hours decreased. In Ireland, the Netherlands and Belgium, this process was stronger.

Here also, the picture for women is largely different. Except for the Nordic countries, all countries show a strong decrease in the number of women without a job, especially in countries where this number was still high in 1985 (Spain, Ireland, the Netherlands, Belgium, Greece and Italy). In Portugal and the UK, the same process occurs but starting from a lower level in 1985. As a consequence, the substantial difference between men and women diminished to a large extent in all these countries. In Ireland, Belgium and in particular the Netherlands, the number of part-time jobs (1-9, 10-19 and 20-29 hours) has grown significantly during the past two decades. In Denmark and Sweden, the number of women without a job remained on the same (lower) level. Although the difference between men and women is (much) smaller than in the other countries, it did not decrease much during the past 10-20 years. Here also the differences between Denmark and Sweden become clear. Denmark has more women without a job and more men and women with a job of 30-39 hours/week.

Figure 4.24 Division of the number of working hours of men and women (25-64 years) in 10 European countries (1985-2003)

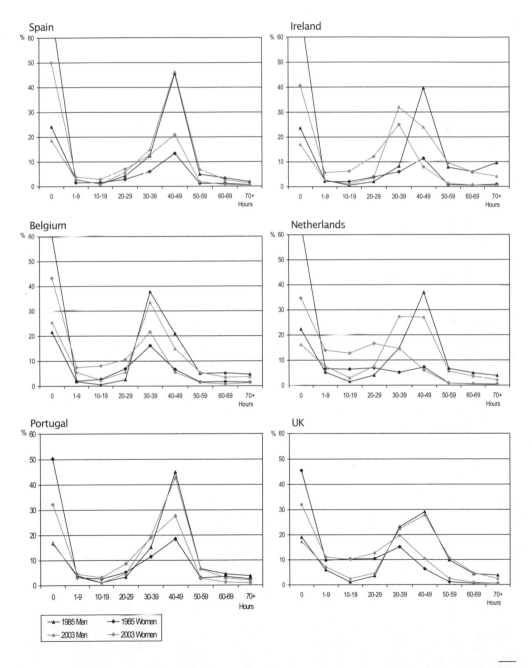

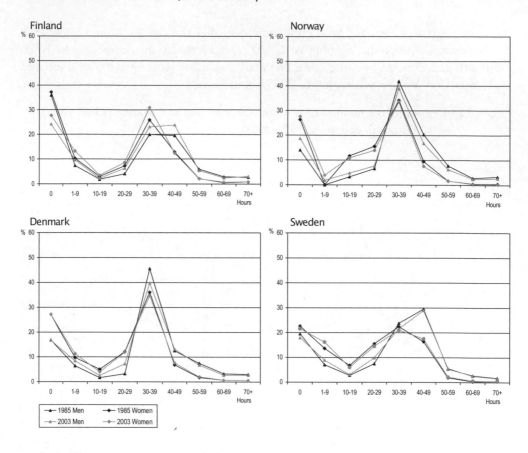

Figure 4.25 shows the division of working hours of men and women with a high and low education in six EU countries in 2003. For both men and women, the same basic difference occurs: highly educated men and women are more likely to have a job than lower-educated men and women. At the same time, the difference between highly educated men and women remains visible, as well as the difference between lower-educated men and women. These subgroups can clearly be linked with the stages of the moderate combination model in Figure 4.15.

Figure 4.25 Division of working hours of men and women with a high and low education in six EU countries (2003)

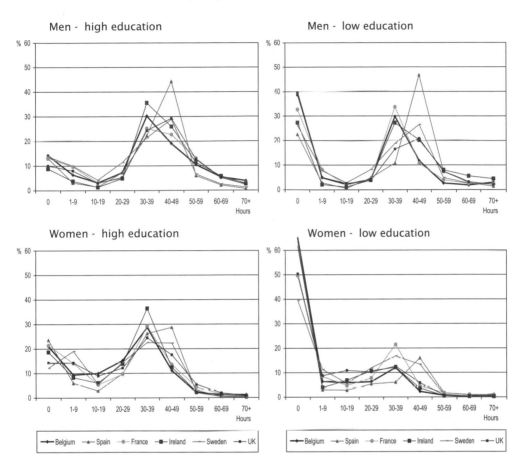

4.3.4.2 *Division of hours of professional work in Eastern European countries*

Figure 4.26 presents the division of working hours of men and women in 1998 and 2004 for Hungary, the Czech Republic, Poland, Bulgaria, Lithuania and Slovenia.

The figures for the Eastern European countries (also for Latvia, Estonia, Slovakia and Romania) are largely similar, which was not the case for the EU–15 countries. In all these countries, the total share of women and men without a job is significantly higher than in the southern, continental and Nordic countries. At the same time, most working men and women have a job of 40–49 hours, which largely differs from most continental and Nordic countries. The share of part-time jobs is still very small, although it has slightly increased in most of these countries.

Figure 4.26 Division of the number of working hours of men and women in some Eastern European countries (1998-2004)

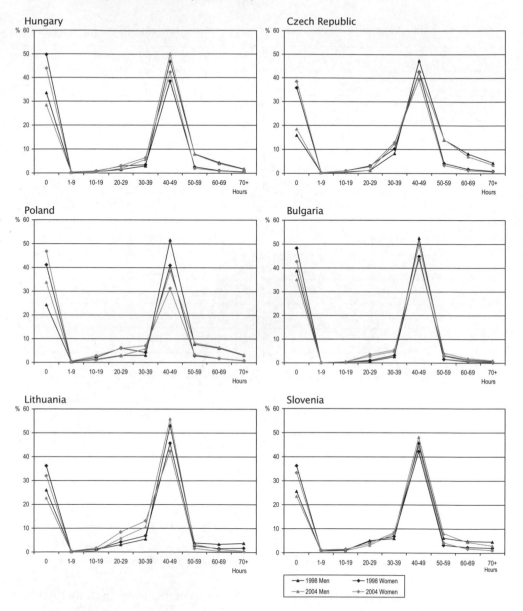

Again, we can see the positive evolution in the majority of these countries, that is, the (small) decrease in the share of men and women without a job since 1998, except for Poland and Romania.

This strong similarity in the division of working hours is probably still largely the result of the employment policy of the former communist regimes in those countries, which aimed at a high degree of equality in the labour market.

The previous figures clearly show that the division of professional labour of men and women has always had a gradual character in all countries, expressing the specific degree of equality and diversity. This means that the values of 'equality' and 'diversity' express two sides of the same coin. The debate on an 'equal division of labour' can only be meaningful when done in terms of the gradual distribution of the number of hours. Gradual equality expresses at the same time gradual diversity in the number of hours. So the scientific and policy debate on diversity is essentially part of the overall debate on societal equality, starting from the basic empirical and normative question: which gradual form of equality/diversity do we actually observe in society and which gradual form of equality/diversity does society want to develop in the future? In this chapter, we show some complementary indicators to answer the empirical question. In the next chapter, we try to answer the normative question by means of some normative future models, starting from the empirical models.

4.3.4.3 *Average number of hours of professional work by age group in EU-15 countries*

Figure 4.27 gives the average number of working hours of all men and women for the different age groups (from 15-69 years) in some EU countries (see also Figure 4.11). The curves of men are at the top; those of women at the bottom. The level of the curves is negatively influenced by the number of people without a job. As said before, the differences between the age groups can also be used as an expression of the evolution during the life course.

Again, both the overall similarity and the gradual differences between the countries become clear. The curves for men are largely similar in most countries with a relatively higher average number of hours in all age groups (during the life course). Yet there are again three main differences with respect to the three age groups. First, we can see the gradual differences in the average number of working hours in the 15-25 age group, with a very low average (less than five hours) in countries like Belgium and Sweden and a relatively high average in countries like the UK, Norway and Denmark. Second, the Nordic countries, the Netherlands and to a lesser extent Spain and Italy have a lower average of about 35 hours/week in the 30-55 age group against an average of about 40 hours in the other countries. In the next section we shall see that for Spain and Italy this is mainly related to the lower participation rate in this group. Third, the width of the figures shows a difference between countries, with the narrowest curve in Belgium, Greece and Italy, expressing on average earlier retirement than in other countries, and the widest curve in Ireland, the UK, Finland, Denmark and Sweden.

Figure 4.27 Average number of working hours of men and women per age group in European countries (1990-2004)

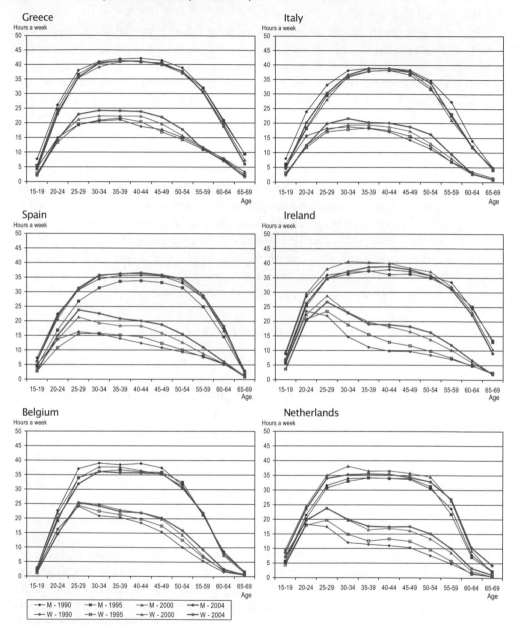

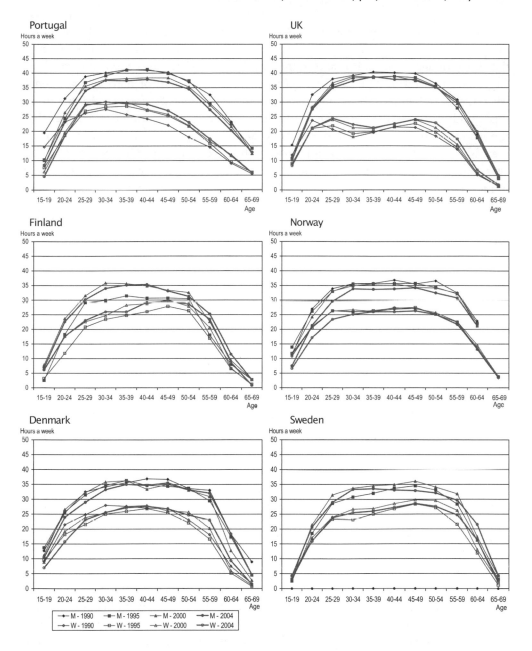

Portugal

UK

Finland

Norway

Denmark

Sweden

| —♦— M - 1990 | —■— M - 1995 | —▲— M - 2000 | —●— M - 2004 |
| —●— W - 1990 | —□— W - 1995 | —△— W - 2000 | —●— W - 2004 |

The picture for women is again largely different. First, the figure clearly shows the differences between the average number of working hours of men and women in the different age groups. But also in the Nordic countries, the difference is still fairly large, although the difference between the participation rate of men and women is very small (see Figure 4.22). Comparing Figures 4.22 and 4.27, one can see that in the more traditional countries the increase in the activity rate of women was larger than the increase in the average number of working hours, expressing the relatively stronger increase in the number of part-time jobs in these countries. In Greece and Italy, the average number of working hours did not increase that much during the past decades, while in Spain, Ireland and the Netherlands, the average number of hours strongly increased, coming from a very low level in 1985. In Belgium, Portugal and the UK, the increase was smaller but these countries already had a higher level in 1985. In the Nordic countries, the situation hardly changed but at the same time one can observe smaller differences between men and women. As for men, there were gradual differences in the average number of working hours in the 15-25 age group. In the southern and continental countries, young women of about 20-29 have the highest number of working hours, which then decreases rather strongly with increasing age. This is, of course, related to the presence of young children in the families and to the attitude of women leaving the labour market or strongly reducing the number of working hours. The Nordic countries show a different picture, without a significant influence of age and children on the average number of working hours. In these countries, the number of working hours is somewhat larger in the higher age groups.

Again, the differences according to the education level can be easily illustrated: lower-educated men and lower-educated women in particular have a lower number of working hours in all countries, in almost all age groups.

4.3.4.4 *Average number of hours of professional work by age group in Eastern European countries*

Figure 4.28 presents the same indicator for the same Eastern European countries as in Figure 4.23, for the period 1998-2004.

The figures for the Eastern European countries (also for Latvia, Estonia, Slovakia and Romania) largely show the same gradual – albeit bigger – differences as for the participation rate in Figure 4.23. In Slovenia and the Czech Republic, the average number of hours of men is still around 40 hours/week, while in the other countries it is about 35 hours/week. Figures for Bulgaria, Romania, Lithuania, Latvia and Estonia are very similar to figures for the Nordic countries, even with a relatively smaller difference between men and women. In Hungary, the Czech Republic, Poland and Slovakia, the difference in the number of working hours between men and women is again much more significant in the younger age group, which largely follows the difference in participation rate in Figure 4.23. In all these countries, we can see the low average number of working hours in the 15-25 age group, expressing both the high percentage of students in this age group and the high unemployment rate of young people that finished their studies.

Figure 4.28 Average number of working hours of men and women per age group in some Eastern European countries (1998-2004)

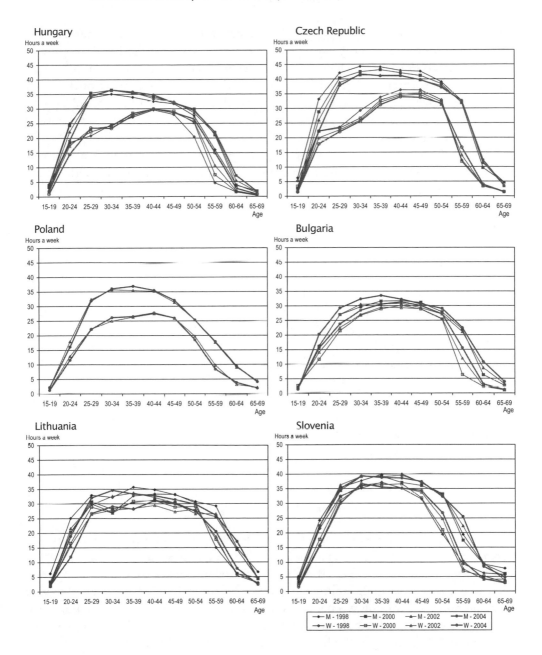

4.3.4.5 *Average number of hours of professional work by age group of men and women having a job in EU–15 countries*

Figure 4.29 gives the average number of working hours of men and women actually having a job, for the different age groups (between 15 and 69 years) in EU-15 countries, for the period 1990-2004. Here, the negative influence of the number of people without a job is eliminated. As such, this indicator gives an extra aspect of the work organisation, that is, the length of the average working day of working people. Again, the differences between the age groups also express to a certain extent the development during the life course.

The curves for working men are largely similar in most countries, with a relatively high average number of hours in all age groups. The only exception is the Netherlands, where men work on average around 35 hours/week. The Nordic countries also show a lower average number of working hours.

Although both the overall similarity and the gradual differences between the countries are clear again, the pattern has changed somewhat. In the southern countries, working men and women do not differ that much with respect to the number of working hours. Consequently, the average level of working hours of women in these countries is relatively high. The difference in these countries is somewhat smaller than in the Nordic countries and much smaller than in the continental and English-speaking countries. In particular in Ireland, the UK and the Netherlands many women have a (small) part-time job, resulting in a substantial difference between men and women. For this aspect, Portugal appears to be a southern European country, while for the other aspects it follows much more the UK or the continental countries.

Again, the differences by education level can be illustrated: lower-educated working women have a lower number of working hours than higher-educated women in all countries, in almost all age groups. The difference between lower- and higher-educated working men is fairly small.

4.3.4.6 *Average number of hours of professional work by age group of men and women having a job in some Eastern European countries*

Figure 4.30 presents the same indicator for the Eastern European countries, for the period 1998-2004. The figures are largely similar, with only small differences between working men and women. The average number of working hours of working men is fairly similar to that in the southern and Nordic countries. The average number of working hours of working women, however, is higher than in most other European countries. Logically, the age groups of 15-19 years and in particular of 60-70 years show more differences than the broad age group of 20-59 years.

Figure 4.29 Average number of working hours of men and women with a job, by age group, in 12 European countries (1990-2004)

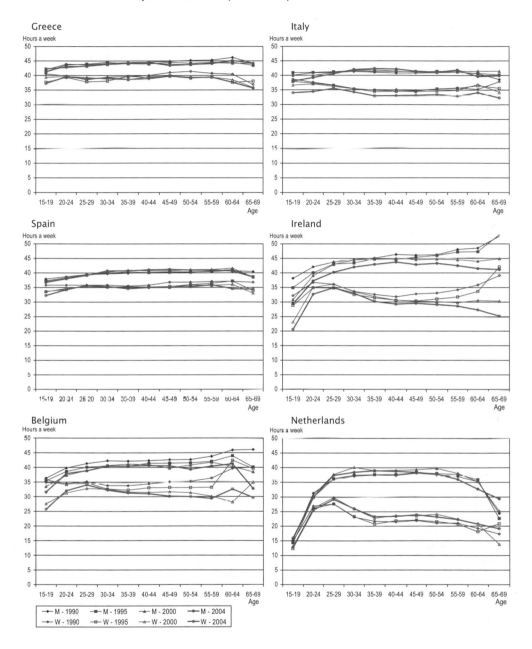

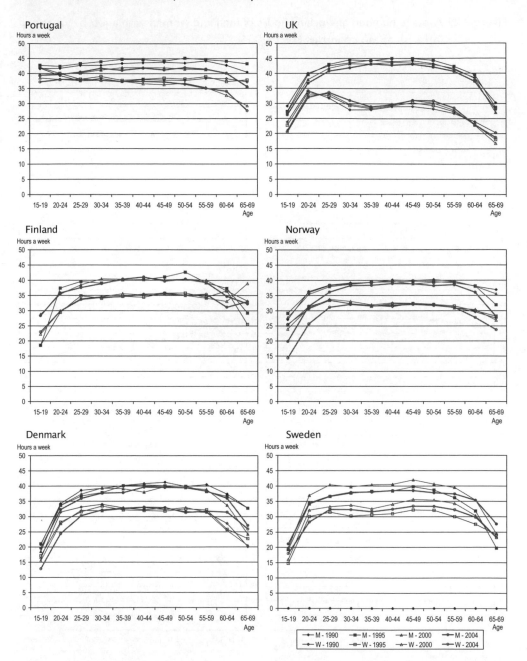

Portugal

Hours a week

UK

Hours a week

Finland

Hours a week

Norway

Hours a week

Denmark

Hours a week

Sweden

Hours a week

M - 1990   M - 1995   M - 2000   M - 2004
W - 1990   W - 1995   W - 2000   W - 2004

Figure 4.30 Average number of working hours of men and women having a job, by age group, in Eastern European countries (1998-2004)

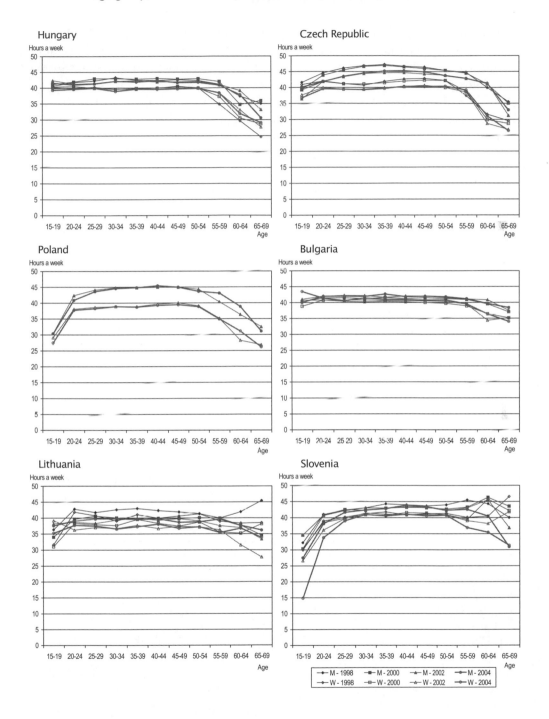

4.3.5 *Hours of household or family work: division of the number of hours and average number of hours by age group*

Similar figures can be produced for the number of hours of family or household work. We present two indicators for family work in some western countries: the division of the number of hours of family work and the average number of hours per age group (see Figure 4.12). The data comes from the international database MTUS (University of Oxford). Time use surveys offer the only useful data to do so, but as said earlier, they are not available for sufficient countries in a systematic way for a longer period. Therefore, we only show the division of family work in some countries in the period 1995-2000. Unfortunately the data was not available for Eastern European countries.

4.3.5.1 Division of the number of hours of family work

Figure 4.31 illustrates the division of the number of hours of family work of men and women in the age group 25-64 years in a number of countries. To repeat, this basic indicator has been used for the construction and presentation of the historical models in Figure 4.14 and for the normative future models in Figure 5.2. As for professional labour, the indicator very clearly expresses the gradual equality and/or inequality (diversity) of the division of the number of hours of family labour of men and women.

The curves for men and women in both periods are in line with the curve of the moderate combination model in Figure 4.14 and with the curve for Belgium/Flanders in 1999 (Van Dongen and Danau, 2003). Again, they show the gradual difference between the countries as was noticed for the division of professional labour.

The curves for women show a greater difference between the countries than for men, which is compatible with the greater difference in the division of hours of professional labour of women (the mechanism of the communicating vessel within families in Figure 2.9).

Figure 4.31 Division of the number of hours of household labour of men and women (25-64 years) in some EU countries (1995-2000)

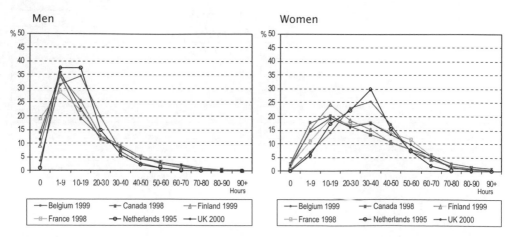

Figure 4.32 gives the division of the number of hours of family work for men and women with a high and low education, in the period 1995-2000. This can be compared with Figure 4.25 for professional labour.

The curves of lower-educated men are only slightly more to the right than those of higher-educated men, indicating the small difference in the number of hours of housework. The curves of lower-educated women are more to the right than those of higher-educated women, showing the more substantial difference in the hours of housework. This is compatible with the difference in the hours of professional labour between the two groups (Figure 4.25).

As for professional labour, the division of family labour between men and women has always been very gradual in all countries, expressing gradual equality and diversity. The values of 'equality' and 'diversity' express two sides of the same coin: gradual equality expresses at the same time the gradual diversity in the number of hours. The scientific and policy debate on equality and/or diversity is the same for professional

Figure 4.32 Division of the number of hours of family labour for higher- and lower-educated men and women (25-64 years) in some EU countries (1995-2000)

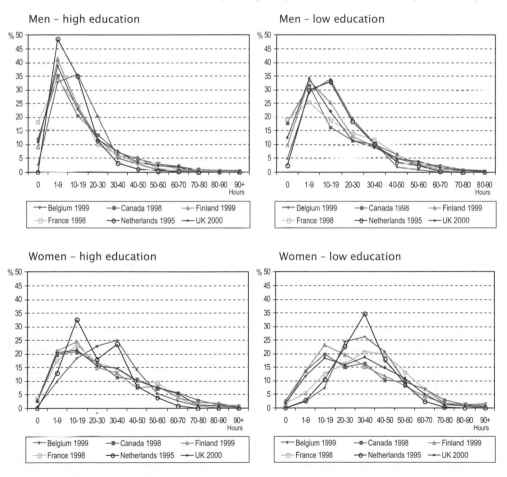

and family labour and has to start from the basic empirical question: which gradual form of equality/diversity do we actually observe in different countries/societies? We can then look at the normative question: which gradual form of equality/diversity is desirable in the different countries, starting from the concept of a democratic division of labour?

4.3.5.2 *Average number of hours of family work by age group*

Figure 4.33 illustrates the average number of hours of family work per week of men and women (Y-axis) for every age group (X-axis) in the same six countries. Largely the same story can be told here as for the division of professional labour. The curves show the gradual similarity and difference between the countries. The curves for women show a more substantial difference between the countries than for men, which is compatible with the greater difference in the division of professional labour of women (the mechanism of the communicating vessel within families; see Figure 2.9).

4.3.6 Hours of leisure time: division of the number of hours and average number of hours by age group

The same figures can be provided for the other main activities, such as leisure time and personal care, using the same time use data. They give some complementary information about the division of time in the different countries. In this section we look at the division of leisure time.

Figure 4.33 Average number of hours of family labour by age group in some countries (1995-2000)

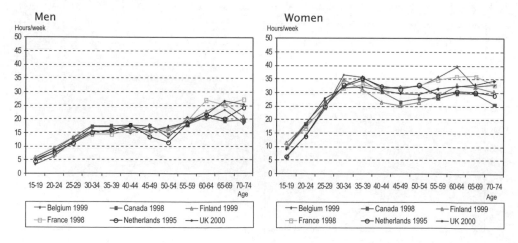

4.3.6.1 Division of the number of hours of leisure time

Figure 4.34 illustrates the division of the number of hours of leisure time of men and women in the age group of 25-64 years, according to the narrow definition of leisure time that we used in Figure 2.6 (Gershuny, 2000; Aguiar and Hurst, 2006).

The curves for men and women in both periods are in line with the curves we found for Belgium (Flanders) in 1999 (Van Dongen and Danau, 2003). They show both the large similarity and the gradual differences between the countries. The curves for women and men in every country hardly differ, except in southern countries like Italy where the breadwinner model was/is still more dominant. Yet in all countries, the curves for men are a little bit more to the right, indicating that men systematically have a few hours more free time per week.

Finally, we can see that the difference between higher- and lower-educated men and women is very small, albeit the curves for lower-educated men and women are a little bit more to the right, expressing the somewhat larger number of hours.

We can conclude here that for leisure time there is no real policy problem or challenge with respect to the difference between (higher- and lower-educated) men and women. Nevertheless, the very large differentiation or inequality in the number of hours within the two groups, mainly due to other factors, can be questioned. In other words, is it desirable and/or useful for society to reduce this difference?

Figure 4.34 Division of the number of hours of leisure time of men and women (25-64 years) in some countries (1995-2000)

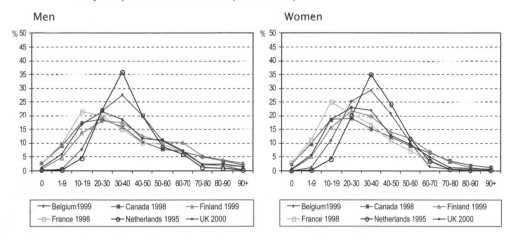

4.3.6.2 Average number of hours of leisure time by age group

Figure 4.35 illustrates the average number of hours of leisure time of men and women for every age group in the same countries. Again, the curves show the large similarity and the gradual differences between the countries. The curves for women show a somewhat larger difference between the countries than for men, but a much smaller difference than for the division of hours of professional and family labour.

Figure 4.35 Average number of hours of leisure time of men and women by age group in some countries (1995-2000)

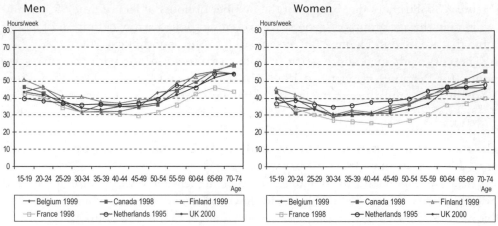

4.3.7 Hours of personal care: division of the number of hours and average number of hours by age group

4.3.7.1 Division of the number of hours of personal care

Figure 4.36 illustrates the division of the number of hours of personal care of men and women in the age group of 25-64 years. As for leisure time, the curves for personal care for men and women in both periods are largely in line with the curves we found for Belgium (Flanders) in 1999 (Van Dongen and Danau, 2003). They show the same large similarity and small gradual differences between the countries. The curves for women and men in every country hardly differ. Here, however, the curves for men are somewhat more to the left than those for women, indicating that men systematically have a few hours less personal care per week.

Again, the difference between higher and lower-educated men and women is very small, but in favour of the lower-educated men and women having somewhat more hours of personal care.

So also for personal care, society has no major policy problem with the difference between (higher- and lower-educated) men and women. However, the question remains whether it is desirable and/or useful to reduce the large differentiation within the two groups.

4.3.7.2 Average number of hours of personal care by age group

Figure 4.37 illustrates the average number of hours of personal care of men and women for every age group in the same countries. Here, the large similarity between the countries is even more striking. The curves for women and men are almost identical, supporting the policy conclusions in the previous section.

Figure 4.36 Division of the number of hours of personal care of men and women (25-64 years) in some countries (1985-2000)

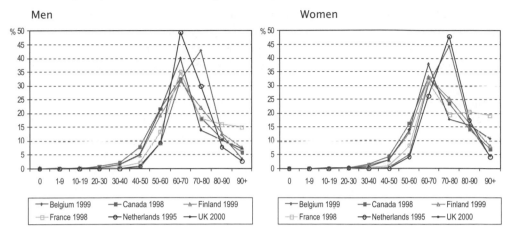

Figure 4.37 Average number of hours of personal care of men and women by age group in some countries (1985-2000)

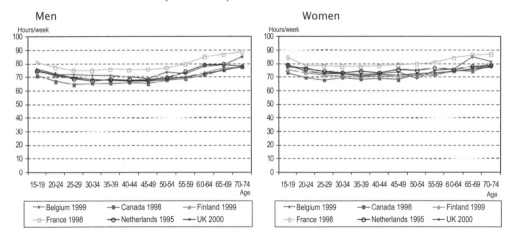

4.3.8 Some other characteristics of professional work (1992-2004)

In this section a number of aspects of the temporal quality of the professional work of men and women are presented for most EU countries (and Norway). For this analysis we use LFS data (Eurostat). We check whether the similarities and differences between the different (types of) countries that we found for the previous indicators also exist for some other aspects of professional work: temporary work, shift work, night work, Sunday work and working at home.

4.3.8.1 *Temporary work*

Figure 4.38 shows the share of working men and women having a temporary job in EU-15 countries in 2004, with a breakdown by age (three age groups). The countries are ranked according to the score of the age group 15-24 years.

The most striking thing is the substantial difference between the age groups. In all countries, many more young people (15-24 years) have a temporary job than older people. This means that in all countries 'temporary' jobs are mostly jobs for the first stage of the professional career. Since all jobs are the result of the interaction of demand and supply, we can strongly suppose that most employees want to have sufficiently stable or permanent work during their career and that most employers largely agree with that basic choice.

As for the participation rate and division of working hours in the previous section, we can again observe a gradual diversity between the countries, but with a different order than the classification distinguished before.

Largely unexpected, both for men and women, Ireland and the UK have by far the lowest percentage of temporary jobs in the age group 15-24 years (about 10%-12%). For women, these countries are followed by Denmark, Greece and Austria, but with a

Figure 4.38 Share of working men and women having a temporary job in EU-15 countries, by age (2004)

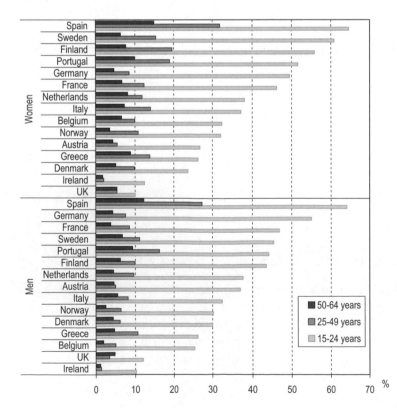

significantly larger percentage (20%–30%). For men, the two countries are followed by Belgium, Greece, Denmark and Norway, again with a larger percentage of 20%–30%.

On top we find Spain, with the highest share of temporary jobs for young men and women (about 65%). For women, Spain is followed by Sweden, Finland, Portugal and Germany (50%–60%). For men, Germany, France, Sweden, Portugal and Finland follow, with a percentage of 50%–60%. Spain also has the highest score for the other age groups, followed by Finland, Portugal, Sweden and Italy. The in-between group with 30%–40% of temporary jobs consists of Norway, Belgium, Italy and the Netherlands for women, and Italy, Austria and the Netherlands for men.

The evolution of the share of temporary jobs in the period 1992–2004 is also very different for the three age groups (not in the figure). For young people, this percentage has increased in most countries, especially in Germany, Italy, the Netherlands and Sweden. Only in the UK, Ireland and Denmark, where the share of temporary jobs was already relatively small in 1985, this share further decreased significantly. In the 25-49 age group, this percentage also increased in most countries, albeit to a smaller extent in Belgium, Germany, Greece, Italy, the Netherlands and Sweden. In the other countries, the share did not change significantly. Finally, in the 50-64 age group, the percentage of temporary jobs did not change significantly in most countries. Only Belgium, Italy and Portugal show a small increase, while Greece and Norway show a small decrease during the past decade.

Figure 4.39 presents the share of working men and women having a temporary job in Eastern European countries in 2004, with breakdown by age (three age groups).

In general, the percentage of young working men and women having a temporary job is much lower in Eastern European countries than in the EU-15 countries, except for Slovenia and Poland, which both show a very high score. In these two countries,

Figure 4.39 Share of working men and women having a temporary job in Eastern European countries, by age (2004)

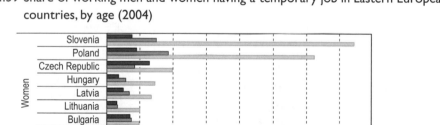

this percentage has increased dramatically during the past few years, while the increase was only small in the Czech Republic, Latvia and Hungary. In the other countries, the percentage was fairly stable. The percentages of older working men and women (>24 years) having a temporary job are comparable with that in the EU-15 countries. These percentages have not changed much during the past few years. Poland and Slovenia also have the highest percentage of temporary jobs for the 25-49 age group.

4.3.8.2 Shift work

Figure 4.40 shows the share of working men and women doing mostly shift work in EU-15 countries in 2004. Again, we can see that the diversity between the countries largely differs from the classification of the welfare states. But the order also differs greatly from the figures for temporary work. The order between the countries is the same for men and women.

In addition, with more than 20% of men and women doing mostly shift work, we find the UK, Greece and Finland. In these three countries the score for women is higher than that for men, and the difference is fairly substantial. At the bottom of the figure, Denmark, France and Belgium show the lowest score (5%-12%). Denmark is the exception, with a slightly higher percentage for women. The group in between, with 12%-20%, includes Germany, Portugal, Sweden, Spain, Austria, Ireland, Italy and Norway.

The evolution of the share of 'mostly shift work' in the period 1992-2004 is very different. For both men and women we see a clear decrease in Denmark, Belgium and Sweden, as opposed to a fairly strong increase in Germany, the UK, Portugal, Ireland, Spain, Italy and Greece. In Finland and Norway there was no significant change.

Figure 4.40 Share of working men and women doing mostly shift work in EU-15 countries (2004)

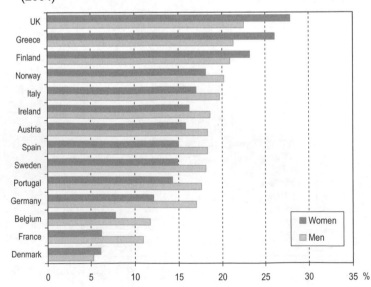

Figure 4.41 gives the share of working men and women doing mostly shift work in Eastern European countries in 2004. As for the EU-15 countries, the figure shows the diversity between the countries. The percentages are somewhat higher than in the EU-15 countries. Again, the order of the countries differs greatly from that for temporary work, except for Slovenia and Poland, again showing the highest score for both men and women, followed by the Czech Republic and Slovakia.

Figure 4.41 Share of working men and women doing mostly shift work in Eastern European countries (2004)

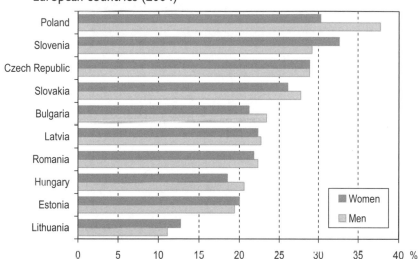

4.3.8.3 *Night work*

Figure 4.42 shows the share of working men and women doing mostly or sometimes night work in EU-15 countries in 2004. For both men and women the countries are ordered according to the percentage 'mostly'. Again, the figure shows that diversity between the countries differs greatly from the classification in the previous section and from previous figures in this section.

With respect to the percentage of 'mostly night work', the scores for men are (significantly) higher than those for women in all countries. The difference is substantial in the UK, Portugal, Austria, Italy and France. In the Nordic countries, Belgium, Greece and Spain, the difference is rather small.

For men, the UK has the highest score of 15%, followed by Finland, Austria, Italy, Portugal and France, having a score of around 10%. At the bottom, Spain, Sweden, Greece, Belgium and Norway show a score of 4%–6%. For women, Finland and the UK are at the top with 8%, followed by Denmark, Portugal, Austria and Italy with a score between 5% and 7%. Spain, Belgium, Greece and Sweden show the lowest scores (around 3%).

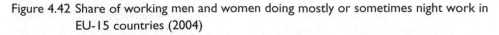

Figure 4.42 Share of working men and women doing mostly or sometimes night work in EU-15 countries (2004)

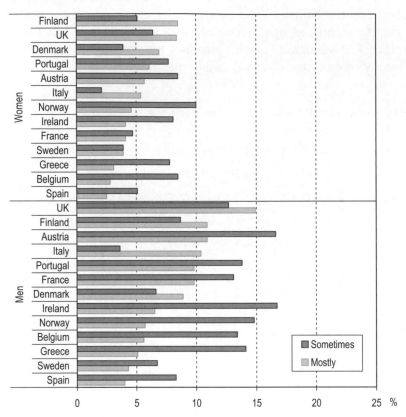

Only in the UK, Italy and Portugal one can observe a significant increase in the share of men and women doing mostly night work during the past four years, with a larger increase for men. In Greece, only women show a small but systematic increase during the whole period. Sweden is the only country with a significant decrease during the past four years. For both men and women, we see a clear decrease in Denmark, Belgium and Sweden in the period 1992-2004 against a fairly strong increase in Germany, the UK, Portugal, Ireland, Spain, Italy and Greece. Finland and Norway showed no significant change.

The scores for the percentage of 'sometimes night work' are, in all countries, also significantly higher for men than for women. Next, in countries with a lower percentage of 'mostly', the percentage of 'sometimes' is much higher than the percentage of 'mostly', which is quite logical. The exceptions here are Swedish and French women. The countries with a higher percentage of 'mostly' are divided into two subgroups. Finland, the UK, Italy and Denmark have a lower percentage of 'sometimes' while this percentage is much higher in Austria, Portugal and France (only women).

For both men and women, we see a decrease in Italy, Denmark, Finland and the UK between 1992 and 2004, and to a smaller extent in Ireland, while Spain, Greece, Belgium and Austria show a significant increase. The combination of the evolution of both percentages shows to what extent the situation has become better or worse, supposing that in general night work is worse than day work and that working mostly at night is worse than working sometimes at night. Greece is the only country with an increase in both percentages, showing that the situation in 2004 is worse than before. The UK and Italy follow, combining a strong decrease in the percentage of 'sometimes' and a strong increase in the percentage of 'mostly'. This process implies a worse situation in 2004. Spain and Belgium combine an increase in the percentage of 'sometimes' with a stable percentage of 'mostly'. The situation in 2004 therefore is a little worse than before. Norway has a more or less stable percentage of 'mostly' and 'sometimes'. Finland, Denmark and Ireland show a decreasing percentage of 'sometimes' in combination with a fairly stable percentage of 'mostly', which illustrates a small improvement. Finally, Sweden combines a stable percentage of 'sometimes' with a decreasing percentage of 'mostly', which implies a larger improvement.

Figure 4.43 gives the share of working men and women doing mostly or sometimes night work in Eastern European countries in 2004. The countries are again ordered according to the score 'mostly'.

As for the EU-15 countries, the diversity between the countries differs from the diversity in the share of temporary jobs. In most countries, men also have a higher score than women. For men and women, Slovakia has by far the highest score of 'mostly' followed by Slovenia, Estonia and Bulgaria. Lithuania has again the lowest score for men and women. Most countries with a lower (higher) score of 'mostly' show a higher (lower) score of 'sometimes'. In almost all countries, the score of 'mostly' has been stable during the past few years.

Figure 4.43 Share of working men and women doing mostly or sometimes night work in Eastern European countries (2004)

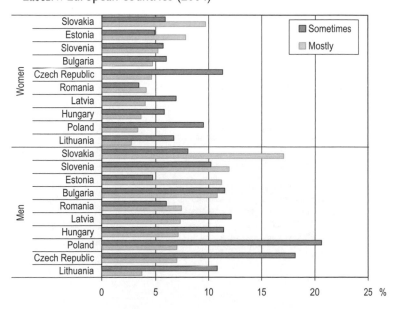

4.3.8.4 Sunday work

Figure 4.44 presents the share of working men and women doing mostly or sometimes Sunday work in EU-15 countries in 2004. Here also the countries are ordered according to the percentage of 'mostly'. No data are available for the Netherlands and Germany. The gradual diversity between the countries is again largely different from all previous classifications.

Contrary to the previous figures, the percentage of 'mostly Sunday work' is very variable. In Ireland, Austria, Italy, Greece, Norway and Portugal the scores for men are higher than those for women. Finland, Spain, France and the UK show hardly any difference between men and women, while in Denmark, Sweden and Belgium the scores for women are somewhat higher than those for men.

The percentage for men is the highest in Denmark (18%) followed by Austria and Finland (17%). The lowest percentage can be found in Belgium (8%), Portugal (10%) and Sweden (11%). The in-between group consists of Ireland, Italy, Greece, Spain, Norway, France and the UK (between 12% and 15%). For women, the same three countries are at the top, with more or less the same scores. The lowest score is for Ireland (9%) and Belgium (10%) followed by Portugal, Norway and Greece (about 11%). In between we find scores of 13%–14% in Italy, the UK, Sweden, France and Spain.

Figure 4.44 Share of working men and women doing mostly or sometimes Sunday work in EU-15 countries (2004)

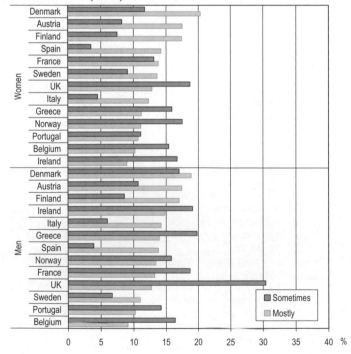

Portugal, Sweden, Ireland and Finland show a significant decrease in the share of men and women doing mostly Sunday work in the period 1992-2004. In all other countries, the share of both men and women has been stable during this period.

The scores for 'sometimes Sunday work' are higher for men than for women in all countries but Norway and Belgium. Next, in the three countries with the highest percentage of 'mostly', the percentage of 'sometimes' is much lower, for both men and women. This is also the case in Spain, Italy and Sweden. In all other countries (with a lower percentage of 'mostly'), the percentage of 'sometimes' is significantly higher, for men and women. Compared to other countries, the score for men in the UK is extremely high, combined with an in-between percentage of 'mostly'.

We can see a clear decrease in Italy, Sweden, Finland, Austria, Denmark and the UK. Belgium shows a small increase during the whole period, while Portugal saw a very sharp increase during the past few years, from about 3% in 2000 to 11% for women and 14% for men.

Again, the combination of the evolution of both percentages expresses the degree of improvement or setback, supposing that Sunday work is generally worse than work during the week and that working mostly on Sunday is worse than working sometimes on Sunday. In no country did both percentages increase in the period 1992-2004. The worst actual evolution, with an increase in the score for 'mostly' and a decrease in the score for 'sometimes' is observed for men and women in Italy and Austria, and for women only in the UK. A stable score for 'mostly' in combination with an increase in the score for 'sometimes' is shown for Belgium. A stable score for 'mostly' and 'sometimes' is visible for men and women in Spain and Greece. A decrease in the score for 'mostly' and an increase in the score for 'sometimes' can be seen in Portugal. A stable score for 'mostly' and a decrease in the score for 'sometimes' occurs in Denmark and in the UK (only women). A decrease in the score for 'mostly' and a stable score for 'sometimes' can be found in Ireland and Norway for men and women, and for men in the UK. Finally, Sweden and Finland show a decrease in both scores, expressing the best evolution from the normative perspective we formulated.

Figure 4.45 presents the scores for the Eastern European countries. Here, also, the ranking of the countries differs from that of previous aspects.

The scores for 'mostly' show more or less the same diversity as for the EU-15 countries. Men have somewhat higher scores than women in most countries. For men, Romania has the highest score, followed by Slovakia, Bulgaria, Latvia and Slovenia, while the Czech Republic and Hungary have the lowest score. For women, Romania also has the highest score, followed by Latvia, Estonia, Slovenia and Slovakia. Hungary currently has the lowest score, followed by the Czech Republic.

As for previous aspects, most countries with a lower (higher) score for 'mostly' show a higher (lower) score for 'sometimes'. Finally, the score for 'mostly' has been fairly stable during the past few years in all countries.

Figure 4.45 Share of working men and women doing mostly or sometimes Sunday work in Eastern European countries (2004)

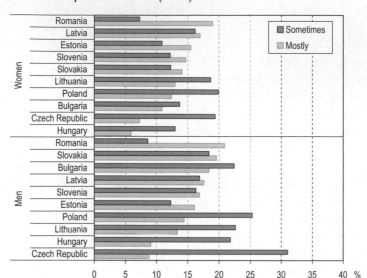

4.3.8.5 Home work

Figure 4.46 presents the share of men and women working mostly or sometimes at home in EU-15 countries in 2004. As before, the countries are ordered according to the percentage of men and women working mostly at home. For the Netherlands, only the data for working mostly at home are available. We must be aware that the percentages also include independent workers.

Again, the gradual diversity between the countries does not follow the diversity in the previous figures. The percentage of men and women working mostly at home is very variable. In Finland, the Netherlands, Norway and Ireland, the score for men is higher than that for women. In Italy and Sweden, the percentages are equal, while in all other countries the percentage for men is lower than that for women. The percentage for men is the highest in Ireland (13%) followed by Finland, Norway, Belgium, France and Austria. The lowest percentage can be found in Spain (1%), Portugal, Greece and the UK. The in-between group consists of the Netherlands, Denmark, Sweden, Italy and Germany. For women, France is at the top, with a score of 13%, followed by Austria, Finland and Belgium. The lowest scores are for Spain, Portugal and Greece. In between we can find the UK, Germany, Italy, Sweden, Denmark and the Netherlands.

Portugal, Germany, Sweden, Denmark, Austria, Belgium and Ireland show a decrease in the share of men and women working mostly at home in the period 1992-2004. In all other countries, the share of both men and women has been largely constant during this period.

Figure 4.46 Share of working men and women working mostly or sometimes at home in EU-15 countries (2004)

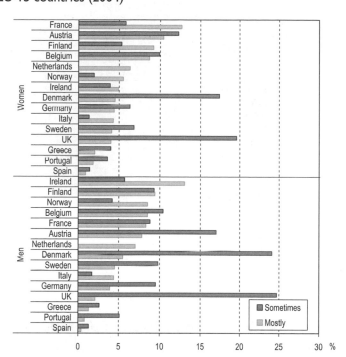

The scores for working sometimes at home are (much) higher for men than for women in all countries, except for Greece and Spain. In most countries, the percentage of 'sometimes' is much higher than the percentage of 'mostly', except in Finland, Norway and Italy for men and women, in Ireland for women and in France for men. In particular in the UK, Denmark and Austria, the percentage of 'sometimes' is very high.

We observe a moderate increase in Spain, Portugal, Ireland, Finland, Germany, Sweden and Belgium and a large increase in Austria and Denmark. The UK and Italy show a small decrease, while the scores are constant in the other countries.

Finally, Figure 4.47 gives the results for the Eastern European countries. Again, the ranking of the countries is largely different from that of the other aspects.

In general, the scores for 'mostly' are significantly lower than for the EU-15 countries, both for men and women. Women have somewhat higher scores than men in most countries. For men, Estonia has the highest score for 'mostly' followed by Slovenia and Latvia, while for women Slovenia shows the highest score followed by Latvia. For men and women, Romania and Lithuania have the lowest score. Here, most countries show a higher score for 'sometimes' than 'mostly'. Finally, the score for 'mostly' has been largely stable during the past few years in all countries.

Figure 4.47 Share of working men and women working mostly or sometimes at home in Eastern European countries (2004)

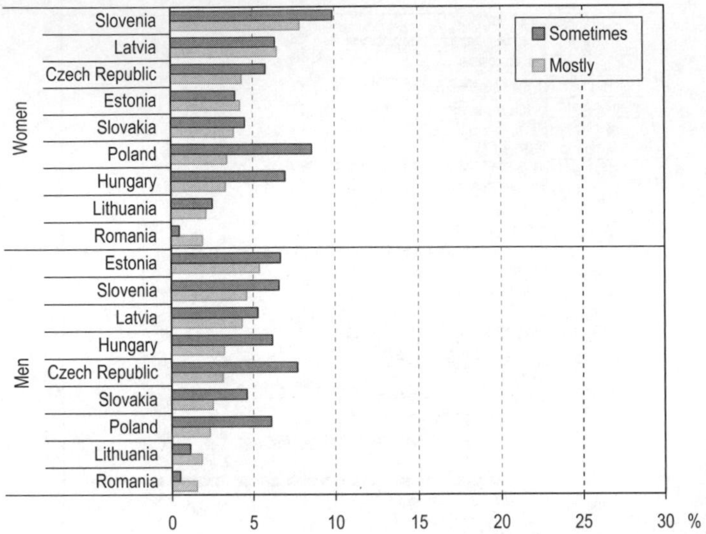

4.4 Summary: evolution of the division of professional and family work

4.4.1 From the breadwinner model to the moderate combination model

This chapter has offered a broad picture of the *actual division of professional and family labour* in EU countries and some other OECD countries. By means of some basic indicators we showed the general development from the strong breadwinner model in the period 1950-70 to a moderate combination model in the period 1985-2005. We started with a wider historical perspective, illustrating the long evolution since 1850, from the old combination model in the 18th and 19th century to the strong breadwinner model in the 20th century, as Figure 1.1 shows in a general way. The second section presented a general historical model for the period 1950-2005, based on the total activity rate and the average number of hours of professional and family labour of men and women, both for the total groups and for different age groups. The empirical model proves to be very well applicable in all countries of the western world. At the same time, the gradual differences between the (types of) welfare states became visible. The third section illustrated the development in the period 1985-2005 by means of some complementary indicators. The indicators give a complementary picture of the development of the division of professional and family labour in the different countries, which is compatible with the longer-term picture in previous sections. Again, we emphasise both the overall similarity of the process in all countries and the (gradual) differences between the different (types of) welfare states.

In general, we note more or less the same basic division of professional labour, family labour, social labour, personal care and free time in all European (and other western) countries. This means that all countries have gone through the same historic basic models: from the old combination model in the 19th century to the (strong or moderate) breadwinner model in the 20th century and to a variant of the moderate combination model at the beginning of the 21st century. This implies that all these countries largely face the same normative challenge concerning the future division of professional and family work, taking into account the differences in welfare level and societal context.

A possible and plausible explanation for this large similarity in the division of basic activities is related to the fact that every person has the same amount of time available in their daily life: 24 hours a day, 168 hours/week, 52 weeks a year, etc. People only differ in the total number of available years in the life course, which can mostly only be determined with certainty by the end of their life. So in their daily division of time during the life course, most people do not bother that much about the potential number of years in their lives. Starting from this, the basic argument can be formulated in the following way.

We can observe different levels of welfare in the different countries, as expressed by the composition of the personal, social, material and financial means at the input and output side of all basic activities. The total welfare is the result of the daily division of basic activities. In all countries, a certain average number of hours (per week, per year) of all basic activities is necessary to realise the output that corresponds with that specific actual welfare level, given the available input elements and productivity level. The output of every activity is the input for the other activities. We emphasise the conceptual starting point of the Combination Model that on average all basic activities equally contribute to the development of the total personal, social, material and financial capital of people, families, organisations and of society as a whole. So, in every country a certain average number of hours of professional labour is required to realise the professional output of that welfare level, with the available professional inputs (technology and productivity level). At the same time, a certain average number of hours of family labour are needed to produce the family output that corresponds with that welfare level, with the available inputs (technology and productivity level). The same can be said for the other basic activities. A striking observation in this context is the almost equal and constant number of hours of total labour (sum of professional and family labour) for both men and women in the period 1960-2000. Unlike all technological progress during the past decades, all men and women in all these countries spent almost the same number of hours on the two basic activities in order to realise the specific output level in each period.

Starting from these observations, one could formulate the strong hypothesis that the division of basic activities between men and women is largely similar in all countries of the world, with a similar diversity as we observed for the European countries. It would be interesting to test this hypothesis in the future by means of basic time use data for some countries in other parts of the world. More or less by coincidence, we received a paper by Ferre et al (2004) dealing with the division of hours of family labour between men and women in Uruguay (2001). The curves for the division of family labour in Uruguay ware very similar to those for Flanders (1999) and other European countries (see Figure 4.32). This suggests that the division of family labour in Latin American countries is quite similar to that in European and North American countries. If this hypothesis could be supported, the policy challenge concerning the future division of professional and family work would also be largely similar for all these countries, albeit within the specific societal and welfare context of the different regions and countries.

The main differences between the division of labour of men and women, both on the micro and macro level, almost completely refer to professional and family work. The other basic activities show no significant differences between men and women. Although the number of hours of total labour was largely constant for both men and women, the difference in professional and family work was very important for the development of individuals, families, organisations and society as a whole, in terms of the right combination of personal, social, material and financial capital.

The unequal division of professional and family has a long history in all countries, albeit with a different course. The basic idea is that the dominance of the breadwinner model was restricted to a fairly short period in the long history. Yet, the breaking down of the old combination model and the development of the breadwinner model during many decades had a big impact on the division of labour in western societies. For decades, the professional human capital of women has been systematically weakened and neglected in business life, both in quantity and quality. At the same time, most men changed their basic attitude towards the division of labour, largely neglecting their engagement for family work, with a loss of family-oriented personal and social competences.

The famous 'economic approach to human behaviour' of Becker (1965) (New Home Economics) is based on a dual model of human activities and on the actual inequality in professional capital between men and women in the period 1950-70, when the breadwinner model was dominant. In that short period one could clearly observe the actual comparative advantages of women in the household and those of men in professional life. But Becker and so many researchers after him largely neglected the long process leading to that big inequality in human capital and the meaning of the combination perspective, saying that each activity offers a specific combination of personal, social, material and financial benefits and that people must perform each activity themselves to a certain extent in order to realise the human benefits.

Although the overall welfare level increased in all countries, this most probably cannot be attributed to the so-called 'advantages' of the unequal division of labour in the breadwinner model. The 'gender specialisation process' did not in itself lead to the enrichment of society, neither in professional life nor in family life. After all, the model is largely inefficient because the professional human capital of women and the household human capital of men were neglected to a large extent, with a very unequal development and division of power in all segments of society. The increase in wealth in the 20th century is mainly the result of the social welfare state and the increase in the general education level, largely initiated by different social movements, technological revolutions and the internationalisation of the market system. Starting from an integrated approach, one can strongly argue that the development of the welfare states in the 20th century was restricted or hampered by the dominant breadwinner model, especially by the unequal and inefficient use of male and female human capital in professional and family life. From that perspective, more attention can and must be focused on the financial burden of the breadwinner model during previous decades for individuals, families, companies and society as a whole. Cuvilier (1979) was probably the first to clearly highlight this financial burden, in particular the (hidden) financial support given to the large group of breadwinner families, largely at the expense of combination families with a modest income. Only in that way could the government prevent a large group of breadwinner families from having insufficient family income and ending up in poverty.

We emphasise again that this critical consideration is completely aimed at the breadwinner model as a societal model or system and certainly not at the individual breadwinner families and their family members. This analysis does not criticise or attack all men and women who have 'opted' for the unequal division of labour of the breadwinner family for different reasons. After all, these families made a legitimate choice within the societal context of that time, starting from their personal and social background. We highlight in particular the often hidden societal costs of the breadwinner model for many groups in society.

Evidently, it is impossible to know for sure whether the period of the breadwinner model was inevitable in the western world. To a certain extent the Nordic countries show that this was not the case in all countries, but the Nordic countries did not escape from the influence of the breadwinner model (Borchorst, 2008; Lundqvist, 2008; Melby et al, 2008). The actual dominance of the model during a certain period in most countries shows that the societal forces in favour of the model were stronger than the counterforces. But this dominance does not imply that the breadwinner model in itself was better for (the overall welfare level in) society. This evaluation depends on the normative approach to society, the market system and division of labour in families and organisations. Unlike the actual dominance of the breadwinner model, we can argue that from a democratic point of view the model was not necessary to realise a higher level of welfare in modern societies. On the contrary, the overall welfare level could and most probably would have been higher with a more equal division of professional and family work between men and women during this period, especially because of the more efficient use of the human capital of men and women in both professional life and family life.

But a critical attitude is necessary again. The evolution in Eastern Europe in the period 1950-90 illustrates that an equal division of labour is surely not a sufficient condition for realising a democratic society with a high welfare level. Moreover, an equal division of labour with insufficient freedom for personal choice and initiative and with a an inefficient allocation of the means of production, cannot lead to a (more) wealthy democratic society. A real democratic welfare state aims at sufficient equality going hand in hand with sufficient freedom, solidarity and efficiency in all segments of society. This normative challenge for the future division of labour in democratic welfare states is the main topic of the following chapters.

4.4.2 The moderate combination model in the different welfare states as the starting point for future models

We conclude this long empirical story with a general overview of the variants or stages of the contemporary moderate combination model in the different countries (see Figure 4.15). As said before, the models are determined by the combination of professional and family work, expressed by the participation of men and women in these activities and by the number of hours per week. The classification is a more differentiated version of the famous classification of Esping–Andersen (1990, 1999) and Korpi (2000) with respect to the division of labour. Most countries can be placed in one group fairly easily; the countries in brackets are less typical of that model and are on the borderline with another model:

- southern weaker combination model (moderate breadwinner model) in Italy, Spain, Greece, Cyprus and Malta;
- continental moderate combination model in Belgium, France, Germany, Austria, Luxembourg, (the Netherlands and Portugal);
- Anglo–Saxon moderate combination model in the US, Canada, the UK (and Ireland);
- Nordic more advanced combination model in Sweden, Denmark, Norway, Finland and Iceland;
- eastern more advanced combination model in Eastern European countries.

The Combination Model in the southern countries of Italy, Spain, Greece, Cyprus and Malta is, in fact, still a rather weak combination model (or even a moderate breadwinner model), with a fairly unequal division of professional and family labour between men and women. As shown, Portugal does not follow this model for most of the basic indicators presented in this chapter. The southern countries still show a high proportion of women staying at home and a small average number of hours of professional labour for the total group of women. Professionally active women, however, have a fairly heavy burden with a large number of working hours. The still largely dual division of labour is a typical heritage of the strong breadwinner model. A few decades ago, this pattern was also visible in the continental countries such as Germany, Belgium and Austria. The past decades show a rather fast development towards a higher participation of women in the labour market, together with an increase in societal provisions for combination families, in particular external childcare for the youngest children. The main question is, then, how fast this process will be followed by a redistribution of family labour in order to have a more equal division of both professional and family labour. These countries have chosen the path towards a more advanced moderate combination model. An important challenge here is whether the traditional pedagogical and family view supporting the actual policy model can be changed in the direction of a more shared education during the next decades.

The continental or western European countries of Belgium, France, Germany, Austria and Luxembourg really represent the moderate combination model as presented in Figure 4.14. The Netherlands and Portugal are located more at the crossing with other models. All indicators illustrate the position of these countries between the southern and Nordic countries. This again shows that Figure 4.10 is largely inspired by the actual development in these countries and therefore must be applied to other countries with sufficient flexibility. During the past 40 years, these countries moved step by step from a moderate breadwinner model to a moderate combination model, investing in a more equal division of labour and more societal provisions for combination families. Although the gap between men and women is still significant, largely reflecting the policy models of past decades (Korpi, 2000; Gornick and Meyers, 2003), these countries are ready to move forward to a more advanced combination model during the next decades. Since these countries also show many gradual differences in the daily division of labour and in their policies, every country has to develop its own short-term policy model in order to move to a more advanced combination model. Again, a major challenge in these countries is the broader introduction and acceptance of a new pedagogical view for the youngest children and a new family view, based on shared education within and outside the family.

The English-speaking countries of the US, Canada, the UK (and Ireland) follow a more advanced combination model than the continental countries, as is illustrated by the higher activity rate of women and the somewhat more equal division of professional and family labour. The more liberal market system and market policy push most women into the labour market. One of the major problems is the lower quality of the jobs of lower-qualified women and men, with a negative effect on their daily life. Yet the division of household labour is somewhat more equal than in the continental European countries, probably due to the lack of leave facilities with sufficient financial compensation, offering fewer opportunities for women to invest in their family life, but at the same time urging men, to a larger extent, to participate in daily family tasks. The gap between men and women is still quite large and one can surely question whether the current policy is a good basis to diminish that gap and to move toward a more advanced combination model during the next few decades. As these countries develop their own policy model towards a better combination model, they will have to deal with the lack of high-quality daycare provisions for the large group of low-income families, starting from a new pedagogical view on education/care for the youngest children.

The model in the Nordic countries of Sweden, Denmark, Norway, Finland and Iceland is already a more advanced moderate combination model. With a very long tradition in social policy and equality policy for men and women (Korpi, 2000), these countries show a largely equal activity rate for men and women. Although the division of professional and family labour is the most equal of all countries, there is still a significant gap between the number of hours worked by men and women. The current combination model is the result of the generous leave policy for parents with children younger than one year and the generous high-quality childcare provisions for children older than one year. The main challenge for these countries is to further bridge the structural gap between men and women, by reforming the current combination of leave and childcare policy. The question here is whether the deeply rooted pedagogical view underpinning the actual policy model in these countries can be changed during the next few decades, in order to create also for the youngest children a strong basis for a shared education.

Finally, the Combination Model in the Eastern European countries can also be called 'more advanced' in the sense that the division of professional labour between men and women is more equal than in the southern and continental countries. This is largely the result of the 'very strong combination policy' followed by the former communist regimes, strongly emphasising the equality of men and women in the labour market. This basic goal, however, came at the cost of the free choice of people and the efficient allocation of human and non-human means. As a consequence, these countries are quite far behind with respect to economic development and general welfare levels. At the same time it is clear that the basic idea of the breadwinner family is still (or again) attractive for a part of the population. The future development of a modern combination model implies the realisation of a division of labour with sufficient freedom, equality, solidarity and efficiency. This process will gradually differ between countries, depending on the overall approach to society and to the division of labour between men and women. In some countries, one can see a small shift backwards to the moderate breadwinner model, while other countries are moving to an advanced combination model. However, these countries will suffer from an overall weaker economic basis and a higher unemployment rate for both men and women.

Most of the countries can be placed in one of the five groups or models quite easily, while some countries are located on the border between one or more groups. This is the case for the Netherlands, Ireland and Portugal. The Netherlands are historically linked with the continental and Nordic model, but the country has increasingly moved towards the Anglo-Saxon model during the past two decades, especially with respect to social and fiscal policy. Ireland is labelled as an Anglo-Saxon model because of its liberal social and employment policy, but it lies on the border with the continental model since the strong breadwinner model has been dominant for many decades. Finally, Portugal is classified as a continental model but is actually on the border with the southern and the Anglo-Saxon model, due to its geographical location and historical influences.

A classification of countries is always relative and restricted because it is based on a few essential factors or indicators. Therefore, we again emphasise the gradual differences between and within the five groups of countries. A classification is necessary and useful to distinguish a number of similar patterns between countries within the multitude of differences.

4.4.3 Complementary empirical models of the division of labour

We must recognise that the empirical story in this chapter is far from complete. The main goal is to offer a sufficiently differentiated and integrated picture of the actual division of labour, starting from the conceptual and normative approach of the Combination Model in the previous chapters. The empirical models offer a solid basis for the elaboration of normative models and policy perspectives for the future division of labour in the next chapters.

Our empirical presentation of the division of labour between men and women is only one of the possible presentations. We have mentioned some other integrating models of the division of labour. Therefore, we finish this chapter with a short presentation of a rather similar empirical model of the division of labour between men and women that is strongly inspired by the TLM model (Anxo, 2004; Anxo and Boulin, 2004, 2005, 2006a, 2006b; Anxo and Ehrel, 2004; Anxo et al, 2004, 2006).

These authors studied the patterns or models of labour market integration in a number of European countries from a life course perspective. In that way they tried to identify four types of welfare states with respect to the time policy or combination policy: the universal breadwinner model (Sweden, Denmark), the modified breadwinner model (France, Belgium), the part-time work model (the Netherlands, UK) and the Mediterranean model (moderate breadwinner model) (Italy and Spain). This classification is largely similar to ours but some countries are placed in another group: Germany, for example, is placed in the same group as the Netherlands and the UK, while in our classification Germany is in the group containing France and Belgium.

Using cross-sectional data from the European Community Household Panel (ECHP) they created a number of family types in terms of partnership, presence of children and age of the children. These 'cross-sectional' family types were then 'placed after one another in a time perspective' in order to simulate the different family stages during the life course. So, family types were used as the expression or simulation of the (normal) successive family stages of men and women. They then presented three labour market indicators for all the family stages: activity rate, average number of hours of professional labour per week of all men and women in the professional population and average number of hours of professional labour per week of all professionally active men and women. The graphical presentation of the three indicators for different EU-15 countries illustrates the patterns or models of labour market integration.

Figures 4.48, 4.49 and 4.50 show the results for Spain, France, the UK and Sweden. Each of these countries represents one of the labour market models mentioned. These figures show the same gradual differences between the European countries: from the southern countries (Spain), the continental countries (France), the Anglo-Saxon countries (UK) to the Nordic countries (Sweden). Figures 4.22, 4.27 and 4.29 in this study present the differences between the age groups of men and women, illustrating the evolution in time for different (types of) countries. But these figures can also be used as an expression of (changes during) the life course of men and women.

Figure 4.48 illustrates the activity rate in the different 'family stages' and can be compared with Figure 4.22. The 'life course models' of Anxo et al (2004, 2006) are clearly complementary to our empirical models. The most important feature and advantage of their presentation by means of the family stages is that the differences with respect to the presence and the age of children are more visible. The figure shows that the activity rate of mothers with young children (family stage 3) is lower in all but the Nordic countries. This difference is less visible in Figure 4.22 since young mothers are located in more age groups, together with young women of other family types. Figure 4.48 is a simulation of the family stages during the life course, but the actual combination of family stages in daily life can differ to a large extent between men and women.

Figure 4.48 Activity rate of men and women during the different family stages in some EU-15 countries (2000)

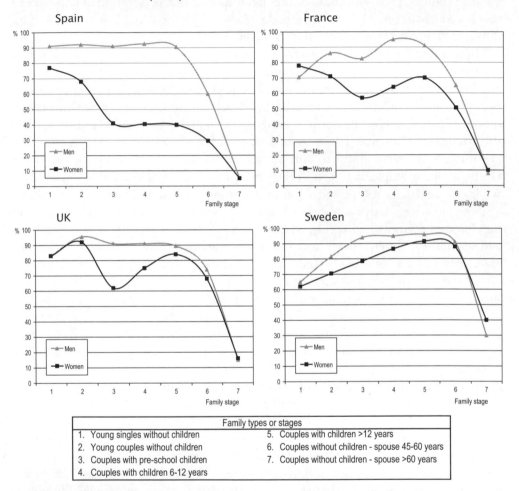

Figure 4.49 presents the average number of hours of professional labour per week of all men and women in the professional population and is comparable with Figure 4.27. The figure illustrates the lower number of working hours of young mothers (family stage 3) in all countries, including the Nordic countries. In the southern countries the number of working hours is also small during the later family stages, while in the other countries the number increases again in these stages and then strongly decreases in the latest stages.

Figure 4.49 Average number of working hours of men and women during the family stages in some EU-15 countries (2000)

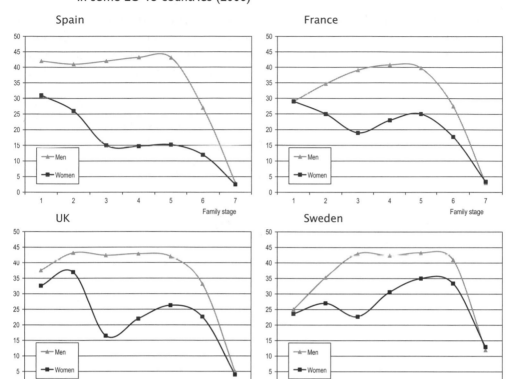

Family types or stages	
1. Young singles without children	5. Couples with children >12 years
2. Young couples without children	6. Couples without children - spouse 45-60 years
3. Couples with pre-school children	7. Couples without children - spouse >60 years
4. Couples with children 6-12 years	

Finally, Figure 4.50 illustrates the average number of hours of professional labour per week of all professionally active men and women, and is to be compared with Figure 4.29. In the southern, continental and Nordic countries all working women have quite a high number of working hours, while in Anglo-Saxon countries young working mothers have a lower number of working hours.

The simulated 'life course models' of Anxo et al (2004, 2006) clearly offer the same basic information about the labour market patterns as our combination models with a life course perspective. But essentially they illustrate an *additional* aspect of the division of professional labour in a compact way and are therefore complementary to the combination models presented in this chapter. This comparison again illustrates that all indicators include a limited empirical message about certain aspects of the complex division of labour. The combination of some strong empirical indicators or models creates a broad empirical picture of the actual division of labour, as the basis for the policy debate.

The disadvantage of these labour market models is that they do not pay attention to the division of family labour (and other basic activities), in relation to the division of professional labour. Therefore, it would be useful to develop these 'life course models' for family labour (and the other basic activities), based on time use data.

Figure 4.50 Average number of working hours of men and women who actually have a job during the family stages in some EU-15 countries (2000)

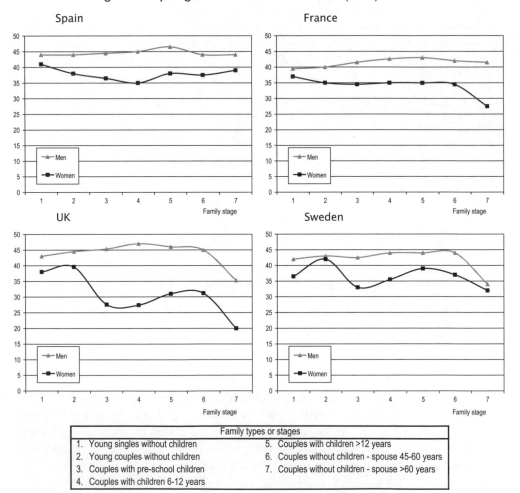

Family types or stages	
1. Young singles without children	5. Couples with children >12 years
2. Young couples without children	6. Couples without children - spouse 45-60 years
3. Couples with pre-school children	7. Couples without children - spouse >60 years
4. Couples with children 6-12 years	

The Complete Combination Model as the basis for an integrated policy in a strong democracy

5.1 Meaning of normative future models or policy models

The previous chapters led to the central policy question for the future: how should the division of professional and family labour in democratic societies be developed? Starting from the conceptual approach and the empirical models of the actual development (see Figures 4.15 and 4.24, Chapter 4), future development can be explored in many different ways, looking at what people think, expect, hope, believe or want to happen in the future. Consequently, an immense number of models or images of future development are possible, and many different scenarios or paths leading to those models (de Smedt, 2005). From a scientific point of view, it is necessary to develop future models that have a strong empirical basis and sufficiently link up with (the empirical models of) actual development. But even then a large number of future models are possible. So, further selection is necessary to avoid a too extensive and too expensive scientific exploration process. After all, future scientific models and scenarios always (have to) serve certain societal goals and must therefore be developed in an efficient way. This process must lead to the most relevant future models that are largely feasible and desirable.

So, we automatically come to the *normative dimension* that is always present in societal life and in all scientific research. Since all scientific models of the past and current world have a normative dimension, background or determinant, this is certainly the case for all scientific models of the future world. This normative dimension can be explicit or implicit, dominant or subordinate, clear or vague, and so on, but it is always there. In the past, many scientists or scientific schools tried to hide the normative component. An *integrated view on science* implies that the normative dimension is explicitly and actively used in a controlled way, as a positive, constructive and selective component for the development of the most relevant future models. With this perspective, we use the terms 'normative future models' or 'policy models'.

This brings us back to the basic normative question that all democratic countries or societies have to answer: which model of the division of professional and family labour should be (further) developed in the future, in the long and short run? This question was visually expressed in Figure 1.1 by means of the long-term transformation to a new basic societal model, which was called the model of a democratic welfare state and a democratic market system. The general starting point is that western democratic countries have opted for the new basic model. During the next few decades this model will become more dominant, but the old model will still have a significant influence.

Therefore, it is not certain which variant of the new basic model will actually be established.

All national and supra-national authorities have to decide on the general policy model to be used as a guideline for the basic policy perspectives and for the specific policy measures that determine and orient the practical organisation of daily life within families, clubs, companies, institutions, and so on. It is necessary, therefore, that all political parties, governments and large societal organisations are very clear about the normative future model they use as a general guideline for their policy. Sciences can support these societal actors by developing useful normative future models, starting from a broad and solid conceptual approach, a strong basic normative view and adequate empirical models of actual development.

In this chapter, we try to answer this basic normative question by means of three normative models or policy models of the daily division of professional and family labour: the strong combination model, the complete combination model and the moderate combination model. More models can be conceived (Van Dongen and Beck, 1999), but this does not increase the clarity and efficiency of the future exploration process and policy debate.

Each of the three policy models expresses an ideal normative view for the future, largely reflecting a major variant of the normative concept of democracy or democratic society, in terms of the relative meaning of basic values for the division of labour between men and women. Since the normative models represent ideal policy views for the long run, they do not (completely) coincide with the actual political or ideological views. They can be used as scientific instruments to screen and evaluate the existing policy models of the major policy actors in society.

Starting from the normative perspective of a strong democracy, we argue that the complete combination model is the most suitable long-term policy model for all western welfare states. It is, most of all, compatible with a fully democratic division of labour in families and organisations and it is also in line with actual development during the past few decades. We conclude this chapter with a brief presentation of the other normative policy models mentioned before.

5.2 Presentation of the normative future models

Starting from the general concept of a 'strong democracy', one can formulate the normative question in more operational terms: which normative future model can serve as an adequate normative guide for future development towards a fully democratic division of professional and family labour and for future policy to realise it? This general policy question contains three specific questions expressing the interaction between the conceptual, empirical and normative dimension of the models. First, which combination of the basic values of democracy (freedom, equality, solidarity and efficiency) do the normative models reflect? In other words, what is the relative weight of these values in the three models? Second, to what extent do the models link up with the actual development of the division of professional and family work? Or, in short, to what extent are they feasible within a reasonable time? Finally, to what extent can the models lead to a consistent set of mutually supportive policy perspectives for the long run, as the basis for policy measures and instruments in the short run?

In general, a fully democratic division of labour between men and women implies a real balance between the four basic values. All basic values have to be realised in a sufficient way simultaneously, both stimulating and restricting one another continually. Equality within and between families is very important but must be realised in a gradual way, leaving sufficient choice for the possible combinations of professional and family work. The main goal is to determine and realise the most desirable gradual division of professional and family labour, expressing the right degree and form of equality and diversity.

Given the general acceptance of the concept of democracy in the different countries, it is understandable that every country at least wants to realise a better combination model in the short run, that is, a more advanced stage of the moderate combination model, as is shown for professional labour in Figure 5.1. A similar figure can be produced for family labour. The figure follows the presentation in Figures 4.14, 4.24 and 4.31, expressing the *basic normative idea* of the gradual equality (or inequality) in the actual and future division of labour in the clearest way.

Figure 5.1 Stages of the moderate combination model (professional labour)

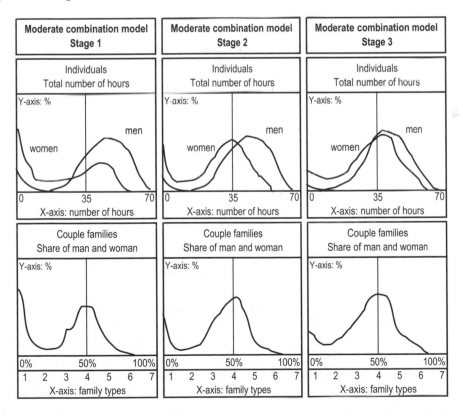

However, the choice for a better combination model in the short run does not answer the question of which final combination model should be used as a policy guideline in the long run. Figure 5.1 does not clearly formulate the long-term orientation. Starting from the actual situation in each country, several paths or scenarios are possible. It is therefore important that the long-term normative model is explicitly formulated and thoroughly discussed in order to serve as a solid guideline for specific policy models in the short run.

Figure 5.2 shows three symmetric normative models for the future division of professional and family labour, placed within a long-term perspective (2030-50):
- strong combination model (SCM)
- complete combination model (CCM)
- moderate combination model (MCM)

The figure follows the empirical models shown in Figures 4.14, 4.24 and 4.31, expressing the desirable division of labour in the long run. To have a more differentiated picture, the models can also be presented by means of the indicators in Figure 4.6 and Figure 4.27. Again, we think that the curves in Figure 5.2 offer the strongest compact expression of the desirable division of labour in the three models.

As the figure clearly shows, all three normative models are symmetric, expressing the importance of gender equality in the EU as a basic value for future policy on the macro level. If necessary, less symmetric variants can be designed for each model. The shape of the curve (smaller or wider) determines the level of equality on the micro level, that is, within the group of men and women and within families. A smaller curve implies a higher degree of equality, while a wider curve implies a lower degree of equality.

The upper part of the figure shows for the three models the desirable division of the number of hours of professional and family work for all men and women in the professional population, with or without a partner, with or without children (macro level). The curves of professional and family work of men and women coincide in all three models, albeit with a different scale on the X-axis: from 0-70 hours for professional labour and from 0-50 hours for family labour (see the typology in Figure 2.12). Although this range of hours largely results from the actual development, it is not absolute and can be modified if necessary. It could be different across the (types of) countries, but it is better to use one version to present all policy models.

The curves show that the division of the number of hours of professional and family work must be symmetric on the macro level, that is, between the whole group of men and the whole group of women. Each curve presents a specific normative answer to the actual unequal division of professional and family work as shown in Figures 4.14, 4.24 and 4.31, which is seen as undesirable from the normative perspective.

The middle part illustrates the desirable division of the total number of hours of professional and family work within couple families (two adult partners living together, married or not, with or without children). Again, the curves of professional and family work of men and women coincide in all three models, with a different scale on the X-axis: from 30-110 hours for professional labour and from 20-80 hours for family labour. The range of hours on the X-axis can also be modified here.

Figure 5.2   Normative future models for the division of professional and family labour of individual men and women and of families (2050)

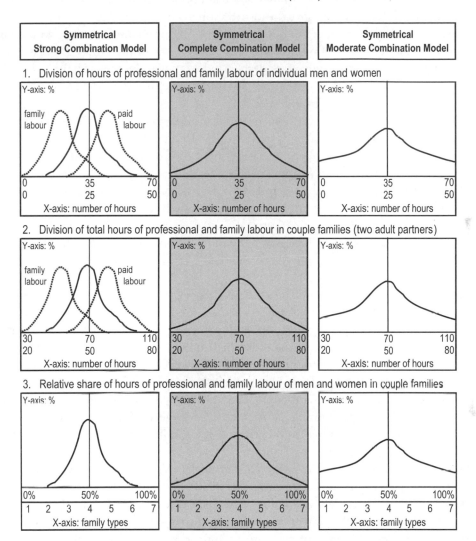

These curves give possible normative answers to the undesirable actual unequal division of the total professional and family work within couple families. Unfortunately, we do not have sufficient internationally comparative data to show the actual division of the total professional and family work. This is an empirical task for the future, offering additional evidence for the actual development of the combination model.

The curves express the additional condition for future policy that couple families need a sufficient total number of hours of professional and family work to realise a decent welfare level. The importance of this condition is illustrated by Cantillon et al (2002), emphasising the high poverty risk for couple families without any professional work and, consequently, without any professional income.

The lower part presents the desirable relative division of professional and family work between the partners of couple families, as an additional condition for future equality on the micro level. The figures give the distribution of couple families (Y-axis) based on the relative share of the number of hours of professional and family work of women in the total number of hours of professional and family work of the family (X-axis). The curves of professional and family work of men and women coincide in all three models, with the same scale on the X-axis: from 0%-100%, reflecting the gradual typology of seven family types, as shown in Figure 2.13.

The different curves give possible normative answers to the undesirable actual unequal division of professional and family work within couple families. Again, we lack comparative data to show the actual relative division of professional and family work between partners. This is also an important empirical challenge for the future.

The degree of equality on the micro level is determined by the width of the curves. A smaller curve around the centre point implies larger equality within the families. The curves show the desirable division of the different family types in society (Figure 2.13): from the strong male breadwinner family at one end (1), to the complete combination family in the centre (4), to the strong female breadwinner family at the other end (7).

The three policy models formulate a different message and orientation for the future division of labour. The *strong combination model* on the left side of Figure 5.2 aims at a high professional participation of all men and women and at a largely equal division of professional and family labour, at the individual and family level, leaving less freedom to choose a more unequal division of labour. The *complete combination model* allows all possible choices, combining a fairly high participation of men and women with a fairly equal division of professional and family labour and giving some freedom to choose a less equal division of labour. The *moderate combination model* offers more space for an unequal division of professional and family labour, sacrificing the equality condition to a larger extent.

The first publications on the combination model (Van Dongen and Beck, 1999; Van Dongen and Franken, 1999), presented five policy models, with a *very strong combination model* on the left side and a *weak combination model* on the right. A very strong combination model aims at very high labour market participation and an equal division of labour between partners, with little freedom for personal choice. A weak combination model starts from much freedom to choose the division of labour, with an unequal division of labour between partners, largely sacrificing the basic value of 'equality' in favour of the value of 'freedom'. The societal discussion with different stakeholders showed that these more extreme policy models were not that relevant anymore. The reduction to three policy models increases the clarity and efficiency of the societal debate. However, when necessary, the more extreme models can always be introduced again.

As said before, the three models are ideal, which means that, to a certain extent, they differ from actual political or ideological views. Yet the general orientation of the actual political or ideological views can be more or less recognised. The models must be used as reflective instruments or long-term guidelines to feed and orient the societal and political debate on the future division of labour in modern societies, within the boundaries of the concept of 'democracy'. Of course, many variants of these models can be constructed, but this does not offer more clarity or efficiency for the debate. Every societal actor (individuals, families, companies, societal organisations, political parties, governments, and so on) can choose only one model as their normative guideline for the future division of labour. It is therefore important that all major societal and political actors explicitly show which normative model they choose as the long-term guideline for their policy view and for the policy programmes in the shorter run. So the political debate can become more transparent and efficient.

During the past few years, criticism has been formulated against the use of such policy models. Some argue that these models are too prescriptive or pedantic, pushing people too strongly in a certain direction and that they restrict or destroy too much the freedom of people to choose the division of labour they prefer. Moreover, some critics suggest that the models are too extreme, implying that they are too far away from the actual situation. The first criticism often reflects the idea that individuals, families, organisations and society as a whole can function without using these kinds of normative models or that in the current situation no such directive normative models are used. However, all societal actors always make use of such normative models (implicitly or explicitly, consciously or unconsciously, consistently or inconsistently, etc) to orient their daily activities and exchange processes with other actors. In that way, every model offers a certain degree of freedom and equality, within the boundaries that are determined by society. The question therefore is not whether or not to use normative models, but to search for the most adequate model, from the basic normative perspective of democracy. We offer three future models to orient and support the policy debate. Everyone can formulate arguments in favour of (a variant of) one of these models and try to make it acceptable for future policy by means of the democratic political process.

The second criticism that the models are extreme is by no means valid. Starting from the empirical models one can easily show that the models in Figure 5.2 are not extreme and are sufficiently in line with actual development during the past decades. Starting from Figure 2.15 one could easily show different extreme models that are conceptually imaginable but most probably are neither feasible nor desirable in a real democratic society.

5.3   The Complete Combination Model as the most suitable model for a strong democracy

5.3.1 Division of labour for men and women in the Complete Combination Model

Figure 5.2 visually expresses (with the grey background) our central normative hypothesis that the complete combination model is the best future model for an adequate long-term policy in a strongly democratic society. Of course, everyone has the right and opportunity to question this hypothesis and to give arguments in favour of another model. Moreover, everyone can question the validity of the normative concept of strong democracy.

The main goal of the complete combination model is that almost all potentially professionally active men and women combine the basic activities in a balanced way during their life course, avoiding one of these being threatened or neglected. During all stages of the life course sufficient time has to be spent on the different basic activities. So, one can fulfil both professional and family responsibility and can realise a suitable combination of personal, social, material and financial capital.

In general, the model says that a sufficient number of men and women perform sufficient hours of paid work per week, during sufficient years of their life course. In other words, the model implies that the extreme choices (zero or very few hours and many more hours per week) are reduced to the minimum level that is necessary and useful in society. The model essentially implies that in the longer run a *normal full-time job* will count as approximately 35 working hours/week. Again we stress that this norm is not absolute. At the same time, the model offers a maximal diversity of jobs, from very small jobs (less than 10 hours/week) to much larger jobs (up to 70 hours/week), according to the needs of families (family members) and organisations. The broad clock-curve implies that paid jobs occur less frequently to the extent that the number of hours differs from this basic norm or average.

It is possible to present the policy models by means of other indicators as shown in Chapter 4. For example, Figure 5.3 shows the desirable total activity rate of men and women in different age groups in the three future models, compared with the situation in the EU in 2004. In the same way, Figure 5.4 illustrates the desirable average number of hours of professional work in the different age groups. The figures clearly show that for both men and women the two actual curves have to shift to the right during the next few decades.

Similarly, the complete combination model demands that sufficient men and women perform sufficient hours of family work per week, during sufficient years of their life

Figure 5.3 The total activity rate of men and women in different age groups in the three future models (2050), compared with the situation in 2004 (EU-15)

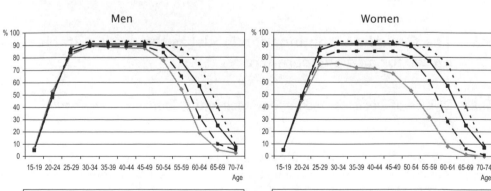

Figure 5.4   The average number of hours of professional work of men and women in different age groups in the three future models (2050), compared with the situation in 2004 (EU-15)

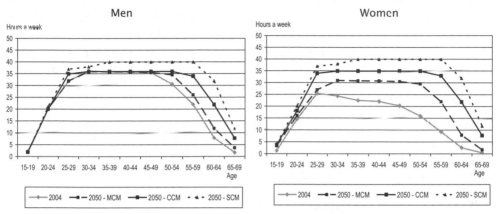

course. Also here, the extreme choices (zero or very few hours and a huge number of hours per week) are reduced to a minimum level. The average *normal household task* implies about 25 hours of family labour a week, with a broad variation from less than 10 hours/week to about 50 hours/week. Again, the clock-curve implies that the household tasks occur less frequently to the extent that the number of hours differs from the basic norm. The variation in the number of hours of household labour is again largely determined by the age (life course stage) and by the presence of children (family stage), and not by the education level or social background. Figure 5.5 shows for some countries that the curves of the actual joint number of family labour of men and women in the different age groups can be a good basis for the future variation in

Figure 5.5   Average joint number of family labour of men and women in the different age groups in some countries (1995-2000)

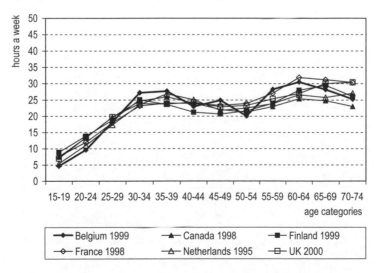

the complete combination model for men and women separately. The central challenge is to redistribute family work between men and women, with an increase in the share of men and a decrease in the share of women.

Furthermore, the total number of hours of professional and family labour of the family (sum of the partners) is also important. The complete combination model implies that in the longer run the number of families without professional or family work should become zero and the number of families with only a small number of hours should be reduced to a minimum. The same can be said for families with many more hours of professional or family work.

Finally, for couple families the relative division of professional and family work is also important, as is presented by the lower part of Figure 5.2. In the complete combination model, the combination families represent the large majority, but also male and female breadwinner families are possible to a certain extent, as expressed by the clock-curve.

Figure 5.6 illustrates in a general way the ideal combination of the number of hours of the basic activities *during the life course* of the average man and woman. The picture is the same for men and women and it can be seen as the answer of the complete combination model to the actual unequal division of professional and family labour in the different countries that was shown in Figure 4.21.

Again, differences are possible according to the life course stage and the presence of children (family stage). The average number of hours of professional labour would increase from 8 hours at the age of 20 years to 35 hours at the age of 30. It would diminish to about 30 hours during the ages 30–50 and then decrease slowly from the age of 50. The number of hours of family work also increases in the 20–30 age group, is the highest at the age of 45 and is then more or less stable until the age of 75. External

Figure 5.6 The average number of hours of the basic activities during the life course for men and women in the Complete Combination Model

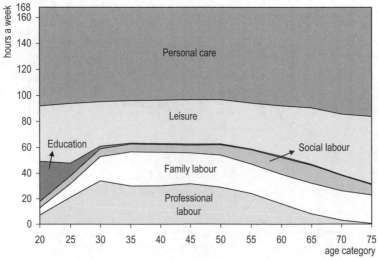

education is especially important until the age of 25, with a strong reduction between the ages of 25 and 30, remaining at a low level during the rest of the life course. Social labour also shows a relatively small number of hours during the life course, with a significant increase after the age of 50, as partial compensation for the strong decrease in professional work. The number of hours of leisure time is relatively low during the 'professional and family stage' between the ages of 30 and 55. The same counts for personal care, but with smaller differences.

Figure 5.7 illustrates the desirable division of the number of hours of basic activities during the life course for men and women in the complete combination model, starting from the presentation in Figure 5.2. Given the importance of the basic value equality, the curves for men and women coincide for every activity.

It is clear that the normative curves are general guidelines for the future division and certainly not absolute prescriptions. More important is the position on the X-axis (number of hours) and the width of the curves, expressing the level of equality.

As mentioned before, the curves for *professional and family labour* are rather wide and low since the complete combination model accepts that a small group of men and women have zero hours of these activities. The curve for *total labour* is smaller with an average of 60 hours/week because the model implies that all men and women have at least 40 hours/week. The curve for free time is still smaller with an average of 45 hours/week, while the curve for personal care is also small and is more to the right, with an average of 75 hours/week. Finally, the curve for social labour on the left side is the smallest, with an average of five hours/week.

Figure 5.7   The desirable division in the Complete Combination Model of the number of hours of basic activities during the life course for men and women

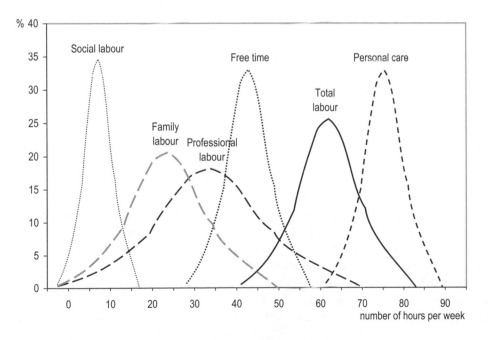

5.3.2 Balancing the basic values in the daily division of labour

The complete combination model offers a real balance of the *basic values* of a strong democracy with respect to the division of labour: freedom, equality, solidarity and efficiency. All values have to be realised simultaneously in a sufficient way, continually stimulating and restricting each other. The central goal is to maximise the level of all values simultaneously.

Gender equality between men and women and within couple families is very important but is demanded in a gradual way, leaving choice for all possible options to a certain extent, expressed by the clock-curve. The basic objective is that men and women will have the same overall division of professional and family work, but with a sufficiently large diversity within the two groups. Moreover, the model implies that in most couple families professional and family tasks are more or less equally divided. The number of (strong) male and female breadwinner families is reduced to a minimum, as far as it is necessary in certain families (for family and/or professional reasons) and as far as it is possible and acceptable in business life and in society as a whole.

On the micro level, all families have sufficient *freedom* to choose the division of labour according to their own historical background and their personal preferences at a certain stage of their life course, albeit within the societal boundaries of the clock-curve. The diversity of family types offered by the model is larger than the actual diversity during the past decades (Figures 4.24-4.26, 4.31 and 4.32). In the old breadwinner model, many women (mothers) were not able or were not allowed to have a (full-time) paid job while most men (fathers) were not able to work fewer hours and to participate sufficiently in household tasks and the education/care of children. In that perspective, the *complete combination model explicitly shows that more equality in the division of labour can go hand in hand with more choices* for men and women and their families, and for employers. The model combines a sufficient level of free choice with a sufficient level of equality, for the division of basic activities. So, it solves the old trade-off in traditional economic theory between freedom and equality and offers a clear win-win situation for all groups involved.

The complete combination model also largely satisfies the *solidarity* principle since both the professionally active rate and the average number of hours of adult men and women is large enough. So the societal cost of the breadwinner families is restricted to a minimum. A small percentage of breadwinner families is always possible to the extent that this is necessary in certain families. In that way, the collective basis is large enough to finance social investments for dependent people or families, including the small group of breadwinner families.

Finally, the *efficiency* principle is also sufficiently met since the personal, social, material and financial capital of all men and women is being used in an efficient way for professional work, family work and the other activities. By fully integrating (almost) all men and women in professional life (labour market), family life and social life in a sufficiently equal way and with respect for individual or family choices, everyone can largely realise their aspired professional position, family engagements and social engagements. In that way everyone will sufficiently contribute to the personal, social, material and financial results or benefits of these activities. At the same time, everyone can make use of all these benefits for their future development. Contrary to the traditional (economic) view, the complete combination model fully integrates the production and distribution of societal welfare within the context of a democratic society, in order to realise the most adequate result. Production and distribution are part of the same overall societal labour process that cannot and should not be separated.

The complete combination model implies that the division of labour between partners remains sufficiently equal during the stages of the life course. Therefore, the internal caring tasks should be combined with external professional and social care. Families with specific needs can opt for a less equal division of labour and diminish the number of hours of professional labour. Since differentiation according to the stage of the life course and/or family type is an essential part of the model, sufficient attention goes to a differentiated supply of jobs: small jobs of 5-20 hours/week for students, larger flexible jobs of 35-45 hours/week with smaller household tasks for young men and women without children, 'normal' jobs of 25-35 working hours with somewhat larger household tasks for parents (also for one-parent families) and for older people who want to diminish their professional labour step by step, and also small jobs of 5-20 hours/week for people on a pension who want to remain professionally active to a small extent. As shown in the lower part of Figure 5.2, the model implies that the moderate and complete combination families are dominant in the large group of *couple families*. Yet the other family types with a more unequal division of labour are also allowed to a certain degree.

The figure in the lower part can also be a guideline for one-parent families resulting from a divorce of a two-parent family, more specifically for the remaining division of labour of their 'former family', ranging from a very unequal 90%/10% division in favour of the father at one end, to a very equal 50%/50% division in the middle, to a very unequal 10%/90% division in favour of the mother at the other end. The complete combination model strives at a gradual system of shared or combined parenthood by the ex-partners, with the remaining division of labour being more or less equal in most of the 'former families'. This does not mean, however, that it can be reached automatically or easily. On the contrary, one-parent families most probably have more problems in realising a sufficiently equal and adequate division of professional and family labour. In this perspective, the complete combination model does not want to promote lone parenthood as such, since it mostly implies a weaker and less stable division of labour, but aims at supporting existing lone-parent families in their daily search for a suitable division of labour.

At the same time, the model can deal with the needs of socially weak and vulnerable people and families, who must also be able to realise an adequate combination of professional and family labour. This implies special attention and support for the different forms of lower-qualified labour. The complete combination model therefore equally aims at a sufficiently high quality of both professional and family labour for all men and women.

The complete combination model is a normative guideline for the *division of basic activities* of men and women, emphasising professional and family work. The model *does not formulate additional conditions for the division of partial activities within these main categories*, for example the division of household tasks and education/care as two partial activities of family labour. Consequently, the *basic conditions for the division of the main activities do not restrict the diversity of the different partial activities*. So, no one has to worry that there is insufficient space for diversity in the concrete daily life of men and women. In fact, the potential diversity in the daily division of partial activities and the division of personal, social, material and financial means is and will remain almost infinite. The complete combination model offers a general normative frame that combines the right and duty for men and women to realise an adequate combination of basic activities. The combination of basic activities enables them to develop their own personal combination of the different partial activities, in space and time. After all, the partial activities determine the concrete contents and results of the daily division of time.

Finally, the complete combination model allows for sufficient changes or transitions in the combinations of basic activities during the life course. These transitions must lead to a new suitable combination of activities to realise a good mix of personal, social, material and financial means, as a solution for the changing opportunities and risks during the life course. At the same time, the model strongly aims at the combination of sufficient flexibility and sufficient security (protection) with respect to the main aspects of the division of labour of all men and women: number of hours, working time arrangement, contract, income, qualification, location, etc. In that way, the complete combination model also answers the basic challenges of the TLM model and the flexicurity model.

5.3.3 A new view on the education/care of children

The complete combination model implies a new *pedagogical view* with respect to the position and education of children in a democratic society. This view is fully compatible with the concept of strong democracy and with the view on the division of labour of adult men and women. The basic pedagogical view of the model says that all boys and girls can enjoy 'shared or combined' high-quality education from birth, both within and outside the family. The concept 'shared or combined education' has a gradual meaning that allows for all variants to a certain extent. In that way, the model goes beyond the traditional pedagogical view of Bowlby and Spitz (Vandenbroeck, 2003), saying that young children need an (almost) exclusive education within the family (by the mother). This view has been the basis for the pedagogical view of the traditional breadwinner models and in a modified version also that of the moderate combination models during the past decades. The application of the view, however, resulted in many variants in different countries with respect to the 'critical pedagogical age' (the age until which children should stay at home) and the quality of education outside the family. Mainly because of the contradictions between the variants in different countries, the basic idea of this pedagogical view has been undermined. Therefore, it can no longer be the basis for a future normative model that stresses equality between men and women, continuity during the life course and integration of activities inside and outside the family.

According to the complete combination model, the child's family must, of course, be able to play its full pedagogical role as a home base and central axis for the child's daily life. But external daytime education/care is also a full part of the broad development of all children from birth, not as a replacement for education within the family, but as a full complement and enrichment of it. Again, the clock-curves of Figure 5.2 can be used to express the gradual distribution of the number of hours and days per week that children of different age groups spend in external daytime education/care, for example from 0-54 hours/week, according to the normative models. Figure 5.8 illustrates this for the three future models: the complete combination model (CCM), the moderate combination model (MCM) and the strong combination model (SCM).

The curve of the complete combination model implies that all children are gradually located around an average of 3-4 days of 24-32 hours/week of external education/care. The actual number of hours and days is then largely determined by the age and other characteristics of the children and by the living and working conditions of the parents. As for the working hours of adults, the model here also implies that the extreme choices are reduced to the minimum level that is necessary and useful in society. The one extreme, with zero or very few hours of external education/care, means that the child is at home all day long, with no or very little education/care by people outside the family. As a consequence, the child cannot enjoy the external pedagogical sources of society nor the interaction with internal sources. The other extreme, with more than 50 hours of external daytime education/care, implies that the child is outdoors all day long, with no or very little caring or education within the family by parents, sisters or brothers. In this case, the child cannot sufficiently enjoy the internal pedagogical sources of the family nor the interaction with external sources.

Between the two extremes, all gradual forms of combined education are possible, offering the children a certain combination of the internal pedagogical sources of the family and the external pedagogical sources of society (extended family, friends,

Figure 5.8   Division of the number of hours and days per week of external education/care for children aged 0-12 years in the future models

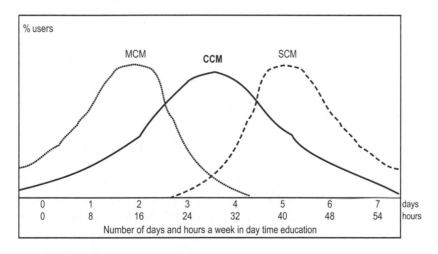

neighbours, daycare, school, clubs, etc). In that way, the complete combination model implies that the division of time of children is fully compatible with the division of time of the parents.

The family and external education/care are seen as two education cornerstones, both quantitatively and qualitatively, that have to support and stimulate each other continuously, in order to offer every child a complete development within society. These two cornerstones are to be supplemented with other activities (personal care, free playing, sports, music, dance, etc) within the large family, neighbourhood, circle of friends and local clubs. So the complete combination model follows the well-known phrase 'It takes a village to raise a child', indicating that, from birth, each child is at the same time a 'member' of different societal entities, which all play their role in the total education process (Vandenbroeck, 2003; Van Dongen, 2004c, 2004d). Again, the complexity model in Figure 2.7 can be used to express this basic idea of the integration of children in the societal context.

5.3.4 The Complete Combination Model of the division of labour in organisations

Professional organisations (commercial companies, non-profit organisations, public institutions, etc) are also permanently changing in time, following the overall developments within society to a certain extent, on the micro and macro level, but at the same time permanently influencing these developments. International competition has increased considerably during past decades, technological changes occur at a high speed, the consumer is increasingly demanding a good price/quality proportion and employees are more conscious and demanding about the daily combination of professional and family life.

To survive in the quickly changing (international) market system, organisations have to be very alert to the necessary renewal of their products and services, the right investments in new technology, the exploration of new markets and the renewal of the daily organisation of work. During the past decades, the change in the daily work organisation has often been placed under the broad (normative) umbrella of a (more) 'flexible work organisation'. We can easily refer to the development of the Flexicurity Model.

At first, the need for a more flexible work organisation was formulated by employers, mainly in order to increase the possibility of adjusting the input of human (personal and social) capital according to the changing circumstances of the production process and the input of material capital.

Next, organisations were increasingly facing the challenge of conceiving and realising a more flexible work organisation in favour of their employees. This implies that the work organisation is sufficiently in line with the insights and new demands of employees concerning the daily combination of professional and family work. Until now, only a small number of companies have already embedded this perspective in their daily practice and then probably only partially or as a secondary perspective in their business concept and strategy (Henderickx and De Prins, 1998; den Dulk et al, 1999; Van Hootegem, 2000 ; den Dulk, 2001; Van Dongen et al, 2001; Evans, 2001;

Poelmans, 2001; Poelmans and Chinchilla, 2001, 2003; Van Dongen, 2004b, 2005a; Galinsky, 2005; Peper et al, 2005; Benko and Weisberg, 2007). This is strongly related to the lack of a coherent conceptual and normative model and the lack (of application) of efficient management instruments to support companies in the realisation of a new work organisation (Benko and Weisberg, 2007; see also Section 6.5).

Although we did not present any empirical models of the development of the division of labour in organisations, one can easily translate the future models in Figure 5.2 into future models for organisations (see Figure 5.9), starting from both the perspective of the employees (upper part) and that of the organisation (lower part).

The upper part is identical to the upper part of Figure 5.2 showing the desirable division of the number of hours of professional work for all men and women in the professional population, with or without a partner, with or without children (macro level). As said before, each curve presents a possible normative answer to the undesirable actual unequal division of professional work (see Figures 4.14, 4.24 and 4.31).

The lower part presents the desirable relative division of professional work of men and women within the organisations. The figures give the distribution of organisations (Y-axis) based on the relative share of the number of working hours of women in the total number of working hours in the organisation (X-axis), with a scale from 0%–100%. This scale reflects the underlying gradual typology of organisations presented in

Figure 5.9   Normative future models for the division of labour of men and women in organisations (2050)

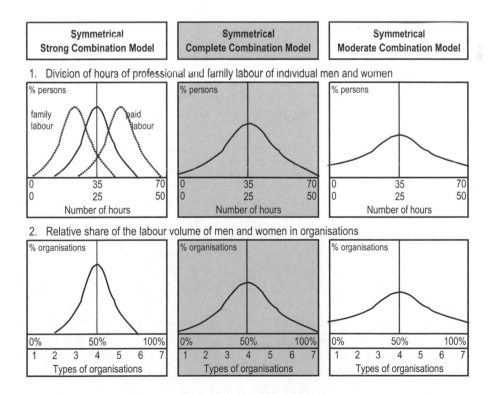

Figure 2.14. Due to the lack of (internationally comparative) data, however, it is very difficult to create solid empirical models for (the division of labour in) organisations. This is a major empirical challenge for future research.

In general, the complete combination model for organisations means that in the long run the professional position of men and women is largely equal, both on the macro and the micro level, as can be expressed by some basic aspects: number of men and women in the organisation, number of weekly working hours and days, shift system per week or per month, flexible working hours, quality of the work, functional levels, payment for different functions, and so on.

On the micro level, all organisations have sufficient *freedom* to choose the division of labour according to their own historical background and their own management view and strategy, albeit within the societal boundaries of the clock-curve. The diversity of organisational types offered by the model is most probably larger than the actual diversity during the past decades. In the old breadwinner model, many organisations did not have the opportunity or attitude to work for a more equal division of labour between men and women. The complete combination model explicitly shows that more equality in the division of labour can go hand in hand with more choices for organisations, as it is for families. Again, the model solves the old economic trade-off between freedom and equality and offers a clear win–win situation.

The complete combination model also aims at a sufficient level of *solidarity* between the different types of organisations according to the gradual differences in efficiency. By investing in a family-friendly and gender-friendly work organisation, the overall flexibility in favour of employees increases and at the same time the overall flexibility for organisations improves.

Again, the *efficiency* principle is also met since the human capital of all men and women is being used in a sufficiently efficient way for professional work, but also for family work and other activities. By fully integrating most men and women in the different professional organisations in a largely equal way and with sufficient respect for individual and family choices, all organisations can improve their daily activities and results.

The basic goal of the complete combination model is that organisations can come to win–win situations for all actors involved: a higher quality of daily life for employees and their families and a more optimal functioning of the organisation. The hypothesis is that a number of problems within the work process (for example, absenteeism, stress, conflicts) can be positively influenced by means of a better combination of professional and family life. So, realising the complete combination model in organisations implies that employers sufficiently meet the needs of families concerning the daily combination of professional and family labour. In that perspective, organisations have to develop a suitable family and business policy, within the boundaries of general government policy and collective agreements. According to the gradual character of the model (clock-curve in Figure 4.5), a broad variety of policies are possible and desirable. The actual level and content of the combination policy of each organisation is largely related to its historical background and some basic characteristics (sector, activities, composition of personnel, technological development, international position, etc).

All aspects of the daily business of the organisation are relevant for the combination policy of organisations:

- *Working time arrangements*: number of working hours, overtime, working time schedule per day and per week, flexible working hours, breaks, shift system.
- *Leave arrangements*: official holidays, system of working time reduction, temporary reduction of working hours with or without specific reasons.
- *Work organisation*: quality of the work, cooperation between employees, dependency of the job, variation in the tasks, number of working places, working at home and support for it, organisation culture and decision making process.
- *Personal and household services*: different forms of childcare, means for commuter traffic and other facilities, personal and family services and financial arrangements.

In the next chapter, which deals with the policy perspectives of the complete combination model, more attention will be paid to specific policies and practical instruments to support companies in the process towards a more family and gender-friendly work organisation. In this context, we have to mention the large similarity between the complete combination model for organisations and the mass career customisation (MCC) model presented by Benko and Weisberg (2007). We shall discuss this model in Section 6.5.

We conclude this section with the basic idea that, starting from the broad conceptual approach to the daily life of men and women in families, companies and other organisations, the complete combination model for individuals and families has to be linked with the complete combination model for professional organisations.

The complete combination model for individuals and families also expresses the differentiated normative supply function for the labour market, based on their needs and opportunities. The complete combination model for organisations, then, is the differentiated normative demand function, based on their needs and opportunities. Given the normative objectives, the two partial models are fully equivalent and are part of one overall model for the division of labour in society. They have to be realised simultaneously so that they support one another continually. In that way, an efficient labour market policy is possible in order to create sufficient suitable jobs that meet both the needs of men and women within their family and professional context and the needs of organisations to realise their societal project. At the same time, the collective system can be financed sufficiently in order to provide all necessary collective services, not least (financial) support for the different dependent societal groups.

5.4   Comparison with the other combination models

As mentioned before, everyone has the right and opportunity to question the hypothesis that the *complete combination model* is the best future model for an adequate long-term policy in a strongly democratic society. Everyone can give arguments in favour of another model and can question the validity of the normative concept of strong democracy. In this way, the set of policy perspectives following from the complete combination model (Chapter 6) can also be discussed. After all, the policy models are neither a goal as such nor an absolute normative message. Above all, they are instruments to support, stimulate and orient the scientific and policy debate on this major societal field. Therefore, it is useful to clarify briefly the meaning of the strong and moderate combination models.

5.4.1 Strong Combination Model

In the *strong combination model* on the left side of Figure 5.2, many more people are located around the centre point of the 'normal' full-time job, with no one having a very small job or no job at all (upper part). The same holds for the family labour of men and women and for the total professional and family labour of couple families (middle part). The lower part shows that all families are located around the complete combination family, excluding the strong male and female breadwinner families (see Figure 2.13).

In a still 'stronger' and probably more realistic variant of this model (curves in dotted line), the curve of professional work is more to the right and the curve of family work is more to the left. This means that the average number of hours of professional work is higher than 35 per week and the average number of hours of family work is lower than 25. This stronger variant is the starting point in this section. For couple families with two adult partners, the curve of the relative division of labour is also smaller (lower part in Figure 5.2). The strong male and female breadwinner families are excluded and the share of the moderate and complete combination families is much larger.

The strong combination model emphasises to a larger extent the value of 'equality' and higher professional participation as the basis for welfare and solidarity in society. The strong male and female breadwinner families are excluded or made impossible. In that way, the free choice of families and the need within society for diversity is sacrificed to a larger degree.

In this model, the available time of parents for the family is more restricted, in favour of professional work. Consequently, children's activities outside the home receive more attention and the role of external education/care becomes greater. The danger exists that parents (on average) are not sufficiently available for their children to give them enough personal attention.

The exclusion of breadwinner families largely restricts the free choice of and diversity between families. The model does not support families that (have to) opt for the breadwinner family model because of special circumstances or problems. Yet one can suppose that a small group of such families will always exist.

Given the importance of individual free choice and diversity in social life, this model does not realise a full balance of the basic values. By strongly emphasising professional labour, other major activities receive less space, for example family work and the education of (young) children within the family. Consequently, the efficiency condition is not sufficiently met since human capacities for other activities are not being used in an optimal way. Finally, the feasibility condition cannot be fully met because the model is less in line with actual development. In other words, the distance between the actual and normative model is larger, which means that it is more difficult to realise.

5.4.2 Moderate Combination Model

The moderate combination model on the right side of the complete combination model gradually offers more space for the free choice of families to work less or more hours than average, sacrificing, to a certain extent, the equality condition. Families are more inspired to choose a more unequal division of professional and family labour. Consequently, the share of both male and female breadwinner families becomes larger. This weakens the feasibility of the model because the distance from the actual division of labour increases. Since professional labour has to make more room for family work, family benefits are lower, less collective means are available to invest in dependent groups (solidarity) and the professional human capital of many men and women is used less efficiently for societal development. Moreover, seeing external daycare largely as a substitute for family care and not as a complement to it, the model gives less room for a fully shared education of young children. In that way, the pedagogical basis for their future development within the family and other entities in society becomes weaker.

5.5 Comparison with other future models

We can briefly compare the normative combination models for the future division of labour (especially thecomplete combination model) with the other normative models mentioned in previous chapters: the combination scenario, the TLM model), the flexicurity model, the dual earner/dual carer model and the universal caregiver model. Finally, we mention the new future model for the division of labour in organisations presented by Benko and Weisberg (2007), with the challenging term 'mass career customisation'. Since it is a practical management approach for organisations, we shall discuss this in Section 6.5 when dealing with the combination policy in organisations as a major policy perspective of the complete combination model.

5.5.1 Combination Scenario

In general, the *Dutch normative combination scenario* expresses the idea that the division of both professional and family labour between men and women should become much more equal in the next few decades, with sufficient diversity between individuals and families. As said in Chapter 1, the combination scenario was presented mainly by means of the new ideal family type with an equal division of professional and family labour between the two partners, as an alternative for the traditional breadwinner family in the period 1960-1980 and for the moderate breadwinner family in the period 1980-2000. As such, most attention was focused on the promotion of that ideal family type, implicitly suggesting that in the longer run (almost) all families should follow it.

So, opponents of the combination scenario presented it as a dogmatic policy model that leaves insufficient space for the necessary diversity between families regarding the division of professional and family labour. They actually presented the combination scenario as a (very) strong combination model, as if it would largely eliminate the free choice of people/families to choose another division of labour and as if it would lead to maximum uniformity between men and women and between families. Although the promoters of the combination scenario by no means had these 'goals' in mind, they did not develop a clear (graphical) presentation of the gradual character of both the actual and preferable future division of labour in the Netherlands (and other European countries). From the presentation in different publications, we can deduct fairly easily that the combination scenario did not refer to the strong combination model, given the great attention to different forms of leave arrangements. However, it is not so clear to what extent the long-term normative message of the model coincides (more) with that of the complete combination model or with that of the moderate combination model.

Political discussion about the combination scenario resulted in different policy proposals in the period 1999-2001. However, the attractive and promising combination scenario was not communicated in an efficient way in order to make it acceptable for a majority in society and – above all – in the political world. After some time, the combination scenario lost its political support to a large extent, so prohibiting further practical elaboration, improvement and communication. After some years, the model almost completely disappeared from the scientific and political scene. The positive international exchange and collaboration between the Dutch and Flemish scientific group dealing with these policy models also vanished after some time. At that time, the TLM model became more attractive in some European countries, especially in the Netherlands.

5.5.2 Transitional Labour Markets Model

As already discussed in Chapter 2, the general normative message of the TLM model looks largely similar to that of the complete combination model, going beyond the perspectives of the traditional welfare state and aiming at a stronger democracy on all levels of society. The basic goal is that both men and women can realise a smoother professional career, with more fluent transitions during the life course and a more equal division of labour between men and women. The different publications, however, do not give a clear (graphical) presentation of the desirable division of labour for men and women. So it is not easy to know which future division of labour is proposed by the TLM model. As far as we know, only Schmid (2002a, p 177, Figure 5.1) presents the future division of labour of the normative TLM model by means of one graphical clock-curve, based on the gradual distribution of the number of working hours of men and women. In general, the clock-curve is similar to the curve of the complete combination model in Figure 5.2, expressing the 'flexible 35-hour week', with possible jobs ranging from 10-60 hours/week. According to Schmid (2002a), the normative model would also be valid with a 'flexible 30-hour week' (jobs from 10-50 hours/week) or with the 'flexible 40-hour week' (jobs from 10-70 hours/week). However, the curve is clearly smaller than the curve of the complete combination model, which would imply that the options of not working, working very few hours or working many more hours would not be possible in the normative TLM model. This presentation largely expresses the basic idea of the strong combination model. Further explanation of the model and its policy perspectives, however, expresses the basic idea of the moderate combination model, enabling a large group of men and women to leave the market for a long time for family reasons, in particular for the education of young children at home.

The different publications and policy discussions during the last two conferences of the TLM network in 2004 (Amsterdam) and 2005 (Budapest) showed that the normative TLM model has, in fact, a very broad scope. Referring to the future models presented in this chapter, the normative TLM model seems to cover more or less the strong, the complete and the moderate combination model in Figure 5.2. This would mean that the TLM model is less sharp and clear as a long-term policy model or guideline, because it covers a larger range of possible normative statements and policy perspectives, with a higher probability of internal contradictions. Most policy perspectives of the three normative combination models presented before can be placed under the normative TLM model. The scope of this model is probably too broad and therefore prevents the model from being a solid basis for developing a consistent set of policy perspectives and policy measures. Therefore, it would be useful to develop a few variants of the TLM model, starting from empirical studies, to have a sharper distinction between and a more coherent formulation of the possible policy perspectives resulting from the normative models. Then, a correct and more complete comparison with the three normative combination models would be possible.

5.5.3 Flexicurity Model

In general, more or less the same can be said about the normative flexicurity model. This model basically aims at a 'more democratic' labour market, offering a combination of sufficient flexibility and sufficient security to both employees and employers. This flexicurity idea also covers the normative view of a more equal division of labour of men and women, with sufficient respect for individual choices during the life course. However, this normative view is vague as the broad TLM model.

Wilthagen and Tros (2004) propose one unique flexicurity policy strategy, as the only good and desirable combination of the different sorts of flexibility and security. In fact, they implicitly show that different normative flexicurity models are possible, for example from a very weak to a very strong variant, but they defend only one version for which they preserve the unique label of flexicurity strategy. As such, we do not have any problem with their defending a specific policy model with that label. But they create a contradiction between the analytical and empirical flexicurity tool and the normative strategy. The analytical and empirical tool implies the existence of different combinations (of levels) of flexibility and security. But if that is the case, different normative combinations of flexicurity are possible and, consequently, the normative concept of 'flexicurity' cannot be used for only one of the possible normative combinations. The danger of reducing the normative flexicurity concept to one of the possible models is that the effective model becomes increasingly broader, in order to capture more normative variants. After all, different groups using the model will claim the unique flexicurity concept to express their specific normative strategy. In other words, a number of 'more or less' different normative strategies, that is, variants of the unique strategy proposed by Wilthagen and Tros (2004), will be placed under the normative flexicurity concept. As a consequence, it will become broader and more vaguer leading to the same problem as that of the TLM model, that is, a high risk of internal contradictions.

So, again, it would be useful to elaborate some relevant variants of the normative flexicurity model, starting from the empirical study of existing flexicurity variants, and fully integrate the combination perspective as suggested by Muffels and Ester (2004). Most probably, these normative flexicurity models would be very similar to the normative combination models.

5.5.4. Dual Earner/Dual Carer Model

It is fairly clear that the basic normative message of the dual earner/dual carer model of Crompton (1999) and Gornick and Meyers (2003, 2004a, 2004b) goes further than the traditional model of the welfare state. Implicitly, the model aims at a more equal division of labour between men and women at all levels of society, in the broad sense of the word. Yet the model seems to start from a weaker version of the normative concept of democracy (with less emphasis on equality and solidarity). This is, most probably, related to the actual societal and political circumstances in the US and the UK, that is, a strong free market system with less support from the government for a family- and gender-friendly division of labour. Starting from the actual situation in the US and the UK, the normative and political ambition of the model, therefore, seems to be more restricted. The basic question here is which policy steps towards a more equal division of labour are feasible within the next 10-15 years, largely referring to the actual division of labour and to recent policies in some western European countries.

Unfortunately, the authors do not give any visual presentation of their normative dual earner/dual carer model (in line with the presentation of actual development). So it is difficult to know which future model is actually proposed. Yet their explanation of the model shows that it is most similar to the moderate combination model in Figure 5.2. Starting from the actual policy model in the US (dual earner/market carer model), they see a certain variant of the actual 'European model' as the most useful future model for the next decade. Although they do not explicitly tell us which of the actual European models serves as their ideal model, they implicitly express their general favour for a mix of the continental and Nordic model. In this context, they emphasise the strong tension between the need for sufficient family time and the need for more equality between men and women, both in the household and labour market.

By starting the explanation of their policy perspectives with family leave policy and by emphasising the desirability of long leave arrangements for the (full-time) education of young children under the age of three within the family, they express the central idea of the moderate combination model in Figure 5.2. Moreover, external daycare for children younger than three years old is largely conceived as a substitute for education within the family and not as a complement to it, thereby largely following the traditional pedagogical view. This basic idea of the moderate combination model is also expressed by the much lower ideal average number of working hours being proposed in their model for families (one or two parents) with children under the age of three than for families with older children (Gornick and Meyers, 2003, pp 96-7).

5.5.5 Universal Caregiver Model

We also mention the policy models that were formulated by Fraser (1994, 2006), mainly from a (feminist) political science perspective. Fraser (1994) also starts from the historical breakdown of the traditional breadwinner model during the second half of the 20th century, as the dominant model in traditional capitalist welfare states, largely expressed by the unequal division of labour and income between men and women. In contemporary welfare states, this model increasingly makes space for new and more equal forms of the division of labour. Her basic normative view aims at real *gender equity,* implying the joint realisation of five distinct norms for different aspects of daily life: the anti-poverty principle, the anti-exploitation principle, three equality principles (income equality, leisure time equality and equality of respect), the anti-marginalisation principle and the anti-androcentrism principle. Moreover, gender equity must be placed next to some other basic values in society, in particular liberty/freedom and efficiency, to have an integrated normative approach to the division of labour within the modern welfare state. This basic normative view implies that the future welfare states have to develop new effective forms of protection for all people, based on a new division of labour between men and women.

She then formulates and evaluates three ideal policy models for the future division of labour. The first model is called the *universal breadwinner model,* which is largely similar to the strong combination model in Figure 5.2, emphasising the equal division of professional and family labour, with a full participation and remuneration of both men and women in the labour market, but with less time for family needs. Most care activities are shifted from the family to the professional market sector (private or public). According to Fraser, the model would have good results with respect to the anti-poverty and anti-exploitation principle, moderate results for income equality, equality of respect and anti-marginalisation, but poor results for leisure time equality and anti-androcentrism. She concludes that this ideal model is far from the current reality (in the US), which implies that it is not really feasible in the long run. Moreover, it does not sufficiently meet all the principles together.

An alternative is the *caregiver parity model,* which is close to the moderate combination model in Figure 5.2 (or even to a weak combination model), allowing one partner (man or woman) to stay at home during a fairly long period of the life course, mostly for the education of young children. The caregivers are then supported financially by the government. Probably, in reality, it is mostly women who will actually play the role of caregiver, so most men will not be challenged to change their division of labour. This model would score well with respect to the anti-poverty and anti-exploitation principle, moderately for leisure time equality, equality of respect and anti-androcentrism, but poorly for income equality and anti-marginalisation. Fraser's conclusion is that this ideal model is also far removed from the real situation (in the US) and therefore not really feasible, and that it insufficiently meets the five principles.

To solve the basic 'combination problem' of both models, that is, the dominance of professional work in the first model and the dominance of domestic work in the second, Fraser (1994) proposes a new ideal future policy model, that satisfies all five normative principles of full equity. As such, the model combines the strong aspects of both unsatisfactory models and transforms their weaknesses into positive elements. Fraser (2006) calls this model the *universal caregiver model,* stressing the fact that the (caring) lifestyle of women must be much more the reference for this model and that men also have to change their lifestyle.

This policy model is largely similar to the complete combination model in Figure 5.2. Although the name of the model does not really suggest it, it aims at an equal division of both professional and family work between men and women, both at the individual and family level. She thinks that this new model is very promising for the future development of societal life. In that perspective, we would propose to call it the *universal breadwinner-caregiver model*, emphasising the equal division of professional and family work between men and women and the necessity for both men and women to adjust their lifestyle and division of labour. This name is also much more similar to the complete combination model and the dual earner/dual carer model. Unfortunately, Fraser only concludes that much work needs to be done to develop this model for future welfare states. We hope that our study is a useful contribution to that major challenge.

5.6   Conclusion

This brief international comparison shows the importance of a clear differentiation and explanation of the relevant future policy models, as the basis for a coherent policy analysis, policy debate and policy process. The Dutch combination scenario was a promising model but it did not succeed on the political level and disappeared mainly because of the inadequate communication of the basic idea. The chance that the current TLM model will last very long as a policy model is not so great in our opinion because it lacks a clear didactical presentation and presents only one policy model that covers too large a normative spectrum. As a consequence, it cannot serve as a strong and coherent basis for the policy debate. So far, the same counts for the flexicurity model that largely follows the normative perspective of the transitional labour markets model. As mentioned, it would be useful to develop a few relevant variants of the basic model in order to increase the policy relevance. The dual earner/dual carer model also lacks a proper didactical presentation, which makes it somewhat difficult to capture. Although the normative spectrum of the model is not too broad, a clear comparison and confrontation with some other relevant future models is missing. Moreover, the elaboration of the model is much more related to the actual models in Europe, taking over some of the major contradictions. Finally, the three breadwinner-caregiver models of Fraser start from a solid normative approach, but they miss a clear presentation and empirical basis. The models are fairly similar to the normative combination models, but they are insufficiently developed. So, the practical usability for the policy debate is rather limited.

The comparison also illustrates that the Combination Model is further developed than the other models, conceptually, empirically and normatively. This is mainly the result of the active development and application of the Combination Model since its introduction in Flanders (Belgium) in 1998, based on many years of (international) research – we have learned a great deal from the other normative models – and several interactive workshops or seminars with different stakeholders. This process encouraged us to further develop and fine-tune the models.

We have shown that, in general, the Combination Model is a useful instrument for studying the division of labour in all welfare states. Furthermore, the normative combination models are useful tools in supporting and orienting the policy debate on the desirable and feasible future division of labour. The consequent use of the policy models actually leads to a more transparent, consistent and efficient policy discussion, a fundamental condition of a strong democracy.

Since the different policy models are largely overlapping and complementary, more international collaboration is desirable, aiming at the further elaboration and streamlining of the models under a general normative umbrella, for example the search for a 'fully democratic division of labour' in future society.

SIX

Policy perspectives for the realisation of the Complete Combination Model

The daily division of professional and family labour between men and women is the beating heart of societal life. Reforming and improving the division of labour therefore requires changes and improvements in many societal fields. The *central hypothesis* in this book says that the Complete Combination Model is the most suitable long-term orientation for future policy in all welfare states that want to develop a full democratic division of labour between men and women, within families and organisations. We emphasise again that everyone can choose and defend another future model of the division of labour.

The realisation of the Complete Combination Model needs an integrated policy, both in the short and long run. 'Integrated' means that the main components are dealt with together in an interactive framework, on all levels and for all relevant actors of society. Realising such a long-term model implies realising a sequence of short-term models with a time perspective of, for example, 10 years, starting from the actual situation in every country. Given the actual stage, all countries have to realise a feasible next stage of the moderate combination model, taking some steps forward in the direction of the Complete Combination Model. Of course, it remains an open question to what extent and how fast the different countries can realise the Complete Combination Model.

In each policy stage, a set of feasible goals has to be formulated with respect to the daily division of labour and means, as the basis for a coherent policy plan covering different societal fields. To facilitate a positive long-term result, the instruments and measures of that plan must be mutually supportive. By the end of each stage, the results must be evaluated to adjust the policy process during the next stage.

It is impossible to elaborate a full policy programme for all countries separately. Therefore, we present a number of possible policy perspectives with respect to the relevant societal fields. On the one hand, these policy perspectives are derived from the Complete Combination Model as a long-term policy orientation; on the other hand, they are the essential instruments to realise the model. These perspectives can be compared with those presented by Schmid and Gazier (2002) and by Gornick and Meyers (2003), following from their normative model. We also refer to Gauthier (1996), den Dulk et al (1999), den Dulk (2001), Peper at al (2005), Roman (2006) and Ghysels and Debacker (2007), among many other publications.

6.1 Promotion of the normative concept of 'strong democracy' and the Complete Combination Model

The main normative ambition of the concept of 'strong democracy' is to realise a new balance between the basic values, on all levels of society: freedom, equality, solidarity and efficiency (see Section 3.3 in Chapter 3). Since perfect democracy can never be established in the real complex world, the main goal is to initiate a permanent process of democratisation in the daily life of all subjects, relative to their actual situation. So we can make a gradual distinction between a very weak democracy on the one hand, and a very strong democracy on the other, expressed by the degree of joint realisation of the basic values at all levels of society. Each basic value is then both a positive lever and a restriction for other values. In other words, one basic value cannot be (partially) realised without (partially) realising the other, and the partial realisation of one basic value prevents dominance by another.

So a first general policy perspective should be the broad promotion of the basic normative concept of strong democracy on all levels of society (local, regional, national, international, global) and of the Complete Combination Model as the best policy model for a democratic division of labour. This broad campaign should focus on the macro level of the market system(s) and on the micro level of families and organisations.

6.1.1 Promoting the basic idea of a democratic market system

First, it is essential to promote the basic idea of a 'democratic market system' on all levels of society (local, regional, national, international, global), as a strong alternative for the old and ambiguous concept of the so-called 'free market system' (Van Dongen, 2004a).

The basic value of 'freedom' is only one value to describe the normative character of a market system. Therefore, it is an indistinct normative label for (comparing) the different sorts of 'more or less' free market systems. During previous decades, the concept of the free market has been used (and misused) by many different ideological groups, from the extreme right to the moderate left, as their general normative orientation. As a consequence, the concept has become too vague and therefore useless for the policy debate in society. To a certain extent, one could try to solve this problem by making a gradual distinction between different types of free market systems, for example from a very free to a very unfree market system. Between these two extremes, more progressive, mostly left-wing groups have introduced the concept of the 'socially adjusted free market', expressing the need to use the concept of (free) market system as such but also to take into account the values of 'equality' and 'solidarity' to a certain extent. However, this concept neither tells us to what extent the social adjustment is or should be realised nor expresses the sort of adjustment that exists or that is needed. To answer this question, one has to introduce an additional gradual concept, for example from a maximally to a minimally adjusted free market system. But this further complicates and confuses the concept and the whole normative discussion. To conclude, describing and labelling different types of market systems by means of only one of the basic values in society can never lead to a clear and usable normative concept.

By using 'democracy' as the overall normative concept for society, from the micro to the macro level, it becomes a *multidimensional* normative concept that always combines basic values in a gradual way. Consequently, the application of the concept is more complete and balanced.

As discussed earlier, the advantage of the gradual concept of 'democratic market system' is the combination of four basic values to describe the actual situation and the situation that is desired. We can refer to Linda Gratton's challenging book (2004), *The democratic enterprise*, in which she makes an empirical ranking of some large multinational enterprises according to their level of democracy, based on the realised score for some basic values. She clearly shows that it is possible to translate the concept of 'democracy' into an analytical matrix that can be used for empirical studies.

A *strongly democratic market system*, then, can be described as a system that creates a strong balance between the basic values (freedom, equality, solidarity and efficiency) on all levels of the market system. All actors in the market system (have to) take into account all four basic values in an equal way, simultaneously, both at the input and the output side of the daily activities, both in the private and public sphere.

To introduce this normative concept during the next few years, it is necessary to further develop the concept and to apply it to the daily functioning of actual markets in the world, both in a descriptive and a normative sense. The descriptive analysis must result in a broad, gradual and more realistic picture of the different types of market systems at all levels of society, based on a number of relevant characteristics, in that way illustrating the gradual differences between very democratic and very undemocratic market systems. The normative analysis has to develop a set of normative standards concerning the different aspects and the functioning of all relevant variants of a democratic market system. By way of illustration, we formulated a number of norms or standards for a 'strong democratic market system' in Section 3.3, more specifically for the place and functioning of the smaller and larger private actors and of the more collective systems in the market system and for the role and functioning of the fiscal system.

6.1.2 Promoting the Complete Combination Model

We have shown that the concept of strong democracy can be made operational by means of a number of normative combination models. We argued that the complete combination model is the most adequate long-term policy model to express the concept of strong democracy and to serve as the basis for a coherent set of efficient policy perspectives and measures.

Therefore, it is necessary to promote the Complete Combination Model widely and continuously, to show and argue the strength of the gradual model. This can influence the attitude of men and women towards the model in a positive way and stimulate positive change in their actual division of labour. This promotion is most effective when it provides a clear and specific message for all age groups, with extra attention for young men and women starting a steady relationship or their own household. The levers and instruments for such a policy are located in all segments of society: the labour market, public services such as schools, day-care centres, service centres for older people, sporting centres, arts centres, the media, etc.

All young people have to be made aware of the importance of an equal division of labour between men and women when they start their own household: their relative professional position (number of hours, sector, profession, wage, etc) and the division of household tasks. They should have enough opportunities to learn and experience to what extent the background, daily duties, attitudes and aspirations of both partners are on the same track, and how this could be improved. Therefore, the 'daily combination of professional and family life' should become part of the normal education course for all age groups.

It is likely that more older men and women still follow the traditional model. If so, they need to be convinced of the importance of the complete combination model for the future development of society, for all generations. At the same time, they must be shown that the model pays sufficient attention to the personal life course and the societal context and that it allows many different combinations to answer the specific needs of different subgroups, as the label 'complete' expresses. They must be able to recognise their own capacities and opportunities to adapt themselves to new circumstances. The essential challenge for them is also the search for new positive combinations of professional labour, family labour, social labour and free time.

6.2   An integrated 'full employment policy'

6.2.1 New meaning of 'full employment'

In the first place, the complete combination model demands that the traditional policy goal of 'full employment' (for the male breadwinner) is replaced by the more general goal of *full employment, both for professional work and family work, for all men and women in the professional population* (all men and women that are potentially professionally active). The basic principle behind this is the combination of the right and duty of all men and women with respect to professional labour and family labour. The right of every man and woman in the professional population to have sufficient professional labour (and professional income) and enough family time is then strongly related to the responsibility or duty to perform sufficient professional and family labour during the life course. The combination of professional right and duty implies that society (government and professional organisations) is responsible for creating and providing sufficient good jobs. The professional 'duty' of the 'supply side' of the labour market (families, men and women), that is, 'supplying' sufficient professional labour and 'demanding' sufficient professional tasks, can only be enforced and realised to the extent that the professional 'duty' of the 'demand side' (professional organisations: commercial enterprises, social organisations and public institutions) is also sufficiently being realised, that is, 'supplying' sufficient good jobs (in terms of personal, social, material and financial benefits) and 'demanding' sufficient professional labour of all qualification levels. The further increase in the supply side (in quantity and quality) is not possible without the further increase in the demand side, and vice versa. It is clearly an 'and/and' story. Both sides must take sufficient initiative, in proportion to the available personal, social, material and financial capital, in that way encouraging and supporting the other side to realise both their duties and rights.

In the complete combination model, *full professional employment* then implies that all men and women in the professional population can have sufficient hours of paid work, with a sufficient quality, during a sufficiently long career. The model implies a gradual division of all jobs in terms of the average number of hours per week: 5, 10, 15, 20, 25, 30, 35, 40, 45, 50, 55, 60, 65, 70 hours. The official 35-hour job can then be seen as the new 'normal' full-time job, with sufficient differentiation according to the life course and family stage. For example, one could reserve mainly small jobs of 5-20 hours/week for students, bigger jobs of 35-45 hours for adult men and women without children, moderate jobs of 25-35 hours for (young) parents and older people finishing their career, and finally smaller jobs of 5-20 hours for retired people who want to remain professionally active to a certain extent. At the same time, a full family task means or demands that all men and women in the professional population have sufficient hours of family work during the life course, also of sufficient quality. In line with professional labour, this implies a gradual division of family tasks in terms of the 'normal' or average number of hours per week: 5, 10, 15, 20, 25, 30, 35, 40, 45, 50 hours, etc. The 25-hour family task can be seen as the norm for a 'full family task' within the complete combination model.

This implies that the sum of professional labour and family labour, what we call here 'total labour', counts on average as 60 hours/week, with a variation of 40-90 hours/week. The combination of the right and duty with respect to professional and family labour demands a clear formulation and recognition of the possible (temporary) *exemptions from professional labour*. The recognised exemptions from professional labour then imply the right to a sufficiently high replacement income. At the moment, several exemptions are already recognised, with financial compensation by means of the social security system: illness, invalidity, pension and forced unemployment (lack of jobs or lack of employability). The complete combination model implies a further improvement in these arrangements, in terms of equality, solidarity and efficiency. However, the general traditional exemption for housewives who (want to) stay at home to do the housework and/or to raise the (young) children, with or without direct financial compensation, can no longer be maintained in (the process towards) the complete combination model. This idea was already formulated by Cuvilier (1979), referring to the high societal (financial) cost of housewives for society, which was – in the end – mainly paid by professionally active women (with a modest income). During the process towards the complete combination model in the next few decades, the still existing exemption for housewives (and househusbands) should be replaced by a specific, temporary exemption due to (very) difficult family circumstances that prevent at least one of the partners combining professional and family work. This recognised specific and temporary exemption, preserved for a relatively small group of families, can then be combined with a sufficiently high temporary replacement income.

We emphasise that the complete combination model does not and cannot physically compel people to take a job if they really do not want one. So everyone (without an exceptional, difficult personal or family situation) can consciously and freely choose not to participate in the labour market. However, the complete combination model confronts these people with their social and financial responsibility and no longer provides collective (financial) support for that conscious 'free choice'. These people then have to bear the financial consequences of their choice themselves. Instead of receiving a net collective support for their choice not to have a job (no fiscal contribution and in many countries extra financial support), they have to pay a personal fiscal contribution for their use of the different collective provisions that are being paid by all professionally active people. In that way, the real societal and private cost of this 'free choice' becomes clear (Cuvilier, 1979;Van Dongen, 1993;Van Dongen et al, 2001). At the same time, the new policy implies that all people staying at home can fully enter the new employment arrangement, with the same support as people looking for a job.

6.2.2 Transformation of the fiscal system

The collective sector, with the fiscal system (including the social security system) at the income side and all public services at the expense side, always has a large impact on the production process at all levels of the market system. Logically, a (major) change in this system (that is, in the relative prices or tax rates) has a great (positive or negative) influence on every subject of society.

All fiscal systems are (implicitly or explicitly) based on a certain normative approach to the division of labour in society. At the same time, every fiscal system supports a certain division of labour. Therefore, it is essential that all countries that want to realise the complete combination model try to develop a fiscal system that is both largely inspired by and sufficiently supportive of the realisation process towards the model. In this section we propose some major changes to the fiscal system that are necessary for the realisation of the complete combination model, starting from the general norms of a democratic fiscal system in Section 3.3.3.

6.2.2.1 Reduction of the total fiscal pressure

The first basic element to be considered is the total fiscal pressure (including social security) in the different countries, that is, the total tax as a percentage of GDP (OECD, 2005). Figure 6.1 presents the evolution of the total fiscal pressure in OECD countries in the period 1965-2003, sorted along the score for 2003. The total fiscal pressure in 2003 varied from 25% in the US to 50% in Sweden. In most European countries the total fiscal pressure was higher than 35% in 2003. In Belgium, Denmark and Sweden it was even higher than 45%, while in Ireland it was only 29%. Among the non-European countries, the US and Japan showed the lowest tax level (about 25%) followed by Australia (32%), Canada (33%) and New Zealand (35%). Until 1995, the total fiscal pressure increased strongly in most (European) countries. After 1995, the percentage decreased in many countries, except in the UK, Italy, Belgium and Sweden.

Figure 6.1   Total fiscal pressure in a number of OECD countries (1965-2003)

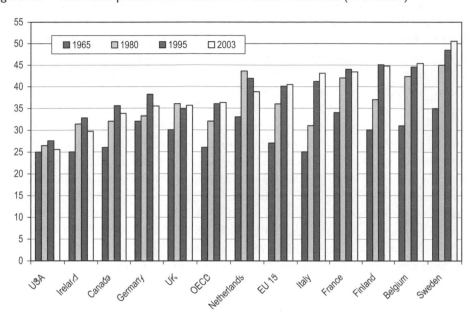

To a large extent, the total fiscal pressure expresses the magnitude of the collective policy of a country. To execute a strong social, collective policy, a certain level of collective means is necessary, since all collective goods and services have their market price. Yet, a (very) high fiscal pressure neither automatically implies that the public expenses are efficient nor that they are inefficient. Sweden has the highest fiscal pressure but is generally known for the relatively high efficiency of its public services. To the extent that public services are efficiently produced and used in the market system, a higher fiscal pressure can lead to higher welfare in society. A strongly democratic society invests sufficient means in collective services to cope with the major societal risks and to support all socially and professionally weaker groups, also allowing them to develop a well-balanced division of activities and (personal, social, material and financial) means. The realisation of the complete combination model, as an expression of a fully democratic division of labour therefore requires a sufficiently developed collective system, ranging between, for example, 35% and 50% of total GDP. The choice for a strong collective financial basis, however, demands an efficient use of the available means, maximally supporting the division of labour in families and organisations.

6.2.2.2 *Reduction of the fiscal pressure on human labour*

The second basic aspect to be dealt with is the relative fiscal pressure on human labour, which is very high in most OECD countries (Van Dongen et al, 2001; European Commission, 2004; OECD, 2005). Figure 6.2 shows the relative share of the main tax forms in the total fiscal revenues in a number of OECD countries in 2003. The countries are sorted along the sum of the share of direct tax and social security contributions, as the two tax forms with the highest burden on human labour. The joint share of direct tax and social security contributions ranges from 54% of the total fiscal revenue in Ireland to 70% in the US and Belgium. We emphasise that in many countries with a low total fiscal pressure, the relative fiscal pressure on human labour is also high.

As mentioned in Section 3.3.3, a high fiscal pressure on human labour/capital leads to a systematic distortion in the market system, harming human-intensive activities in all organisations and sectors and also human-intensive organisations and sectors as such. This has a negative impact on employment in human-intensive market activities. To support the process towards the complete combination model efficiently, fiscal pressure on human labour has to be diminished systematically, until a good balance has been reached between the relative fiscal pressure on human and non-human labour/capital. In that way, more means can be invested in human-intensive activities (jobs) in all segments of society, both in quantity and quality. Most of these activities are located in human-intensive organisations that offer all kinds of human services for individuals, families and companies, such as childcare, education, care for older people, personal and household services, medical and social services, cultural activities, social and financial consulting and administrative tasks.

At the same time, this transformation is one of the foundations of an *effective environmental policy*, that is, to minimise waste of natural resources and material goods. In that way, a better balance will be created between the qualitative level of the material/technical and human capital in all production sectors.

Figure 6.2   Relative share of the basic tax forms in the total fiscal revenue in a number of OECD countries (2003)

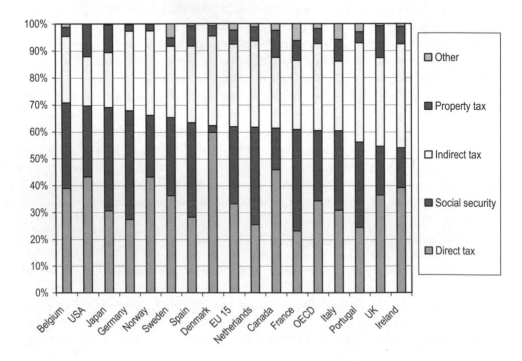

Additionally, the collective human and material damage of the different societal activities must be correctly included in the fiscal tariffs, both for prevention and correction. In that way, a number of hidden inefficiencies can be avoided or corrected and all market actors become more aware of the real societal costs and benefits of their activities.

6.2.2.3 Transformation of the tariff system of personal income tax and social security contributions

In all countries, several objectives concerning the combination of professional and family life and gender equality have been introduced into general policy. Yet the fiscal policy pursued during the past decades (mainly income tax and social security contributions) was, in many countries, still largely inspired by the traditional breadwinner model. The fiscal system mostly supported breadwinner families, largely at the cost of combination families (with a modest income), and it often implicitly resulted in the (temporary) withdrawal from the labour market of mostly low-skilled women.

The realisation of the complete combination model in the long run requires a thorough transformation of the tariff structure of the fiscal system, especially the personal income tax and social security contributions. Here we present a *possible new tariff system* for personal income tax and social security contributions, for all people who are professionally active. We first explain the basic system and then introduce some variants on the basis of the system of fiscal time credits.

Basic system

The new tariff system is based on the combined use of four possible criteria: total professional income, average real number of paid working hours per week (or per year), professional income per working hour and the relative division of professional labour between two adult partners (in couple families).

The *total professional income* of men and women remains the major basis for the calculation of the total fiscal contribution for professional income, provided that the real professional income is known by the fiscal administration. This condition is not new and offers no more problems than before. However, any improvement in this matter is certainly welcome in most (or all) countries.

An additional criterion is the *average real number of paid working hours per week*. Within the gradual distribution of the complete combination model, the official 35-hours job is used as the new norm for a 'normal full-time job'. Around this new norm, a gradual tariff system is possible with slowly increasing tariffs (in percentages) to the extent that the real number of working hours per week of men and women differs from this norm. The new tariffs should be determined in several steps, depending on the actual effect of the new tariff system on the process towards the complete combination model. Figure 6.3 shows this principle, setting the basic tariff for the 35-hours job at 100% and gradually increasing (downwards on the Y-axis) the tariff for jobs with fewer hours per week (left side of the X-axis) or with more hours (right side of the X-axis). In that way, the fiscal system continually encourages the development of the gradual division of professional labour in the complete combination model.

The third possible criterion is *professional income per working hour*, as the expression of the real earning capacity of men and women. This criterion is essential for a (more) correct relation between progressive tariffs and real earning capacity. The fiscal tariffs (percentages of the total income) then gradually increase with the professional income per working hour. So, people (and families) with a low earning capacity will pay less tax for a certain income level. For example, a person earning €2,000 for 40 working hours/week will pay less tax than a person earning €2,000 for only 30 hours/week. This criterion is always combined with the former.

If necessary and useful, a fourth criterion can be used for couple families (married or unmarried), namely the *relative division of professional labour between two adult partners* (lower part of Figure 5.2). The reference point for the fiscal tariffs then is the (almost) equal division between the partners, for example 45%-55% or 55%-45%. The tariffs increase to the extent that the division between partners is more unequal.

The application of this criterion shows that the division of professional labour between the partners is the central starting point and not the division of professional income. After all, many partners have an unequal earning capacity, given education level and other competences. The complete combination model primarily aims at a sufficiently equal division of basic activities between partners, regardless of the differences in earning capacity. The division of time is the basis for the different aspects of total well-being. A normal, full job is also important for people with a lower earning capacity, while full engagement in family labour is also important for people with a higher earning capacity. The complete combination model aims at an equal reward for men and women

Figure 6.3 Basic principle of the new tariff system for income tax and social security, according to number of working hours

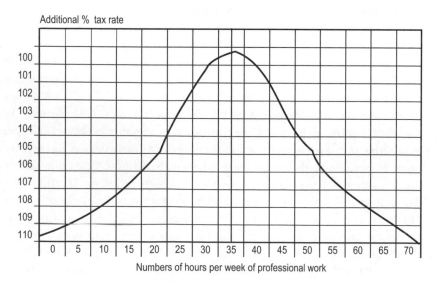

with an equal qualification level. The combination of an equal division of labour and an equal reward for equal work will, in the long run, lead to an equal earning capacity between men and women.

Based on these principles, a new integrated progressive tariff system for income tax and social security contributions can be constructed for all professionally active people. For all people without any professional work, the existing system has to be used with progressive tariffs on the basis of total personal income. Figure 6.4 shows a simple version of such a new system.

For each category of working hours (legend) a curve of the net professional income per hour is given (upper curves, with scores on the Y-axis, related to the number of working hours). These curves are the result of the difference between the diverse levels of the total professional income per hour (X-axis) and the progressive tax rate per hour (lower curves, with scores on the Y-axis) for each category of working hours (legend). The progressive tax rates (percentages) that are the basis of the tax curves are not given in the figure.

The curves of the total net professional income per week (per month, per year) can be calculated by multiplying all values of the professional income per hour with the corresponding number of working hours per week (per month, per year). These curves are not shown in the figure. The professional income per hour (X-axis) varies here from €0-110. A very small group of people still has a (much) higher income per hour. If necessary, the scale on the X-axis can be adjusted.

In this figure, jobs of 34–36 hours/week are taken as the new normative basis for all men and women in the professional population who are single or live in a couple family and who have no dependent people in the household (mostly children). These jobs have the lowest tax rate per working hour for the different possibilities of total professional income per hour (X-axis): the bold tax curve is the lowest of all. Consequently, this reference job leads to the highest net income per working hour for every possible total professional income per hour: the bold net income curve is the highest of all. Starting from the basic principle of the system (see Figure 6.3), the tax curves for smaller and bigger jobs are higher, according to the difference in hours with the reference job. In the same way, the curves of the net hourly income are lower for all smaller and bigger jobs.

The tariff system is based on a progressive tax rate for total professional income per working hour, expressing the real earning capacity of employees, as an indicator of their real productivity, that is, the capacity to produce at least their total wage cost for the employer by means of their labour. The curves of the tax per hour and of the net professional income per hour cross each other at a certain value of the total professional income per hour (X-axis). From that income level, the tax per hour is more than the net professional income per hour.

On the curve of net professional income per hour, one can determine the net minimum income per hour that is necessary to earn a sufficient total net income, when working certain minimum hours per week. In this example the net minimum income per hour is €7. In that case, a zero tax rate counts for a total income per hour of €7. For higher values of the total income per hour, a progressive positive tax rate is counted,

Figure 6.4   New tariff system for income tax and social security: net professional income per hour as a result of tax per hour and total professional income per hour

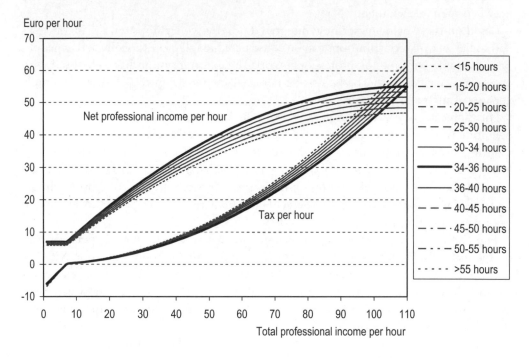

starting from a very low rate for incomes that are a little higher than €7. For all lower levels of total income per hour, a progressive *negative* tax rate is used, resulting in a net income subsidy for a certain number of people, in order to offer them a sufficiently high total income.

The basic goal of this system is that all men and women are correctly located on the gradual productivity ladder in the production system, based on total professional income per hour, expressing their real earning capacity or productivity. All men and women are then encouraged to increase their productivity and to climb on that ladder to a certain extent, leading to higher personal and societal gain. Yet this incentive is stronger for men and women with low to very low productivity, in order to increase their personal gain and to minimise wage subsidies (or to increase fiscal revenues).

This fiscal tariff system encourages all organisations/employers to employ the right person (with a certain qualification) at the right place (on the productivity ladder) in the production process. In that way, they can employ people in an efficient and maximal way, according to their need for (demand) and the availability (supply) of certain labour qualifications. At the same time, the system permanently stimulates the employability of all people with a relatively low to very low productivity, increasing the benefit for the employees involved, but also for the organisations and the government. As such, it is an integrated and efficient policy for both the demand and supply side that can replace the actual package of ad hoc fiscal employment arrangements for vulnerable social groups that exist in many countries.

Modifications by means of fiscal time credits

The presence of dependent children demands more time for parental education/care within the family, combined with external education/care. The same counts for other dependent people (older people, people with a long-lasting illness or disability). To answer this need the fiscal tariff system can be adjusted for families with dependent children and/or other dependent people, lone-parent families and one-person families. These families (with one or two partners) can be given a *fiscal time credit*, with full entitlement to security provisions. The fiscal time credit implies that the gradual tariff system starts from a reference job with a lower number of hours. Figure 6.5 shows the idea by means of variants of the tariff system for different family types. The bold curve 1 is the basic tariff curve shown in Figure 6.3. On the left side, a few other tariff curves are presented for families with children.

Figure 6.5   Variants of the tariff system for income tax and social security, for other family types and specific occupations

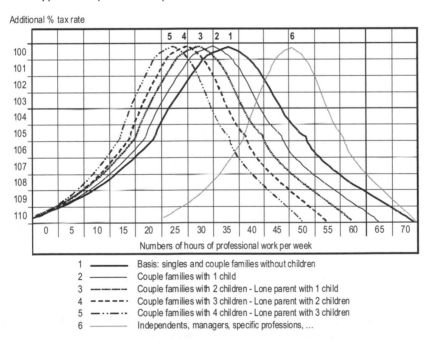

1	————	Basis: singles and couple families without children
2	————	Couple families with 1 child
3	·—··—··—	Couple families with 2 children - Lone parent with 1 child
4	- - - - -·	Couple families with 3 children - Lone parent with 2 children
5	—··—··	Couple families with 4 children - Lone parent with 3 children
6	————	Independents, managers, specific professions, …

The objective of the fiscal time credit is that adult partners with dependent children or other dependent people preserve enough working hours per week, and at the same time are more available for the dependent people, according to the total needs, and still have enough time for other activities. People with one healthy child, for example, could receive a time credit of two hours/week, resulting in a reference job of 32–34 hours/week with the lowest fiscal tariff. The tariff system is then presented by curve 2 at the left side of the basic curve. Referring to Figure 6.4, the 32–34 hour job would have the lowest tax curve and the highest income curve for parents with one child. This tariff system stimulates them not to work less than 32 and more than 34 hours/week, but they remain free to choose otherwise (in agreement with the employer), albeit with a somewhat higher tariff according to the real number of working hours. Couple families with two healthy children enjoy in this example an additional time credit of two hours/week leading to a reference curve of 30–32 hours/week. Curve 3 at the left side of the basic curve represents this tariff system. Curve 4 and curve 5 show the tariff system for couple families with three, four or more children.

An additional time credit can be granted for 'being a single parent', in the strict sense of the word, when one parent is (almost) fully responsible for the actual education/care of the children. This time credit gives extra support to the single parent in order to be more available for the child(ren), but at the same time maintaining enough working hours per week and enough time for personal and social activities. In our example, the tariff system of a lone parent with one child corresponds with the tariff system of a couple family with two children. The tariffs of a lone parent with two dependent children then corresponds with the tariff system of a couple family with three children and so on.

In this line, an additional time credit can also be offered for the presence of a dependent older person or a person with an extra need for family care (child or adult), for example due to a long-lasting illness or disability. This fiscal time credit can be combined with that for the presence of healthy children. So the tariff system of a couple family with one child with a disability corresponds with the tariff system of a couple family with two healthy children.

For specific professional groups with intrinsic long working hours, such as self-employed people or top managers, a negative tax credit could be used. In our example, a reference job of 45 hours/week is presented. This tariff system corresponds with curve 6 at the right side of the basic curve. Of course, more variants of this curve are possible.

Discussion: desirability and feasibility of the new tariff system

One can question the usefulness of such a gradual fiscal tariff system. However, in one way or another, the application of such criteria is necessary for the fiscal system to become an effective lever for the process towards the complete combination model. After all, a fiscal system is always based on a number of normative criteria, expressing a certain normative view on society and the division of labour. Until now, many fiscal systems contained some criteria to support breadwinner families, that is, the unequal division of labour between men and women, with many negative aspects on the micro and macro level. The realisation of the complete combination model requires a consequent and consistent fiscal system that correctly and efficiently applies such normative criteria.

At first sight, many people will also doubt the feasibility of this fiscal tariff system. However, the translation of the new basic tariff system of Figure 6.3 and the different variants (see Figure 6.5) into an efficient fiscal calculation programme is not that difficult. A few basic data are to be introduced for every individual and family in order to get the correct fiscal tariff. Some existing fiscal exemptions, deductions or reductions can be integrated in the new tariff system and the useful remaining exemptions, deductions or reductions can be taken over without problems. With an online calculation programme, every person, family and company can make simulations in order to find the optimal division of labour.

It is clear that such a reform must be realised in several stages, as presented in Figure 5.1. In the first stage, the remaining breadwinner facilities must be converted into new instruments that support the process towards the complete combination model. In a period of 5-10 years these facilities (and the financial means) can be converted into new facilities that support the realisation of the complete combination model. At the same time, the quality of low qualified jobs must be improved, preventing them from being a threshold for people with a weak professional position to take up a job. These people must also be able to experience a job that not only offers a (low) income, but also sufficient personal and social benefits.

6.2.3 Integrated policy for 'maximal employment' and 'minimal unemployment'

The complete combination model needs an integrated policy with sufficient consistency between the different policy fields. The policy perspectives have to support one another mutually. With a new tariff system for personal income tax and social security contributions as presented above, the employment policy is based on the complete combination model. The new tariff system encourages all families and companies to convert (step by step) to a more equal and family-friendly division of professional and family labour. The tariff system has a direct impact on the daily allocation of human labour within the organisation: employers and employees have a common interest in searching together for the most beneficial combination of working hours. This choice is also a 'correct' choice since it is automatically linked with the responsibility of families and organisations to realise effective solidarity within society. After all, the new system leads to a sufficiently strong financial basis for the government, in order to fully invest in financially dependent groups, such as children, older people, people with a disability or a chronic illness, people lacking an adequate education and people with an exceptional family burden. In that way, the new tariff system offers a good basis for adjustments in several societal fields.

The system of fiscal time credits is most relevant and useful for all families with at least one paid job, who themselves, to a certain degree, can determine the number of working hours, in mutual agreement with their employer. The presence of children or being a lone parent can restrict professional labour to a certain extent, both in quantity and quality, but in most cases these factors do not make professional labour completely impossible. Other severe personal or social circumstances have a more drastic effect on the possibility of finding and maintaining a job: a chronic illness, a severe disability, exceptional family problems or very inadequate education/competences.

The complete combination model aims at an optimal participation of people with severe personal and family problems in professional, family and social life. So, society has to decide to what extent these problematic situations can be a basis for (temporary) exemption from professional labour and give a right to a decent replacement income (in quantity and duration). People who are no longer able to perform any professional labour because of severe personal or social circumstances are then no longer seen as members of the professional population. In that case, society should help these people to adjust their division of time, enabling them to participate sufficiently in family and societal life.

In the Combination Model, 'total unemployment' includes both people looking for a job and those staying at home for a long time (see Figures 4.17–4.20). Total unemployment is the negative result of shortages/problems at the supply side (unemployed people themselves) and at the demand side (the lack of good jobs in professional organisations). Therefore, the differential unemployment profiles of unemployed people should be the basis for the differential employment policy of governments and counselling labour market offices.

An efficient employment policy for the supply side (individual men and women, families) is a necessary condition to increase the employment rate, but it is not a sufficient condition. It has to go hand in hand with a dynamic demand-side policy to create sufficient new suitable jobs, on all levels of society. The general decrease in the relative cost of human labour is a major policy perspective for the preservation of existing jobs and the creation of new jobs in all human intensive activities. But at the same time, a broad societal investment programme is necessary on all levels of society, in order to create new useful and beneficial market activities. In a democratic society, both the public and the private sector are responsible for shaping this process. Such a combined employment policy needs sufficient coordination between the different policy levels (local, provincial, regional, national and international). So the EU has to take sufficient initiatives to reform and streamline the fiscal systems and employment policies in order to encourage all professional organisations to realise the same basic policy goals.

At the supply side, most attention must go to a policy that activates all unemployed people in all age groups to find and continue with a suitable job, including all people looking for a job or staying at home (mostly housewives). At the same time, it is essential to prevent older professionally active people from leaving the labour market too early by means of different pre-pension plans. For students, the Complete Combination Model promotes the combination of full study with a small part-time job, leaving space for sufficient variants. Also here, the clock–curve can again serve as a good policy guide.

The first problem to tackle is the inadequate education for a certain part of the professional population. Indeed, society has to invest in better education for these people, increasing their competences and employability, that is, their opportunity to find a suitable and durable job.

Efforts to increase employability are important for people without a job, but also for all people with an unsatisfying and unstable job, both to help avoid job loss andto improve their professional situation generally. In most countries, this employability policy is increasingly being developed and will most probably produce concrete results during the next few decades. Efforts in this field must, of course, be kept in balance with efforts in other fields.

In all EU countries, most unemployed people are financially compensated in a certain way and to a certain extent. People officially recognised as looking for a job mostly receive a replacement income for being unemployed, based on some conditions (previous work and income, family situation, etc). In a democratic society, the replacement income should be high enough to realise a decent living, but at the same time it should not discourage people to look for a suitable job.

People staying at home (mostly housewives) pay no or only little personal tax and social security contribution for the collective provisions they use and in many countries they receive some additional indirect compensation. In that way, they are also financially supported by society to a large extent. However, this financial support is mostly far from sufficient to replace a normal professional income.

A central goal of the complete combination model is to eliminate as far as possible the 'unemployment traps' (in the broad sense of the word), to prevent unemployed people from settling themselves into a long-lasting unemployment. Most direct unemployment compensations are based on professional income earned via professional labour. Yet society does not demand unemployed people to perform (a minimum of) societal work during the period of unemployment. This is quite understandable since society does not offer sufficient adequate jobs and cannot expect unemployed people to create their own jobs. But in that way, the unemployment trap is perpetuated. An efficient employment policy encourages unemployed people to look for work but it also encourages both public and private employers to offer suitable jobs for all these people.

The complete combination model wants to breach this vicious unemployment circle in a positive way, combining the right to a decent job and income with the duty and effective willingness to perform sufficient societal labour. As long as the new fiscal system is not realised and society cannot offer sufficient normal jobs, unemployed people are entitled to a decent replacement income. But the unemployment benefits should then be used as a collective input for the creation of useful societal tasks, for families and all sorts of organisations. These societal tasks could be called 'bridge jobs', that is, largely subsidised jobs that have to act as a bridge between effective unemployment and a (more) normal job. In that way, every unemployed person can have a bridge job of about 20-25 hours/week in a family or organisation and then receive a decent basic income. The bridge job can be seen as the 'basic societal labour' that guarantees societal participation and a basic individual income for everyone. In contrast with the traditional basic income model (Van Parijs, 1992, 1995; Ackerman et al, 2005) that provides a 'basic income' for all people, with no or only a weak link to societal labour to be performed, the complete combination model primarily provides a 'basic job' for all (unemployed) people, combined with a decent guaranteed basic income.

The system of bridge jobs is a useful system during the (long) transition period towards the new fiscal system described above. As such, it has a number of advantages, for people actually looking for a job, for their family and for societal organisations.

At the demand side the concept of bridge jobs is the logical result of the duty of all people in the professional population to perform sufficient societal labour during the professional career. A bridge job is not voluntary work but really professional labour; yet it is not a 'normal' job because, in the current fiscal system, it is financed by means of a special subsidy system. In the new fiscal tariff system proposed earlier, the dual distinction between normal and subsidised bridge jobs is replaced by the gradual location of all jobs on the productivity ladder.

A bridge job is the translation of the (conditional) professional duty of unemployed people, but it is not based an coercion from the side of the government or any other institution. This system gives every unemployed person the possibility of choosing between a certain number of bridge jobs offered, according to interest, education, physical capabilities and so on, for example with a minimum of three offers. This condition, consequently, demands sufficient diversity in the supply of bridge jobs.

Moreover, a bridge job is in principle a temporary, part-time job, for example of 20-25 hours/week. So, all people with a bridge job have enough time to search for a better, 'normal' job, preferably in combination with additional schooling or training.

The system of bridge jobs largely eliminates the employment trap, since all unemployed person have to evaluate their situation from a new point of reference. Being offered some suitable bridge jobs, they have to compare the quantity, quality and the earnings of a possible normal (part-time) job with the minimum quantity, quality and earnings of the bridge jobs offered. When they refuse to take up a bridge job, they have to face the situation without personal replacement income and with an extra fiscal contribution for the collective services used, as described before. So the earnings gap between the situation with and the situation without a (bridge) job becomes bigger, increasing the incentive to take up a (bridge) job. At the same time, the earnings gap between the situation with a bridge job and the situation with a normal job has to be big enough to encourage these people to search for a normal and better job. Of course, such a bridge job is less optimal than a normal job but it is (almost) always better than having no job at all.

All unemployed people taking up a bridge job will receive a higher income than the basic unemployment replacement income. This will improve their welfare level and purchasing power, giving an extra incentive to (local) companies and markets. People with a bridge job also receive additional support and education in order to find a better, normal job. Then, three possibilities occur. First, the bridge job can positively evolve towards a normal job, improving the situation of both the person and organisation involved. Second, the person finds a better, normal job elsewhere, improving their personal situation and leaving the bridge job for another unemployed person. Third, when neither of these possibilities occurs, the person can keep the bridge job for a longer period. After all, the basic goal is that all these people remain active in the societal production process. As long as they are unable to find a normal job, they can keep the bridge job and contribute to society and to their own family welfare. At the same time, they invest in their own personal and social capital to a certain extent, increasing their opportunity to find a normal job later on.

Starting from the right, duty and willingness to work, the system always offers the possibility to choose between a few bridge jobs offered by society, according to the interests, competences and restrictions of the person involved. Compared with the actual choices available for most long-standing unemployed people, this system offers more diversity and choices. But being realistic, the choices for these people are always limited, as it is for most people having a normal job. At the same time, these people fully experience a more balanced daily combination of professional, family and other social responsibilities. In that way, they can experience that a paid job offers them not only the necessary monetary income but also other opportunities to fully participate in society.

Basically, the system of bridge jobs offers equal treatment for all unemployed people, irrespective of their education, the duration of unemployment and the reasons for the unemployment. Consequently, the system does not stigmatise socially weaker groups that are more confronted with long-lasting unemployment.

From the start of this system, all people staying at home (mostly housewives), should be strongly encouraged to participate, enjoying the same basic rights and duties. In that way, they can be integrated in the labour market step by step. For people who can find a job but really do not want to have one, however, the system of bridge jobs cannot offer a solution. They have to face the social and financial consequences of that free choice, as mentioned before.

At the demand side all organisations would be able to create such bridge jobs, with a very low total labour cost, up to a certain percentage of the total actual number of full-time equivalent jobs. For families and non-professional organisations, this restriction is not necessary. This broad scope is the best guarantee for sufficient diversity in the supply of bridge jobs.

The organisations offering such bridge jobs are encouraged to transform them into normal jobs, for example in a period of one to five years, depending on the increasing production capacity of the people involved, which then enables a gradual increase in the total labour cost (personal income and fiscal contributions). In that way, a real activating policy is carried out, integrating unemployed people in a societal organisation and strongly increasing the chances of creating new normal jobs. Of course, this process will follow the ups and downs of the market system to a large extent.

Finally, this system offers many societal organisations the opportunity to realise a number of useful supportive tasks that are now being postponed or neglected, or possibly shifted to present employees, increasing pressure on them. In that way, the performance of these employees and of the organisation as a whole can be improved. This can then lead to an increasing respect for such (mostly simple) supportive tasks. The condition then is that both employers and employees really try to convert these bridge jobs into normal jobs as far as possible.

6.2.4 Adequate leave arrangements as a bridge between professional and family life

The basic goal of the complete combination model and the proposed transformation of the fiscal system is that men and women can plan their professional career in an efficient way, both on the individual and family level. An essential condition is that the basic working time arrangement is sufficiently in line with the needs of family life during the different stages of the life course.

Given the 'normal working time' in a certain period and country, all men and women and all families need an adequate set of leave arrangements, as an answer to their specific needs. During previous decades, different systems of leave arrangements have been developed in different countries, answering to a certain extent the different family needs.

Here, we concentrate on 'family leave arrangements' that have to offer more time for family work, especially related to the presence of (young) children: maternity leave, paternity leave, parental leave, forms of career interruption and family leave for more specific family reasons (breastfeeding, illness, death of a family member).

For an extensive overview of the actual forms and conditions of the leave arrangements in western countries, we refer – among others – to Gornick and Meyers (2003), Ferrarini (2003), Haas (2003), Kamerman et al (2003), den Dulk et al (2005), Deven and Moss (2005) and Riedman et al (2006). These studies show that the different family leave systems are largely in line with the overall combination policies in the different types of welfare states as distinguished in Section 4.4 (see also Esping-Andersen, 1990, 1999 and Korpi, 2000).

The southern weaker combination model still emphasises family responsibility for the education/care of young children. So the government implicitly still supports the traditional breadwinner family to a large extent, giving little support to the different combination families. The continental combination model stresses the free choice of families with respect to the care of young children and therefore supports longer leave for the care of young children in the family, albeit with a fairly low financial compensation. In previous years, the emphasis was on shorter leaves, combined with additional childcare. The combination model in the English-speaking countries also emphasises the care of young children in the family, but leaves the responsibility largely to families and employers. The Nordic advanced combination model promotes the equal division of family work, providing a generous leave arrangement for both mothers and fathers, to take care of their children at home until the age of about one year, with a relatively high financial compensation.

So all the actual combination models still largely follow the traditional pedagogical view that the youngest children should be (exclusively) cared for within the family, implying that at least one of the parents has to stay at home during a certain period, varying from approximately one year in the Nordic countries to approximately three or four years in other countries. However, this pedagogical view and its practical translation into a system of long family leave can never be compatible with the central goal and effective realisation of gender equality as formulated by the complete combination model. This view, still dominant in most countries, albeit in different variants, strongly contributes to the perpetuation of societal inequality between men and women. In the Nordic countries, more young mothers than young fathers take parental leave, with good compensation, and, on average, women take much longer leave. This difference is clearly visible in the systematic gap in the average number of hours of professional work between men and women, in all age groups (see Figure 4.27). Most other countries have developed a sort of dual system, with, on the one hand, still a fairly large group of breadwinner families where young mothers stay at home for quite a long time and on the other hand, an increasing group of combination families with combined education/ care of the young children, already starting from the age of three to six months.

As a normative model, the complete combination model implies a logical shift in the basic orientation for both parents and (young) children. The model starts from a new view on the 'normal daily working time arrangement' for men and women, as part of an equal division of professional and family labour. It also starts from a new pedagogical view emphasising 'shared or combined' high-quality education/care, both within and outside the family, that starts a few months after childbirth, albeit with sufficient variation, largely depending on the characteristics of the children. The child's family must play its full pedagogical role of home base, but external daytime education/care is also a full part of the total development of (almost) all children, as a full complement and enrichment of education/care at home.

Following the normative model for the division of time of parents (see Figure 5.2) and that of children (see Figure 5.8), the complete combination model aims at preserving and improving the basic family leave arrangements around the time of childbirth, for both mothers and fathers, in order to support the intense personal and family changes during the first few months. At the same time, the model aims at encouraging a sufficiently equal division in professional and family responsibilities between men and women. This implies that the long and complete leave facilities have to be reduced to a minimum, to be used as the last solution when all other options prove to be impossible in the short run. The more the new division of labour (see Figure 5.2) is being realised, the less families will need a long leave arrangement as a solution to their family problems. In that situation, more families will need specific family leave to answer specific short-term problems. So it is desirable to transform existing long parental leave arrangements into a general *flexible system of family leave*. This family leave is, then, complementary to the other leave arrangements, not to interrupt jobs for a longer period, but to better support people combining their job and family work. After all, the daily combination of professional and family labour is a permanent challenge for every individual and family, a permanent process of learning by doing. A long full-time leave arrangement mostly does not solve the actual problem regarding the division of professional and family work, but mostly bypasses the problem, postponing the problem to a later date. And in many cases, the problem becomes more serious because these families (largely) eliminate the daily learning process.

This additional 'family leave' can be realised as a time credit, consisting of two components: a fixed basic time credit that is granted to all people, combined with a variable time credit, based on professional work performed in the past and to be performed in the future (as a time loan to be paid off afterwards by means of a certain amount of professional work). So, this new family leave can be combined with a high, gradual financial compensation, diminishing the compensation with an increasing length and quantity of the leave. As a consequence, many more families will be able to use this type of family leave. Finally, since long-term leave is reduced to a smaller group, the re-entry of this group in the labour market can be more easily guaranteed.

6.3 Adequate provisions for dependent children

The transformation of employment policy, the fiscal tariff system and leave arrangements need to be combined with adequate societal provisions for (financially) dependent people in the households, mostly children. In this section, we first deal with the need for a direct collective financial allowance for dependent children (with or without special needs), from birth until the moment of financial independence, as an additional direct financial compensation for the cost of raising children. Then we treat external daytime education/care as a direct basic service for young children and their parents, and as an indirect service for organisations. Next, the gradual need for additional childcare facilities is discussed: before and after daytime education/care, during weekends and holidays and during periods of illness. Finally, some basic perspectives are formulated with respect to the future development of the system of secondary and higher education.

6.3.1 Direct collective allowances for dependent children

First, a strong democratic society should give sufficient direct financial support to families with children. This financial support must enable every family to cover part of the daily private costs of children. In most countries, financial support for (families with) children is realised by means of a complex system of fiscal arrangements, direct allowances, lower prices for services, and so on, with insufficient transparency and consistency. Following the logic of the complete combination model, it is possible to develop a consistent and fairly simple system of basic child allowances that are fully compatible with collective investment in external education/care for children. The basic idea is to create one large collective fund to give all children a monthly child allowance, until the moment they are financially independent, mostly when they start their first full-time job. In the first stage, the fund collects all (or most of the) existing direct collective financial expenses for children. The total amount available can be distributed between all children, according to some basic conditions. Afterwards, the fund can receive extra means, if society wants to increase basic allowances. With such a system, all children have their own social and financial statute, with increasing responsibility to spend this money as they grow older. At a certain age, for example 18 years, they receive full juridical responsibility for spending this money. The practical responsibility can still be shared with the parents to a certain extent.

It is desirable that the basic allowance can be combined with the limited income of students via small jobs, for example starting from the age of 16. In that way, students can increasingly realise their own financial independence, together with their parents. Since in the Complete Combination Model basic child allowance is financed by means of progressive fiscal contributions, it becomes an additional adequate tool of social policy. After all, it offers each generation the necessary extra support for their personal development, irrespective of the success or failure of the parents. It is a combined social transfer, from families without children to families with children, from families with fewer children to families with more children and from richer families with children to poorer families with children. From the side of the children, one can see the basic allowance as an extra reward for their 'education work', to develop their human capital in an optimal way, as the basis for the welfare of future society.

The basic allowance should increase with the age of the children since, on average, the daily cost of children increases with age. Within each age group that is distinguished (yearly, every two years …), all children must receive the same basic allowance, expressing the basic equal right of all children. Any difference according to the income of the family is not desirable, since all children have an equal right and since the system is financed by means of correct, progressive fiscal contributions by all adults.

Every country has to determine the optimal level of basic allowances, in combination with the collective investment in external education/care for children. The two instruments can be combined as a communicating vessel, with the general rule that a lower private cost of external education/care is combined with a lower child allowance, and vice versa. In practice, different scenarios can be constructed, given the level of the total collective investment and a minimum and maximum level for the private cost of external education/care and for basic child allowance.

We emphasise that the complete combination model conceives child allowance as an *additional* support for total family income, to be combined with the professional income of the parents. The model intends to promote the different combination families, which implies that parents with children preserve their professional responsibility as much as possible. If, in some families, one of the parents wants to stay at home full time, without fulfilling the societal conditions for exemption from paid labour, child allowances are of course guaranteed, as a support for the presence of dependent children. However, this parent will have to pay a fiscal contribution for the personal use of collective provisions.

6.3.2 External daytime education/care as a basic provision for all children and parents

This section deals with the overall development of provisions for the external education/care of the youngest children in different countries. Starting from the overview in Gornick and Meyers (2003, pp 185-235), Blau (2001) and den Dulk et al (2005), we formulate the policy perspectives that follow from the new pedagogical view (see Section 5.3.3) and the new division of labour between men and women (see Section 5.3.1) of the complete combination model.

Gornick and Meyers (2003) show that provisions for the external education/care for children younger than 12 years are largely in line with the overall combination policy in the different types of welfare states as distinguished in Section 4.4, with the same gradual differences as for the leave arrangements.

As said before, all countries still largely follow the traditional pedagogical view that the youngest children should be (almost) exclusively cared for within the family, implying that at least one of the parents stays at home during a certain period, until the 'critical pedagogical age', that is, the age after which 'society' accepts that (almost) all children are partly educated outside the parental family. However, this critical pedagogical age strongly differs between countries: approximately one year in the Nordic countries, two to three years in Belgium, France, Spain and Italy, four years in the Netherlands, Luxembourg, Greece, Ireland, the UK, Canada and the US, and five years in Germany and Austria. This 'critical pedagogical age' is usually the starting point of a general provision of (almost) costless external daytime education/care, mostly under the umbrella of the education system (pre-school , nursery or toddler school, primary school) and in some countries under the umbrella of the social welfare system (day-care provisions).

After this critical pedagogical age, external education/care is seen as a necessary and valuable complement to education/care at home, stressing the importance for the development of children and giving entitlement to all children/parents to use the provision. Before this age, this entitlement is not available, since external education/care is largely seen as a necessary replacement for education/care at home, mostly because of the labour market participation of mothers. This replacement day-care is less oriented at the personal development of the children.

In most countries, compulsory primary school starts at a somewhat higher age, varying from four years in Luxembourg, five years in Germany, the Netherlands, Canada, the UK and the US, six years in Belgium, France, Spain, Italy, Greece and Norway, to seven years in Finland, Denmark and Sweden (Gornick and Meyers, 2003).

The southern weaker combination model emphasises family responsibility for the care of the youngest children, with little support for external education/care, which is largely seen as a replacement for family care in combination families. Although the number of places has been increased during past decades, the supply is strongly behind that in other European countries. The day-care system is far from an effective lever for more labour market participation for women or for a more equal division of labour between men and women.

The continental combination model stresses the free choice of families with respect to the care of young children and still conceives childcare more as a substitute for care at home and not so much as a complement to education/care at home. Therefore, the provision of external childcare largely follows the actual demand of the combination families, as a result of the increasing labour market participation of women. Although this demand–driven childcare system is fairly well developed in some countries (France, Belgium), it is only a weak motor for the further development of an equal division of labour between men and women and, consequently, for the further development of the childcare system itself.

The combination model in the English–speaking countries aims at improving the labour market position of women, but leaves external education/care largely to the private initiative of families and employers. The market for external day-care of young children has increased to a large extent, but it suffers from two major problems: low quality of services, expressing the basic idea that it is above all a replacement for family care, and the relatively high cost price for lower and middle-income groups, perpetuating and increasing the pedagogical gap between social groups (Blau, 2001; Gornick and Meyers, 2003). Therefore, the contribution of the childcare system to a more equal division of labour between men and women and to the improvement of the labour market position of lower and middle-income groups is also fairly low in these countries.

The Nordic combination model promotes the equal division of family work, providing generous childcare arrangements for children, from the age of about one year, with a relatively low financial cost for parents. As said before, the Nordic childcare system cannot be further developed as long as the pedagogical view, that the children should be (almost) exclusively cared for within the family until the age of one year, does not change. During the past decade, this Nordic variant of the traditional pedagogical view seems to become a major threshold for the further development towards a more equal division of labour between men and women.

In general, the traditional pedagogical view is still influential in all countries, leading to different partially developed systems of external education/care for the youngest children, in comparison with the (almost) fully developed education systems for the somewhat older children. These childcare systems are largely demand-driven and consequently strongly determined by the level of labour force participation of mothers. Therefore, they can never be compatible with the central goal of gender equality in society, as formulated in the complete combination model. Consequently, they cannot be a strong lever for the realisation of a more equal division of labour.

To realise the complete combination model, families, organisations and society as a whole need to become aware of the positive value of external education/care for children in all age groups, as a complement to and an enrichment of education/care within the family. This requires a general child-oriented policy, mainly based on the right of all children to enjoy a complete education, both within and outside the family, starting fairly soon after birth. A well-balanced combination of good education/care within both the family and external living arrangements (extended family, families of friends and neighbours, minder family, day-care centre, school, club, etc) offers a strong basis for the development of children and for the daily combination of professional and family work of parents. After all, being young is a major factor of societal and financial dependency, for which society bears a large collective responsibility. The government therefore is responsible for investing in sufficient and decent external education/care facilities for all children (Van Dongen, 2004c, 2004d).

The complete combination model conceives external education/care for the youngest children (younger than three or four years) as a basic provision to support education/care within the family. Consequently, it is necessary to develop a general basic package of external education/care for the youngest children. One could call it 'daytime education/care for babies and toddlers', in the broad pedagogical sense of the word and adjusted to the needs of each particular age group, integrating all aspects of the development of children. Organisationally and financially, such education/care for babies and toddlers should be maximally streamlined with existing education of older children in schools. When, as in a number of countries, the basic school is (almost) free of charge for parents, generally financed with fiscal means, daytime education/care for the youngest children should also be (almost) free of charge for the parents.

On a societal level, external daytime education/care for the youngest children, combined with education/care at home, is much more efficient than the full-time, almost exclusive care at home by one of the parents (Van Dongen, 2004c, 2004d), both pedagogically and financially. Shared education/care is pedagogically more efficient since it can combine specific *pedagogical* sources or means (personal, social, material) in a complementary way, leading to mutual support and enrichment. Education/care within the family offers specific pedagogical sources that are not available in the external education/care and that can never be replaced by external pedagogical sources. At the same time, external education/care offers specific pedagogical sources that are not available in the family and that are necessary for the complete development of children. The complete combination model aims at a combined high-quality education/care in both the family and external living arrangements, with a good balance of time spent within and outside the family. Therefore, as shown in Figure 5.8, the gradual forms of combined education/care can never be called extreme since they are always located between the real extreme forms of education/care: full-time education/care within the family on the left or full-time education/care within an institutional setting on the right side of the curve. Combined high-quality education/care is also financially more efficient since it is much cheaper than full-time education/care at home by one of the partners, due to the much higher productivity of professional external education/care. Parents staying at home for the full-time education/care of their young children take care of only one or two children, while a professional educator/caretaker is responsible for about 5–20 children, depending on the age and other characteristics of the children. At the same time, the complete combination model permanently ensures sufficient availability of the parent(s) for the children by restricting both the time spent by parents on professional work and the time of children spent by children in external education/care.

According to the model, almost all young children would make use of external education/care in the long run, with quite a large variation in the number of hours and days, according to personal, family and professional circumstances. As shown in Figure 5.8, the use of daytime education/care can also be presented by means of a clock-curve. Most children would stay two to four days/week in daytime education/care. A small group of children would stay in daytime education/care less than two days/week (left side of the curve) and a small group of children more than five days/week (right side of the curve). This distribution maximally corresponds to the desirable division of professional labour of the parents (see Figure 5.2) and the desirable availability for their children.

The curve of the strong combination model in Figure 5.8 is more to the right (dotted line) with an average of almost four days per week per user, which is approximately equal to the current use of primary education in most countries. The curve of the moderate combination model is more to the left (dashed line), with an average of two days per week per user, which largely corresponds to the actual average in most European countries.

In general, the complete combination model guarantees sufficient high-quality daytime education for every child, with respect to the personal characteristics and to family and professional circumstances. In that way, the model avoids as much as possible any discrimination between children, parents and families.

In all countries that want to realise the complete combination model, external daytime education/care for the youngest children has to be streamlined with external daytime education for older children, with respect to education finality, financial arrangement and day-to-day organisation.

Educational streamlining in the first place implies that the narrow notion of 'care' is replaced by the broader notion of 'education/care'. This means that external education/care has to deal with all aspects of the development of children, to offer a sufficiently broad pedagogical approach, as the basis for a positive interaction with education/care at home. One major advantage is the early detection and tackling of possible developmental problems.

Financial streamlining implies that the private cost of basic external daytime education/care (including the necessary daily travel cost) is (almost) the same for all age groups, in order to minimise the financial thresholds at all stages of the life course of children and parents. The most efficient way is to finance (almost) the total cost of external daytime education/care with collective means, since general daytime education/care is the most collective service in society, with a low risk for unequal use and for abundant consumption. It is also essential to realise a sufficiently high productivity level for all age groups, with a gradual productivity ladder (number of children/places per full-time equivalent), according to the pedagogical needs of the different age groups and of subgroups with specific personal and social problems/needs.

This implies a thorough *organisational streamlining* of the different forms of external daytime education/care. In the first place, a large increase in the number of daytime education centres for the youngest children is necessary in (almost) all countries, albeit with differences according to the actual situation. So, during the next few decades, substantial societal investments in new infrastructure and organisational settings are necessary. It is most desirable to locate the education centres for the youngest children close to existing basic schools. Therefore, basic schools should receive sufficient resources to establish high-quality education centres for the youngest children that can then be integrated educationally, organisationally, financially and spatially. In these broad education settings, it is useful, of course, to develop new combinations of professional labour and supportive voluntary labour of parents, grandparents, older people and so on, in order to maximise the efficiency of the organisation.

6.3.3 Additional childcare facilities for all children and parents

In addition to the basic package of daytime education/care sufficient possibilities for *additional external childcare* must be available for all children/parents: before and after daytime education/care, during (long) holiday periods, weekends and periods of illness.

These facilities must be maximally streamlined with basic provisions for daytime education/care, enabling parents to harmonise their professional and family work as efficiently as possible. Consequently, it is essential to restrict the daily and weekly number of hours of additional external care to a level that is pedagogically acceptable. To avoid excess consumption, parents should pay a certain contribution for this additional childcare. This contribution should be income-related to support lower-income families. Additional (financial) support is also desirable for parents who need much additional care, due to inevitable special working hours. This could largely come from the side of the employers, who then support the system in a direct and efficient way. The need for additional care can, to a certain degree, also be limited by better streamlining the school hours of children and the working hours of parents. The complete combination modeloffers many possibilities for alternative working hours for many parents.

With a general supply of (almost) costless daytime education for the youngest children, many grandparents have much time for their own social activities and for additional childcare, usually before and after school hours, during weekends and in periods of illness. Additional care is also possible by means of cooperation with neighbours and friends. Also local clubs (sport, arts, etc) can offer some additional activities after school hours, depending on the availability of infrastructure, instructors and transport facilities. Furthermore, companies can contribute by means of specific facilities for their personnel, for example evening care, night care and weekend care for children of parents with a special working time schedule. The investments of the companies for these specific provisions will then be more effective and efficient. Finally, to answer the remaining needs of families, the government can organise complementary provision in every community.

6.3.4 Secondary and higher education as a basic provision for young people

The system of secondary and higher education also has to be improved in order to contribute as much as possible to the realisation of the Complete Combination Model in a democratic society. *Secondary education* is an important part of the development of the human capital of all young people aged between 12 and 18. For a large group it is the final stage of formal education and therefore a major basis for their professional career and for their family and social life. In a strong democracy, here expressed by the Complete Combination Model, all young people should be able to participate in secondary education in order to develop their human capital in an optimal way, as the basis for their personal development. Therefore, it is logical that secondary education is also seen as a basic collective provision for all children of that age group. Consequently, the financial contribution of families for secondary education should be (almost) the same as for basic education, in proportion to the total cost price. For a number of young people with less educational capabilities and a very low motivation to attend school, one should provide a combination of part-time work and part-time job-related training, for example from the age of 15 or 16. The basic aim is to bring them into a more satisfying societal setting with direct professional benefit and permanent on-the-job-training.

Higher education is a central part of the development of the human capital of many young people older than 18. So higher education is also a highly productive activity to realise the future human capital of a large group in society. In a strong democracy, all young people with sufficient capacities should be able to participate in higher education, in order to develop their human capital in an optimal way. Therefore, it is logical that the financial cost for families is similar to that of secondary and basic education. It is essential to minimise social selection due to the financial restrictions of the families involved. Supposing that higher education leads on average to a higher professional position and income, the students will, after all, pay back the societal investment during their professional life, by means of correct progressive fiscal contributions on their professional income, as the new fiscal tariff system proposes. So, a democratic society creates a strong intra- and intergenerational equality and solidarity, with sufficient rights and duties for young people. To realise this policy perspective, of course, most countries will have to systematically increase the collective means for higher education during the next decade. However, they can be sure that these investments will have a higher return later, for the young people themselves, for their families, for the professional organisations and for society as a whole.

6.4 Adequate provisions for adults

This section deals with a number of societal provisions that are also important for the realisation of a democratic division of labour between men and women. We formulate some general policy perspectives in the context of the complete combination model, in line with the other major policy perspectives.

6.4.1 Lifelong education as a basic provision for adults

A strongly democratic society offers all children and young people a strong basic package of external daytime education to develop their basic human capital for their current and future life, according to their interests, capabilities and efforts. The basic education is an important driving and orienting factor for the future division of labour of most young people, but the result is never perfect or final. Once they have chosen a certain division of professional, family and social labour in the first stage of their adult life, they are confronted with the (gradual) restrictions and shortcomings of their competences. These restrictions are related to the needs and expectations within the context of professional, family and social life. So every adult permanently needs some additional education or learning to cope with the increasing needs in professional, family and social life. Many of these additional competences can be acquired during professional, family and social life, with or without some informal guiding by a more experienced person. However, more specialised competences require more formal, organised education or teaching by qualified people, often in the context of a specialised organisation.

Therefore, a strongly democratic society offers all adult people sufficient possibilities and incentives for additional lifelong education in order to cope with changing education needs in their professional, family and social life. 'Sufficient' refers to the quality and quantity of the additional external education and must be seen in relative terms, depending on the actual level of the human capital of a person and the future needs for a decent division of labour. In this perspective, (young) adults with a really inadequate education for one or more of the basic activities must be strongly supported and guided during (the first stages of) their adult life, in order to develop a fairly decent division of labour in the future.

This additional education can be financed by a shared contribution from the government and the organisational setting where the additional education is (mostly) needed, that is, families, professional organisations and/or social organisations. A basic condition is that all adult men and women are financially able to follow sufficient external education during their adult life.

6.4.2 Mobility infrastructure

Mobility is a central element of the daily combination of family and professional life in all countries. Mobility has to offer physical connection between the location of the basic activities. Therefore, the mobility problems of many men and women have to be dealt with systematically. The central policy challenge here is to improve the quality of the mobility and to decrease the daily cost of mobility in terms of money and time, for families, organisations and the government. This is related to the availability and effectiveness of the different public and private travelling means and to the mechanism that regulates quantity, quality and the relative prices for the different actors. In all western countries, a number of effective adjustments are necessary in order to improve the mobility system in the future. Since we cannot go into detail here, only a few major perspectives are formulated (Van Dongen and Danau, 2003; De Ceuster, 2004; De Borger, 2005).

One of the main challenges is to control and reduce private travelling by car in the regions with a relatively high population density and consequently a higher risk of frequent and long-lasting congestion. A sufficiently large number of people using their car every day must be encouraged to use other transport means that also offer sufficient comfort. One way of dealing with this is increasing the variable cost of car use, in particular the variable cost connected with traffic congestion and pollution. Consequently, the direct private cost of people that have or want to use a car will increase significantly, but this will be largely compensated by the decreasing cost of congestion.

At the same time, the supply of decent, fast and frequent collective transport means must be strongly increased (train, tram, bus), especially during rush hours, between and within urban centres. Enough attention should be paid to improving the connection (in space and time) between the different means of public transport. All these forms of public transport must of course be affordable for all income groups, in order to increase actual use.

Furthermore, systems of carpooling, collective school and business transport, and so on, can be encouraged. The use of bicycles and motorbikes, combined with public transport, should also be encouraged, especially for those who have to cover only a short distance, both by means of a better and safer infrastructure and by efficient financial incentives. To encourage working people to shift from the car to the bicycle or motorbike, they could be offered a basic monthly commuting premium, increased with a variable premium per km. The basic bonus can and should be sufficiently high because these people have to cope with a number of hindrances and because they significantly reduce the high total marginal cost of congestion during rush hour.

More attention should also be paid to the possibility of working at home, especially to save time for certain daily family tasks (for example, taking the children to school, preparing meals, shopping, etc) and to diminish the traffic burden for other people. Again, financial incentives can be used to realise the most adequate working place arrangement for employees. At the same time, it is useful to support families that are both able and willing to move closer to the workplace, for example families with one adult and families where both partners have a job in the same place or region. Yet one should pay attention to the possible loss of social capital by moving closer to the workplace, for example the availability of parents and other family members for family support, childcare, etc.

In general, it would be useful to fundamentally reform the financing of commuter traffic. Because in most countries the cost of commuter traffic is divided between employees, employers and the government, without much coordination and coherence, the three actors mostly try to shift part of the cost to each other. This system does not stimulate a search for the most efficient combination of travelling means. It would therefore be more efficient to treat commuter traffic as an integral part of the production process and the total production cost of an organisation. The advantage is that organisations are encouraged to find the most efficient combination for all employees and for the organisation as a whole. Moreover, they would employ more employees (with the necessary qualifications) who live nearer to the workplace, so reducing the overall daily need for and cost of commuter traffic. In general, the total financial and time cost of commuter traffic for companies, families and the government would diminish, creating a win–win situation for all actors involved.

6.4.3 Household services

The process to the complete combination model implies the further development of household services, that is, 'market services for households', to support combination families in their daily combination of professional, family and social activities. The most important services are: house cleaning, laundry and ironing, repairing clothes, house maintenance, garden, furniture and appliances, shopping and preparing meals. The goal of the complete combination model is certainly not to maximise the use of marketed services in families, minimising internal household production. After all, the model aims at a good balance between professional and family labour for all men and women. The basic aim is that all families are able to buy a number of services that are most useful and supportive for their specific division of labour and also most compatible with the preferences and competences of the family members. In that way, the complete combination model enables a great diversity in the concrete combination of internal production and the use of external services.

Most of these household services are very human intensive, with a high share of lower-qualified labour. In the new fiscal tariff system proposed earlier, these activities enjoy a relatively low tax rate in order to stimulate professional organisations to offer a broad variety of human services. It is also important to encourage families and companies to have (again) a higher appreciation for these human–intensive societal tasks, which are often lower qualified. This appreciation must become visible in a higher willingness to pay a sufficiently high price (per hour) for these services. In that way a lot of (new) normal employment opportunities can be created for lower–qualified people.

6.4.4 Opening hours of shops, services and public offices

According to the complete combination model, (almost) all adult people are both producers and consumers/users of market goods/services. On the one hand, they want to have good working hours (to produce market goods/services) that can be combined with their personal and family life. On the other hand, they also want to have sufficient time for buying and using market goods/services (for their family work, personal care, leisure activities, etc) that can be combined with their professional life. No society will ever realise a complete match of both sides of the exchange process during the same 'normal working week and workday', or, in other words, a complete collective rhythm of time. Neither is the other extreme possible or desirable, that is, a society without any collective rhythm of time. Since many people actually have a normal working time, many activities have to be done largely beyond that normal working time: recreation activities (doing sports, going to the cinema or theatre, going to a pub), household activities (shopping) and personal care activities (going to the hairdresser or the doctor). People who are professionally active outside the normal working time can do these activities during normal working hours to a large extent.

So every society has a certain level of 'collective rhythm of time' between the two extremes. In this study, we presented a very general comparative picture of temporal flexibility, showing the gradual differences between the countries, but not following the basic classification of the welfare states. In general, overall temporal flexibility did not increase that much in most of the European countries. In other words, the majority of (full-time) employees still have a fairly normal job during normal working time. More specialised internationally comparative analysis in this field is certainly desirable.

Even with the restricted empirical data available, it is necessary to deal with the normative policy question: which level of 'collective rhythm of time' is desirable in a strongly democratic division of labour, as proposed by the complete combination model? Basically, the model aims at a gradual division of professional labour between men and women, around the new 'normal' 35-hour week, emphasising the need for a good balance between professional and family responsibilities. Moreover, it implies that most men and women have more or less 'normal' working hours during the traditional working week, yet with sufficient flexibility towards the needs of the organisation they work for. This implies that most men and women and most families have sufficient time during the normal working week for their weekly shopping and administrative duties during the normal opening hours of shops, commercial services and public offices. Many people can even spend some time on family work, personal care and leisure activities during the normal working time. At the same time, the model allows for a certain share of men and women working more than 35 hours/week and/or beyond the normal working hours, as an answer to a number of daily needs of both families and organisations. In that perspective, the complete combination model also demands sufficient flexibility from employees to realise flexible opening hours outside normal working times. But this flexibility must be clearly demarcated and restricted, to enable these employees to plan or manage sufficiently this flexibility in the job with respect to the needs of their personal and family life.

6.4.5 Adequate provisions for older people

This study mainly deals with the daily life of adults in their professionally active life, that is, the life stage after the normal education course until the moment of (pre-)pension. Yet, as it is for children, there is a major connection and interaction with the daily life of older people. Figure 2.6 in Chapter 2 clearly shows that all older people are faced with the same basic challenge, that is, to realise a good combination of basic activities that offers an adequate combination of personal, social, material and financial means. Their daily life is also located within the complex network of families and all other sorts of societal organisations. Most older people are still living within their own family network, as a parent, grandparent and/or great-grandparent. In this network, they are both caregiver and caretaker. In the previous section, we emphasised the potential role of caregiver to (the family of) their grandchildren, by offering childcare. In addition, they can support the family of their adult children in many other ways: household tasks, financial support, personal contact and advice, etc. Finally, they can also provide services to other groups in society by means of social or voluntary work.

When they become older, the role of caregiver decreases while that of caretaker increases, resulting in a higher dependency on younger generations, especially the professional population. As for children, this changing dependency is important for the daily life of the older people themselves, but also for the daily life of the professional population and young generation. Of course, it is not the intention here to describe the changing daily life of older people, yet it is useful to formulate briefly the major policy perspective of the complete combination model in this field.

As for children and adults, the model emphasises the balanced combination of professional care, family care and social or voluntary care, in order to realise a strong and flexible care system. Furthermore, an adequate gradual combination has to be found between different forms of care inside and outside the home. Finally, the model aims at the right level of productivity in all these forms of care, expressed by the proportion between the number of full-time equivalent caretakers and the number of full-time equivalent caregivers. For example, this means that expensive professional one-to-one care (both at home or in an organisation) should be reduced to its necessary level. This care should be replaced as much as possible by care in (small) groups, preserving or even increasing the quality of the care given.

Every older person should be able to receive the necessary professional care of sufficiently high quality, at an acceptable price, both for the person involved and for society. At the same time, everyone deserves sufficient direct family care, as long as family members are available. However, these family caregivers must be able to combine this care with their other basic activities in order not to become too dependent themselves. So care given to an older family member should not replace the professional work of the caregiver too much. The third part consists of voluntary care coming from people and organisations outside the person's own family. Again, voluntary caregivers that still have a job must be able to combine this care with their other basic activities, to sufficiently preserve their independence. So their voluntary care is always restricted in quantity. Therefore, an important part of voluntary care can and should come from other older people in their (immediate) surroundings. This mutual care between older people has enormous potential, because of the great availability of time and all sorts of competences and experiences. As well as the partial professional, family and voluntary care offered by younger generations, the mutual older social care can be efficiently organised in many combinations, to answer the different needs as well as possible. We could call it forms of 'integrated societal care', integrating different forms of labour in efficient organisational settings.

Therefore, the complete combination model stresses both the right and duty of older people to combine their role as caregiver and as caretaker, in a gradual way, starting from their actual dependency level and need for care and from their capacity to offer care. Again, the clock-curve can serve as a useful guideline for the daily division of family and social work, as it did for the division of professional and family labour of adults and for the division of education and family work for children. To realise this combined right and duty, society must create an adequate physical and organisational infrastructure in all fields of societal life. In all western societies, this has been realised to a certain extent during past decades. Yet there is still a fairly dual approach in most countries, emphasising traditional home care on the one hand and traditional residential care on the other. Between these two approaches, different professional and voluntary organisations offer several services to individual people. However, the great potential of the different forms of integrated care, with a large share of mutual social care between older people, has not been developed that much. The major new policy perspective of the complete combination model for the daily life of older people is therefore the creation of broad, integrating 'activity centres' or 'service centres' in all local communities. These activity centres must offer a sufficiently broad package of activities/services in an adequate infrastructure and an efficient organisational setting, combining professional, family and voluntary labour of all generations in the most efficient way. Evidently, these centres can/should work together with other societal organisations, such as education centres, sporting clubs, arts clubs, and so on.

6.5   Adequate combination policies in organisations

6.5.1   *Combination management in organisations*

All professional organisations increasingly face the challenge of realising a more flexible work organisation in favour of their employees. Until now, only a small number of companies have already embedded this perspective into their daily practice, and then probably only partially or as a secondary perspective in their management strategy (Henderickx and De Prins, 1998; den Dulk et al, 1999; Van Hootegem, 2000 ; den Dulk, 2001; Van Dongen et al, 2001; Evans, 2001; Poelmans, 2001; Poelmans and Chinchilla, 2001, 2003; Van Dongen, 2004b, 2005a; Galinsky, 2005; Peper et al, 2005; Benko and Weisberg, 2007). In fact, companies do not sufficiently use the issue of 'family life' as an effective positive lever to improve their internal organisation and market position. Many working men and women want more flexibility and autonomy, according to the needs of their families. Therefore, the labour organisation strategies pursued by employers and employees should be brought together more closely, for example by extending modern business theories with the dimensions of gender equality, the combination and life course perspective and the family context of employees.

The implementation of the general policy framework of the complete combination model implies the translation of policy goals into specific instruments for families and firms to improve their actual situation. All companies must be encouraged in a systematic way to adjust their internal organisation and management to the needs of gender equality and the family life of their employees. This implies that the government and social partners should strongly promote the realisation of an effective 'combination management' in all professional organisations. This must be combined with consequent investment in the professional position of all men and women, at all levels of the company, in order to maximise the use of their human capital. In this perspective, the general approach of the 'balanced scorecard' (www.balancedscorecard.org) should fully integrate these new perspectives in order to introduce and apply them systematically in business life. Since the organisational conditions and needs of companies are very diverse, a gender- and family-friendly work organisation demands a constructive win-win approach, integrating mutual interests from the very start and aiming at the most adequate combinations of the needs/goals of the organisation and of employees.

An efficient combination policy on the level of the company implies that the right mix of combination facilities is being developed, starting from the needs, preferences and possibilities of employees and organisations, both in the long and short run. The basic goal is to search for win-win situations as the basis for effective action plans. The central question, then, is which facilities can and should be offered and to what extent? Which facilities are essential, which are supportive or complementary? Within the complete combination model, the first goal is to offer employees the most suitable working time arrangements within their career perspective, which are, at the same time, feasible and productive for the short- and long-term project of the organisation. In the first place, organisations should offer a sufficiently large variety in jobs with respect to the number of working hours and days in order to maximally meet the demands or needs of the employees. When the preferred working time arrangements of employees are (largely) realised, they need fewer additional facilities and will be more willing to meet the organisational conditions. Next, the most supportive and complementary leave arrangements should be sought to meet family needs as far as possible. It is essential, however, that organisations minimise the administrative and organisational cost for the correct implementation of specific leave arrangements. Additionally, some facilities regarding the workplace should be offered, for example working at home or nearer to home, with the right material and financial support, the introduction of team work, more variation and rotation in daily tasks, and so on, to improve the quality of the job. Finally, organisations could provide a selective number of useful services, starting from the specific needs of the different subgroups: facilities for commuting, specific and complementary childcare provision, personal services (sports, cultural activities, internet connection), household services and financial facilities.

As before, we emphasise the large similarity between the complete combination model for organisations and the mass career customisation (MCC) model or framework that is presented by Benko and Weisberg (2007). Both authors have a major managerial function in a large company in the US and have developed the approach from their daily experience and the comparative study of the work organisation in different sorts of companies. They start from the unsatisfying results of the 'work-life policies' promoted during the past few decades, also referred to as 'flexible work arrangements' (FWA). These FWA largely coincide with the business policies of (the different variants of) the moderate combination model in different countries. According to the authors, the FWA have a number of limitations: they mostly offer only short-term solutions for individuals or small groups, they are mostly limited to lower-level employees, they do not anticipate longer-term changes in family and personal commitments and they do not include longer-term planning of the career change/progression of employees (within the organisation). They present the MCC framework as a new, integrated and multi-dimensional approach that takes into account all major aspects of the professional career, in relation to the personal life course and family stages. With the MCC, employees and employers can discover the different options to design and achieve the optimal career paths that are compatible with personal and family life and that also support the further development or growth of the organisation, both in the short and longer run. Starting from this basic approach, they present a practical management instrument to encourage and support companies in the transformation process to the new MCC model. This brings us to the next issue, dealing with specialised audit or management instruments to realise an adequate combination policy in organisations.

6.5.2 Promoting the application of specialised Family and Business Audits in organisations

Each organisation can and should develop a more adequate 'combination' or 'family and business' management in order to compose integrated 'package deals' for every group of employees, maximally meeting both the needs of employees and their family and the organisational conditions of the company. To realise such a management process, organisations can make use of specialised professional counselling, by means of the implementation of specialised audit instruments that have been developed during the past few years. We can refer to the German 'Audit Beruf und Familie' (Leist, 2005), the European Audit Work and Family (Leist, 2005), the instrument 'When work works' (Galinsky, 2005) and the mass career customisation approach developed and applied in the US (Benko and Weisberg, 2007), and the Flemish 'Family and Business Audit' (FBA) (Danau and Van Dongen, 2002; Van Dongen et al, 2002; Van Dongen, 2005b). Governments should offer companies effective incentives to apply such specialised instruments in order to implement an effective combination management. In this section we briefly present the Flemish FBA.

In the period 2000-2005, the Flemish government financed the development of the FBA (Danau and Van Dongen, 2002; Van Dongen and Danau, 2002). The basic goal of the FBA instrument is to start a process of change and improvement in an organisation with respect to the daily combination of professional and family life. The FBA covers a number of steps in the normal management process of the organisation. The process and results of the FBA have to be integrated in the existing overall process, leading to a more effective and efficient management.

A *first central characteristic* of the FBA instrument is the horizontal or integrated approach to the issue. Several relevant stakeholders are involved in the FBA process in an active way: employees, top and line management and the unions. Next, the FBA deals with a wide range of aspects of the labour organisation, which we can classify in four major categories: (1) working time (schedules), (2) leaving arrangements, (3) work organisation, quality of work and organisational culture, and (4) material and financial provisions or facilities. Combining the diversity of actors and aspects, the FBA leads to a broad, integrated picture of the current situation and of future choices and perspectives. This picture shows the differences and similarities between the actors involved and becomes the basis of the search for concrete win-win situations, both for the organisation and employees.

The *second characteristic*, complementary to the first one, is that the FBA is a sufficiently general instrument that can be applied in all kinds of organisations, but at the same time it can offer sufficient differentiation to deal with the specific situation and perspectives of every organisation. In that way, the FBA offers a basis for comparison or benchmarking between individual organisations or categories of organisations, but it also enables made-to-measure results for every organisation.

This leads to the *third characteristic*, that the instrument can and must be executed efficiently, in terms of human time and effort, material means and financial costs. Therefore, the FBA aims at a productive combination of a highly quantitative approach and a target-oriented qualitative approach. The former mainly implies an efficient way to gather, analyse and report the necessary data, respecting the input and the position of actors involved, and minimising the total cost in time and money for the organisation. The latter must lead to a constructive processing and translation of the results towards a management process.

These three conditions imply that the adequate application of the FBA is only possible with guidance by a qualified external audit office, to ensure sufficient neutrality and independence toward the actors involved and to realise constructive cooperation leading to effective results. All stakeholders must be able to formulate their position, experiences, opinions and choices in a context of mutual trust and confidence.

The FBA consists of three major parts, each containing a number of steps. The *preparation* includes all practical steps that are necessary for the optimal implementation of the FBA: contact and information, presentation, planning, cost–benefit analysis and agreement. The *diagnosis* makes a picture of the daily situation within organisations and families with respect to the reconciliation of professional and family life. The goal of this approach is to minimise the cost in time for the people involved and to maximise the response and quality of the data for all these actors. The main part covers the different aspects or arrangements of the daily work organisation within the company: working time arrangements, leave arrangements, workplace and work organisation, personal and family-oriented provisions, aspects of the quality of the job and aspects of the organisational culture. For each of these aspects, information is gathered about the actual use by the employees and about their preferences for the (near) future. The top and line management are asked to give their view with respect to the desirability and feasibility of different facilities or arrangements. In this way, the differences and similarities are identified that can serve as the basis for further reflection and discussion, and for defining the priorities of future action. The *management process* starts from the results of the diagnosis and aims at developing recommendations regarding the different arrangements. Internal discussion leads to a specific management proposal for the organisation. Starting from this proposal, the organisation can develop and implement an action plan.

By the end of 2002, a prototype of the FBA was available, resulting from a number of case studies in all sorts of organisations. To implement the FBA on a larger scale in Flemish companies, a follow-up project was started in 2003 in order to optimise the instrument. In October 2006, two commercial consultancy organisations received a licence to apply the FBA in Flemish organisations during the next few years. By the end of 2008, this strategy will be evaluated and adjusted. Hopefully, a wide implementation of the FBA is possible in the future.

6.5.3 Life course planning for employees and their families

The application of such management instruments can and should be combined with additional life course planning for individual employees and their family, starting from their personal and family background. It is desirable that all employees/families can enjoy sufficient professional guidance from the start of their professional career, in order to develop a sufficiently harmonious combination of their professional and family life during the different stages of their life course. Such guidance should take place on a regular basis (for example, every two to four years) and additionally, if necessary, at critical moments during the life course, related to special events such as a new steady relationship, the birth of a child, unemployment, a promotion, a severe disability, chronic illness, etc. This guidance can be offered by different actors involved: the human resources manager in the organisation, trade unions, public (un)employment offices and independent qualified counsellors. They can make use of specific counselling instruments to support families with the management of their daily division of time. We refer to Wallin (2006) for an example of such an instrument.

6.6 Adequate data systems and research concerning the daily life of men and women

We end this overview of policy perspectives with a basic scientific condition for the development of an adequate policy programme to realise the complete combination model in the long run. This condition refers to the availability in sufficient countries of integrated data systems and research about the daily life of men and women, within the context of their family and professional life and within the overall societal context. Adequate data is necessary to construct decent quantitative measures or indicators as the basis for useful empirical models. These models are necessary to picture the actual development of the daily division of professional and family life in the different (types of) countries, with sufficient attention to both the similarities and differences.

In general, there is a need for an international integrated data system with respect to the division of activities and means of men and women, both on the macro and micro level, that is, within families, firms and other organisations. Such a dataset must give basic information about the life course perspective: past professional career and family life (retrospective data), the actual combination of professional and family life (cross-sectional data, including time use data) and future plans or intentions (prospective data). At this moment, such an integrated survey does not exist in Europe. Existing international surveys such as the Labour Force Survey (LFS), the Luxembourg Income Study (LIS), the European Survey on Income and Living Conditions (SILC), the Gender and Generation Survey (GGS) and the European Working Conditions Surveys (EWCS, Eurofound) do not sufficiently answer this need.

A major policy challenge therefore is to produce an integrated international survey that can meet these basic objectives. Since the division of professional, family and social labour, the division of income, flexible work organisation, education and care for children, and so on are major policy issues at the national, European and global level, from a broad normative perspective (equality, diversity, solidarity and efficiency), it would be useful to create a maximally unified survey in as many countries as possible. In this context, we emphasise the need for integrated data about the daily time use of children aged 0-18 years in order to have a more differentiated empirical picture of their daily life, in connection with that of their parents.

The data restriction, however, should not be an excuse to postpone the policy discussion and the basic policy choices concerning the most adequate future policy model for the division of professional and family labour. In a strong democracy, all major policy actors have to be explicit and clear about that basic choice. This is the first step in the long realisation process towards a really democratic division of labour on all levels of society.

SEVEN

Major results

7.1   Background and goal of the study

This study is the result of a long, interactive research process conducted over the last 20 years. During this time, the 'combination of professional and family work' has become a major policy issue in modern democratic welfare states. It is a central motor of the daily life of men and women within their families and within other organisations. An efficient 'combination policy', therefore, needs a consistent and effective policy programme for all relevant societal fields.

Chapter 1 explored the background and the *central goal* of this study, that is, to show that the Combination Model is a useful instrument for all democratic countries, first, for the study of the daily division of labour between men and women, and second, for the development of an integrated policy programme. The Combination Model is a broad scientific instrument based on the permanent interaction between the conceptual, empirical and normative dimension/approach. It was not developed in isolation in Flanders/Belgium, but alongside *similar integrating models* that were put forward in other countries, starting from the same basic challenge but situated against the specific societal and scientific background. We first examined the transitional labour markets model that was launched by Günther Schmid, mainly from traditional labour market research in economics and sociology (Schmid, 1997, 1998, 2002a, 2002b; Schmid and Gazier, 2002; Schmid and Schomann, 2004). Next, we looked at the flexicurity model that was introduced by research groups in the Netherlands and Denmark (Wilthagen and Tros, 2004; Wilthagen et al, 2004; Madsen, 2006; van den Heuvel et al, 2006). Within the context of the US we focused on the dual earner/dual carer model that was launched by Crompton (1999) and that was further explained and applied by Gornick and Meyers (2003, 2004a, 2004b). This model was partially inspired by Fraser's future models (1994, 2006): starting from a critical evaluation of the universal breadwinner model and the caregiver parity model, she introduces the universal caregiver model as a new promising future policy model that combines the strong elements of the two former models. We also mentioned the mass career customisation model presented by Benko and Weisberg (2007), from the perspective of organisations.

During the past years, the Combination Model has consequently been examined further and applied to a broader societal context. This study shows that the model offers a solid basis for an integrated policy for the future division of professional and family labour in all democratic countries, since they are facing the same basic challenges regarding this major societal issue.

7.2 Conceptual approach of the Combination Model

Chapter 2 examined the *integrated approach* of the combination model regarding the daily life of men and women in a modern, complex society, focusing on the division of professional and family work as a major part of it. The conceptual approach is the result of a long scientific process combining and integrating different important concepts of social sciences. As a consequence, it is never definite; at most it is temporarily rounded off. The approach is a concrete expression of a fundamental change in the scientific approach to human behaviour, society and nature during the past few decades, namely from the basically dual models of humans and society to integrating complexity models. Figure 1.1 tries to visualise this major change in the basic model of society. Many economic and sociological approaches to human activities are still largely influenced by this dual view, as illustrated in Figures 2.1-2.3. To understand the complexity of daily life, new models must be developed that are sufficiently clear for all societal actors.

In an integrated approach to daily life, all actors (individuals, families, companies, associations, public institutions, and so on) and all their activities are described within the same theoretical framework that includes all basic components of the societal system. The Combination Model is a practical term or label for an integrated conceptual approach to the division of time between men and women, as part of a more general approach to the dynamic and complex societal system. In this context the new approach to the market system is also essential, conceiving the public sector as a full market actor.

Figures 2.4-2.8 are, as such, fairly simple, but they clearly express the meaning of the new basic model for individuals, families and all sorts of organisations within the national and international market system. The basic starting point is that all human activities are productive labour processes that function according to the same mechanism of demand and supply and can offer a societal surplus value. This is a fundamental difference with the traditional dual approach in social sciences, with a great impact on our thinking about the daily functioning of society. The presentation of the life course as a permanently changing combination of basic activities illustrates the main renewal of the approach to daily life, without getting lost in an overly detailed and complicated classification and presentation. The integration of the combination perspective (for each age group) and the life course perspective in the development of the complex societal division of labour is a fundamental step forward in understanding and being able to clearly present the complex division of individuals' time in a complex society during their complex life course. So, the integrated approach offers a common conceptual basis for better mutual understanding and for long-lasting exchange and cooperation between the different scientific disciplines. This leads to innovation and improvement within the existing disciplines and encourages their streamlining and integration in the future.

7.3 Normative approach of the Combination Model

Chapter 3 starts from the major *normative question* that all (European) countries are facing: which is the most desirable division of labour between men and women for the future? Fraser (1994, 2006), Crompton (1999), Gornick and Meyers (2003) and many other researchers start from the same question, largely motivated by the fact that the actual unequal division of labour in the US and Europe is unacceptable. The search for new conceptual and empirical models is therefore always strongly influenced by the normative view of society as a whole and of the specific research issues. Together with these researchers we emphasise the need for a new normative future vision for the division of labour, which is compatible with the new normative approach and can serve as a strong guideline for future scientific research and future policy. A coherent normative approach is an important basis for the elaboration of coherent future models and for achieving a broad societal and political consensus about the future model in the long run.

We present a *broad normative approach* with a number of possible variants, broadening the concept of 'democracy' to a general normative concept for (the functioning of) society and all its components and actors. Democracy expresses a certain combination of the basic values that are or have to be realised to a certain extent in all segments of society: freedom, equality, solidarity and efficiency. So, different forms of democracy can be shown on a continuum, from a very weak democracy at one end to a very strong democracy at the other. Following this line of reasoning, one can also speak of a democratic division of labour in families and organisations, a democratic market system and a democratic fiscal system. Next, the concept of 'strong democracy' is proposed as an adequate normative basis for future society, emphasising the need for the joint and well-balanced realisation of the four basic values in all segments of society. The advantage is that the basic values are always combined and continually stimulate and restrict one another. A sufficiently democratic future model can never be dominated by one of these basic values.

A *strongly democratic division of labour* offers all men and women enough freedom to develop a specific division of labour but also realises sufficient equality and solidarity between men and women, families and organisations. That equality and solidarity can never be maximal or absolute but always has the form of a gradual clock-curve (see Figure 5.2). Finally, the division of labour has to be sufficiently efficient, with an adequate combination of the basic activities that can render a surplus value. Democracy without efficiency is a contradiction in itself and therefore unfeasible since the other values are not realised in a sufficient way. This is an important principle for future society as a whole and for the market system(s) in particular.

The new concept of *democratic market system* was then presented as a strong alternative for the traditional concept of 'free market system' that is, in fact, useless because of the unverifiable and arbitrary interpretation of the concept of 'freedom'. With the multidimensional concept of democracy, a verifiable and useful distinction between different actual and desirable market systems is possible. A strongly democratic market system aims at a full balance between the basic values: all actors in the market system must continually realise the basic values together, at the input and output side of all activities.

We emphasise that this normative approach is neither definite nor absolute. It is a practical approach/instrument for the development of the future models of the division of labour in society. We therefore invite all interested people to contribute to the further elaboration of an adequate normative approach for a strongly democratic society, on either a local, national or international level.

7.4 Actual development of the division of labour

Chapter 4 deals with the actual development of the division of professional and family work in European countries and some other OECD countries. As mentioned before, we show the main evolution of the division of labour, focusing on both the differences and similarities, against the background of the famous classification of welfare states of Esping-Andersen (1999) and the newer version from Korpi (2000). We largely leave out of consideration some differentiating factors, to better visualise the general evolution in the different countries. The strong similarities in the division of labour between the European countries are an important basis for future policy at the European and national levels.

First, we presented the wider *historical background of the division of labour* to have a better understanding of development since the middle of the 20th century and to think about the most desirable development for the next few decades. The brief sketch of the development from the 'old combination model' during the 19th century to the 'new breadwinner model' in the 20th century shows that the traditional picture of the division of labour between men and women has to be abandoned. Still many people (including scientists and policy makers) think that, historically, the male breadwinner family has always been the dominant family type. We have shown another historical picture, however. Using a broader historical perspective, we argue that the breadwinner family has been more the exception than the rule. Most couple families have always needed more than one job and subsequently more than one income to survive. The 'strong male breadwinner family' originally comes from the highest societal circles that could afford for women (usually mothers) not to contribute to daily professional work. Since 1850, the male breadwinner ideal became increasingly dominant in the societal view on the division of labour. During many decades, more women were being expelled from the labour market, not least by the growing societal and political promotion and support of the new breadwinner ideal. Only in the last stage of that long process did the new breadwinner ideal also become attractive to the lowest social classes. The realisation of the breadwinner model implied the expulsion of many mothers from the labour market and therefore went hand in hand with a high societal cost, mainly because of the destruction and inefficient use of their professional capital for many decades. This expulsion process occurred in all countries, albeit with significant differences in intensity and timing.

Against this historical background, the evolution from the male breadwinner model to a moderate combination model in the second half of the 20th century has another meaning. It is not an evolution towards a completely new and unknown situation as presented so often before, but to a large extent it is a recovery and reformation of the professional position of women within the context of the new democratic societies after the Second World War. The often negative interpretation of the different 'new' societal developments (increasing labour market participation, growing divorce rates and the dismantling of the classic family, a more equal division of labour within families, decreasing fertility, increasing use of external day education/care, and so on) should therefore be questioned. These 'new' developments are not that new and certainly not that negative, but in the light of the process towards a (more) democratic division of labour, they are quite positive developments that are still largely hindered or jeopardised by a number of remaining systems, mechanisms or arrangements that were dominant in the period of the male breadwinner model.

By means of a number of *simple empirical models* we illustrated the general positive development of the division of labour, from the strong male breadwinner model in the period 1950-70 to the moderate combination model in the period 1985-2005, with sufficient attention to the variants in the different (types of) countries and for the still fairly unequal division of professional and family work. These models were then briefly compared with the models of Crompton (1999) and Gornick and Meyers (2003). The indicators are largely complementary, each of them presenting a specific aspect of the division of labour, in order to create a sufficiently broad picture of actual development.

The general indicators for the evolution between 1960 and 2005 show that the gap between men and women concerning the division of labour has, to a large extent, already diminished. The *total activity rate* of (young) women is in many countries close to that of men, but in the southern countries this gap is still quite substantial. The differences in the *number of hours of professional labour* of men and women also decreased systematically. So, the 'optimistic' perspective becomes visible, which means that the improving professional position of women during the past decades went hand in hand with an increasing participation of men in family work. The evolution in the period 1980-2005 illustrates more the 'pessimistic' view, saying that the move to a more equal division of labour has slowed down since 1980 and that the gap is still too wide in 2005, when seen from the perspective of a democratic division of labour. Therefore, one can conclude that the 'moderate' combination policy or the 'multiple track policy' of most countries during the past decades has reached its limits. After all, the necessary (new) facilities for modern combination families have been counteracted to a large extent by the remaining facilities for male breadwinner families. Democratic countries that really want to close the gap between men and women during the next few decades must therefore follow a new policy orientation that aims at eliminating the existing contradictions and thresholds.

While all countries still show significant differences between men and women for professional and family labour separately, the *total labour of men and women* is on average divided largely equally. Moreover, the total labour of men and women remained quite constant during the period 1960-2000. This illustrates that the division of time is durable, notwithstanding the large and fast technological changes and the strongly increasing welfare in European countries. One of the main challenges or tasks of all governments, therefore, is to take action to further diminish the gap between men and women regarding professional and family work.

To give a better picture of the gradual equality or inequality of the division of labour, we presented a more differentiated historical model for the period 1950-2005 based on the *division of the number of hours*. The model contains three partial models for three successive periods: the strong male breadwinner model in the period 1950-70, the moderate male breadwinner model in the period 1970-90 and the moderate combination model in the period 1990-2005 (Van Dongen et al, 2001; Van Dongen and Danau, 2003). These models are largely compatible with the models of Crompton (1999) and Gornick and Meyers (2003). Since insufficient internationally comparative data for the period 1950-85 are available, we presented some complementary indicators for the period 1980-2004. The central idea here is that the general development of the division of labour of men and women is largely similar in all countries, unlike the gradual differences between these countries.

The first indicator illustrates the *general labour situation* of men and women with six categories: professionally active, looking for a job, staying at home, on a pension, study (pupils/students) and a group 'other' (mainly people with full disability. This indicator gives a good picture of the evolution of the relative position of these groups. For Belgium and the Netherlands we showed the evolution since 1947 (Figures 4.17 and 4.18), emphasising the similarities. The main difference concerns the share of people on a pension and staying at home, largely due to the difference in official retirement age. Total unemployment strongly decreased with the systematic decrease of the group of housewives, but it is still much larger than official unemployment. Sufficient attention must be paid to the cost of these forms of unemployment, for the unemployed people themselves, for their family and for society. The international comparison for the period 1998-2004 (Figures 4.19 and 4.20) emphasises the gradual differences in the share of the group of housewives, from a quite high share in the southern countries to a low share in the Nordic countries.

Next, we showed the *general division of the basic activities of men and women* in a number of countries in the period 1989-2000, by means of the average number of hours per week for the different age groups: professional labour, family labour, social labour, external education/care, personal care and leisure time (Figure 4.21). This indicator illustrates the largely similar structure of the division of time by means of the combination of basic activities for the different age groups. So the indicator also expresses the life course perspective of the Combination Model. A major result for all countries is that the differences between men and women are mainly visible for professional and family work. Again we emphasise the gradual differences between the countries as the expression of the various combination policies. Yet it is remarkable that in the Nordic countries the number of hours of professional and family work still show substantial differences between men and women. The number of working hours of young women is larger than that of older women, especially due to the generous leave arrangements for young parents. In the continental countries, the number of working hours of young women is greater, but it decreases significantly with older age.

Some indicators of the division of *professional labour* were then presented. The *professional activity rate* of men and women per age group (Figure 4.22) shows the fast change in the southern and continental countries, with a strong increase in the activity rate of women in all age groups. In the Nordic countries, the difference between men and women has been low for some time, but it seems to be very difficult to further close the gap. At the same time, the differences between the Nordic countries become visible. For this indicator, the Eastern European countries are closer to the Nordic countries, but there are significant differences between these countries. The difference in the activity rate of young people aged 15-19 years is striking. The high rate in the Netherlands, the UK and especially Denmark has a significant positive influence on the total activity rate in these countries.

A crucial indicator for the presentation of the future models is the *division of the number of hours of professional labour* during the past 20 years (Figures 4.24-4.26). The division of working hours of men hardly changed during this period. In some countries, the curve shifted somewhat to the left, expressing a decrease in the number of working hours for some of the men. One can see the small increase in the number of bigger part-time jobs (25-35 hours/week) for men. This indicator offers a different picture for women. Except for the Nordic countries, all countries show a significant decrease in the share of women without a job, especially in countries where that share was still high in 1985. As a consequence, the substantial difference between men and women has been partly eliminated in these countries. In Ireland, Belgium and in particular the Netherlands, the share of part-time jobs has strongly increased during the past two decades. In the Nordic countries, the share of women without a job remained more or less the same. The difference between men and women there is (much) smaller than in other countries but it has not further decreased during the past few years. Again, we note the slight differences between the Nordic countries. In contrast, the Eastern European countries show more similarity than the other countries, most probably as a result of the strict employment policy of the former communist regimes that aimed at a high level of equality. The share of women without a job is not significantly higher than in the southern or continental countries. The share of part-time jobs is still very small but it has increased somewhat during the past few years.

This indicator clearly shows the gradual equality or inequality (diversity) of the division of professional labour for men and women. The values of 'equality' and 'diversity' therefore explicitly express two sides of the same coin. The policy debate on an 'equal division of labour' is only meaningful in terms of the gradual distribution of the number of hours. The debate on diversity is part of the overall debate on societal equality, starting from the basic empirical and normative question: which gradual form of equality/diversity do we actually observe and which gradual form of equality/diversity does society want to develop in the future?

In addition, we presented the *average number of working hours of all men and women for the different age groups* (from 15-69 years) (see Figure 4.27). The figures are very similar to those of the activity rate, also illustrating the general similarities and the gradual differences between the countries. The curves for men are largely similar in most countries, with a relatively higher average number of hours in all age groups (and during the life course). The main differences concern the number of hours of young people, adults and older people. The picture for women again shows more diversity. The most substantial differences between men and women occur in the southern countries, followed by the continental countries. But again, the position of women improved the most in these countries. Young women have a higher number of working hours than the other age groups in these countries and this number decreases significantly with older age. This is, of course, related to the presence of (young) children in families and to the attitude of women leaving the labour market or greatly reducing their working hours. In the Nordic and Eastern European countries the number of working hours of older women is higher than that of the younger women.

In the Nordic countries the difference in the number of working hours between men and women is still quite considerable for all age groups, although the difference in the activity rate is small for all ages. However, the situation has hardly changed during the past few years, illustrating that in these countries the specific combination policy has reached its limits. The generous leave arrangement for raising children younger than one year at home has largely impeded these countries from filling the remaining gap between men and women.

The *average number of working hours* of men and women having a job for the different age groups expresses the actual length of the working day. The differences between men and women are quite small in most countries (Figure 4.29). In Ireland, the UK and the Netherlands, many women have a (small) part-time job, so the difference in the number of hours remains substantial. Belgium takes an in-between position for this indicator. Portugal is clearly a southern country for this aspect, while for the previous aspects it is more similar to the UK and the continental countries. Portuguese women combine a high activity rate with a high number of working hours. In the Eastern European countries, the number of working hours of men and women is somewhat higher than in the other countries.

For *family labour* two indicators are presented that are based on the international database MTUS. The first is the *division of the number of hours of family labour* (Figure 4.31). This indicator was also used for the presentation of the historical models (Figure 4.14) and the normative future models (Figure 5.2). The indicator clearly illustrates the gradual equality and inequality (diversity) of the division of family labour between men and women. The curves for men and women correspond with the moderate combination model (Figure 4.14). The curves for women show greater differences between the countries than those for men, which corresponds with the more substantial differences in the division of professional labour of women. The same can largely be said for the second indicator, the *average number of hours of family per age group* (Figure 4.33), namely the general similarity of the curves in the countries involved. The difference is again greater for women than for men. The two indicators for the division of family labour between men and women largely gives the inverse picture of the division of professional labour, resulting in a more or less equal division of total labour between men and women.

The same indicators are given for *leisure time* and *personal care*. The strongly equal structure of the division of time in the different countries becomes again visible (Figures

4.34-4.37), with relatively small differences. For these activities only small differences between men and women can be observed. From the perspective of gender equality, the division of these two activities poses no real policy problem. Nevertheless, one can question the very large difference or inequality within the two groups, mainly due to other factors: is it necessary, desirable and/or useful to reduce this substantial difference?

Finally, we presented some temporal characteristics of professional labour in the European countries: temporary work, shift work, night work, Sunday work and working at home. Here, the diversity between the different countries was again visible, but this diversity did not follow the existing classification of the welfare states, and moreover, it was quite different for all aspects. These characteristics therefore do not reflect the basic classification of welfare states with respect to the division of professional and family labour.

In general, all countries have the same basic division of professional labour, family labour, social labour, personal care and free time. They have largely gone through the same historical dominant basic models, from the old combination model in the period 1800-1900 to the male breadwinner model in the period 1900-80 and then to a variant of the moderate combination model in the period 1980-2005. All countries are facing the same basic normative challenge with respect to the division of professional and family work between men and women during the next few decades, taking into account gradual differences in the historical development and current situation. In all countries, a certain average number of hours (per week, per year) of all basic activities is necessary to realise an output that corresponds with the specific actual welfare level, given the available input elements and productivity level. The output of every basic activity is the input for the other basic activities. A striking observation is the almost constant number of hours of total labour (sum of professional and family labour) for both men and women in the period 1960-2000, unlike the technological progress during the past decades. On average almost the same numbers of hours are spent on the two basic activities together in order to realise the specific 'output level' of each period.

The largely similar basic structure of the division of labour in the European (and other western) countries is an important starting point for a (more) integrated combination policy in a democratic Europe, preserving, of course, sufficient space for diversity between and within the different (groups of) countries. So, the empirical policy models prove to be useful for all (European) countries.

The basic idea is that the male breadwinner model was dominant during a relatively short period in the long history. But the unequal division of labour had a more substantial negative impact on society than was thought until recently. During that period the professional capital of women was insufficiently developed and employed in business life. At the same time, the family-oriented human capital of men was almost completely neglected. One can conclude that, from a modern democratic view, integrating the basic values of freedom, equality, solidarity and efficiency, the male breadwinner model itself did not really contribute to the relatively higher welfare in western societies. On the contrary, we are convinced that a more equal division of labour between men and women would have resulted in a higher welfare level in (most of) the European countries, especially because of the more efficient input of the human capital of men and women in both professional and family life. But a strongly equal division of labour is not sufficient for realising a democratic society with a high welfare level. A real democratic society aims at sufficient equality that goes hand in hand with sufficient freedom, solidarity and efficiency of all segments of society.

The empirical story ends with an overview of the variants or stages of the contemporary moderate combination model in the different countries. The classification is a modified version of the classification of the welfare states of Esping-Andersen (1992, 1999) and Korpi (2000), based on the actual division of professional and family labour between men and women:

- southern weaker combination model (or moderate breadwinner model) in Italy, Spain, Greece, Cyprus and Malta;
- continental moderate combination model in Belgium, France, Germany, Austria, Luxembourg, (the Netherlands and Portugal);
- Anglo-Saxon moderate combination model in the English-speaking countries of the US, Canada and the UK (and Ireland);
- Nordic more advanced combination model in Sweden, Denmark, Norway, Finland and Iceland;
- Eastern more advanced combination model in Eastern European countries.

Since a classification is always relative, we emphasise the gradual differences between and within the five groups of countries, each representing an empirical model of the division of labour. A classification is useful to recognise the basic similar patterns and the differences between these countries. Most countries fit rather well in the classification, while some countries are located on the border between two or more groups, for example the Netherlands, Portugal and Ireland. The empirical models allow us to present the development of the division of labour in the (western) world in a comprehensible way, as an empirical basis for future policy models.

The overall empirical picture in this study is one of the many possible ways to show actual development. Therefore, we finished the chapter with a short presentation of a similar empirical model of the division of labour between men and women that was strongly inspired by the TLM Model (Anxo, 2004; Anxo and Boulin, 2004, 2005, 2006a, 2006b; Anxo and Ehrel, 2004; Anxo et al, 2004, 2006). They illustrate the patterns of labour market integration in the different types of European welfare states from a life course perspective. Starting from a family typology (based on cross-sectional data) that imitates the 'normal family stages' during the life course, three graphical indicators of labour market participation are shown for these family stages. Their life course models illustrate more clearly the differences between men and women regarding the presence and the age of children. In our models, these family-related aspects are less visible since they are spread over more age groups. Their life course models show an additional aspect of the division of professional labour and are complementary to our models. It would therefore be useful to create similar life course models for family labour and other basic activities, based on time use data.

7.5   Policy models for a democratic division of labour

The policy discussion about the future division of labour was the central topic in Chapters 5 and 6. The conceptual and normative approach and the empirical models led to the basic normative question: which is, in the long run, the most desirable and suitable division of professional and family labour between men and women for democratic countries and which policy perspectives are necessary to realise that future model? Since the new model becomes more dominant in western democratic countries and the influence of the old model further diminishes, policy makers have to choose a policy model that can serve as a guideline for the main policy perspectives in the long run and for concrete policy programmes in the short run. Without a clear policy model for the long run, however, the short-term policy is largely adrift and can follow any direction, without any guarantees that the most desirable direction will be actually chosen.

In Chapter 5 we tried to answer the normative question by means of three normative combination models for the future division of professional and family labour, reflecting the main normative views in society (variants of democracy) and the practical link with actual development: the strong combination model, the complete combination model and the moderate combination model.

A really *democratic division of labour* between men and women implies a maximal balance between the basic values of freedom, equality, solidarity and efficiency. All values have to be realised in a sufficient way simultaneously, both stimulating and restricting each other. Individuals and families must have sufficient freedom to choose the division of labour according to their own historic background, within the societal boundaries. Equality between men and women and within families is very important but it must be demanded in a gradual way, leaving open all possible options to a certain extent.

We defended the strong hypothesis that the complete combination model is the most desirable and suitable long-term policy model for all democratic welfare states. It is compatible with a fully democratic division of labour in families and organisations and it is in line with actual development during the past few decades. It will serve as the best guideline for an integrated and efficient policy regarding the division of professional and family labour during the next few decades. In this perspective, the complete combination model was briefly compared with similar policy models abroad: the combination scenario, the TLM model, the flexicurity model, the dual earner/dual carer model and the universal caregiver model. We noted that the normative TLM model and flexicurity model are too broad and too vague and allow too many contradictory policy perspectives. The other normative models are fairly well delineated but they are insufficiently worked out and visualised. We therefore emphasise the need for more international cooperation that could lead to the further development and integration of existing policy models, under the umbrella of the general normative concept of a democratic division of labour.

The *main goal of the complete combination model* is that almost all men and women in the professional population (new broad definition) combine their professional, family and other activities in a balanced way during their life course, avoiding one of the basic activities being threatened or neglected. During all their life course stages men and women have to spend enough time on all basic activities, so they are able to fulfil both professional and family responsibilities and to successfully combine their personal, social, material and financial capital.

In general, the model implies that enough men and women perform sufficient hours of paid work per week during a sufficient number of years over the professional stage of their life course. The model essentially implies that in the longer run a *normal full-time job* will count as approximately 35 working hours/week (or about 40 hours/week including on average about five hours for travelling and working overtime). We stress that this norm is not absolute, however. At the same time, the model offers a maximal diversity of jobs, from very small jobs (less than 10 hours/week) to very large jobs (up to 70 hours/week), according to the needs of families (family members) and organisations. The broad clock-curve implies that jobs occur less frequently to the extent that the number of hours differs from the basic norm or average. This implies that the extreme choices (zero or very few hours and many more hours per week) are reduced to the minimum level that is necessary and useful in society. The differences in the number of hours are largely determined by the age (life course stage) and the presence of children (family stage) and no longer by the education, social or income position.

Similarly, the model demands that enough men and women perform sufficient hours of family work per week during a sufficient number of years of their life course. The average *normal household task* implies about 25 hours of family labour per week with a broad variation from less than 10 hours/week to about 50 hours/week. The clock-curve implies that household tasks occur less frequently to the extent that the number of hours differs from the basic norm. The variation in the number of hours of household labour is again largely determined by age (life course stage) and by the presence of children (family stage), and not by education level or social background.

For couple families, the relative division of professional and family work is also important, implying that combination families represent the large majority. But to a certain extent male and female breadwinner families are also possible, as expressed by the gradual clock-curve. The clock-curve can also be a guideline for the remaining division of labour in the 'former family' of lone parents, from a very unequal 90%/10% division in favour of the father, to a very equal 50%/50% division, to a very unequal 10%/90% division in favour of the mother.

The complete combination model is a *general policy guideline for the division of the basic activities* of men and women, emphasising professional and family work in this study, starting from the concept of democratic division of labour. The model does not *formulate additional conditions for the division of partial activities within these main categories*, for example the division of household tasks and education/care. The basic conditions for the division of main activities do not restrict the diversity of partial activities. The model offers a general normative frame, combining the right and duty for men and women to realise an adequate combination of basic activities. This combination enables them to develop their own personal combination of different partial activities, in space and time. After all, the partial activities determine the real contents and results of the daily division of time for individuals and families.

The model allows sufficient changes or transitions in the combinations of basic activities during the life course. These transitions must lead to a new suitable combination of activities to realise a good mix of personal, social, material and financial means, as an answer to the changing opportunities and risks during the life course.

The complete combination model implies a *new pedagogical view* with respect to daily life, the education and societal position of children in a democratic society, which says that all children can develop a well-balanced division of activities within the different living arrangements of society, leading to a good combination of personal, social, material and financial means at every stage. They can enjoy a 'shared' or 'combined' high-quality education from birth, both within and outside the family. The different living arrangements have to offer sufficient quality and protection, allowing children to grow up to their best potential, with attention to differences in age, sex, family type, capabilities, and so on.

The children's family must play its full pedagogical role as a home base and central axis for the children's daily life. But education at home is permanently linked with education in other living arrangements such as the large family, circle of friends, neighbours, clubs, day-care centres, schools, and so on. External daytime education/care is a full part of the broad development of all children from birth, as an enrichment of education/care at home.

Intra-family education/care and external education/care are two educational cornerstones, both quantitatively and qualitatively, that have to continually support and stimulate each other. They are supplemented with other activities within the large family, neighbourhood, circle of friends and local clubs. So, the complete combination model follows the well-known phrase 'It takes a village to raise a child', indicating that from birth each child is a 'member' of different societal entities at the same time, which all have to play their specific role (in quantity and quality) in the total education process.

Finally, the normative future models are also applied to the *internal labour organisation in companies*. In general, the *complete combination model for organisations* means that in the long run the professional position of men and women is largely equal, both on the macro and micro level, as can be expressed by some basic aspects: the number of men and women in the organisation, number of weekly working hours and days, shift system per week or per month, flexible working hours, quality of the work, functional levels, payment for different functions, and so on. On the micro level, all organisations have sufficient freedom to choose the division of labour according to their own historical background and their own management view and strategy, albeit within the societal boundaries of the clock-curve in Figure 5.9. The complete combination model explicitly shows that more equality in the division of labour can go hand in hand with more choices for organisations, as it does for families – the model wants to realise concrete win–win situations for employees and employers alike. To do so, organisations must develop an adequate combination policy, within the borders of general government policy and the collective agreements between the social partners. The clock-curve suggests that a broad range of facilities or provisions is both possible and desirable. An efficient combination policy focuses on the right combination of the aspects of business life, both in the long and short run: working time arrangements, leave arrangements, social organisation and the location of the job, negotiation and decision making, facilities for childcare and commuter traffic, personal and household services and financial arrangements. To conclude, we emphasised the similarity between the complete combination model for organisations and the mass career customisation (MCC) model presented by Benko and Weisberg (2007). Starting from the unsatisfying results of the 'work–life policies' of the past few decades, they present the MCC framework as a new multi-dimensional approach that allows employees and employers to discover different options to design and achieve the optimal career paths that are compatible with personal and family life and that also support the further development of the organisation, both in the short and long run.

7.6 Policy perspectives for a democratic division of labour

Chapter 6 presented the main policy perspectives for the relevant societal fields, starting from the complete combination model as a long-term policy orientation. Here we give a short overview.

7.6.1 Promoting the normative concept of 'strong democracy' and the Complete Combination Model

First, it is essential to widely promote the basic idea of 'strong democracy' and a 'democratic market system' in all segments of society, as a strong alternative to the old and ambiguous concept of the so-called 'free market system' (Van Dongen, 2004a). It is therefore necessary to further develop the concept and apply it to the daily functioning of actual markets in the world, both in a descriptive and a normative sense. The descriptive analysis must result in a broad, gradual and more realistic picture of the different types of market systems and division of labour at all levels of society, thereby illustrating the gradual differences between democratic and undemocratic market systems. The normative analysis must develop a set of normative standards for the relevant variants of a democratic market system. By way of illustration, we formulated some basic norms for the functioning of the collective system in a democratic market system.

In line with this, the complete combination model must be widely promoted as the most suitable long-term policy model to express the concept of strong democracy and to serve as the basis for a coherent set of efficient policy perspectives and measures. The model must be permanently presented in a positive way, emphasising the power of the gradual division of labour as expressed by the clock–curve. The goal is to influence the attitude of (young) men and women towards the model in a positive way, stimulating the positive feedback with the actual division of labour. Everyone must become aware of the need for a sufficiently equal division of professional and family labour between men and women, from the very start of one's own household. Therefore, it is useful to introduce the 'daily division of time between men and women' as a permanent part of the education programme of young people.

7.6.2 An integrated 'full employment policy'

Above all, the central policy goal of *full employment for all men and women in the professional population* has to be continuously promoted. The right of every man and woman to have sufficient professional labour (and professional income) and enough family time is strongly related to the responsibility or duty to perform sufficient professional and family labour during the life course. As a consequence, both public and private professional organisations are responsible for creating and providing sufficient decent jobs. Given the available means, both sides of the labour market must take enough initiative, continually encouraging and supporting one another, in order to realise both their duties and rights.

This policy goal demands a clear formulation of the possible (temporary) *exemptions from professional labour*. The complete combination model implies a further improvement of existing leave arrangements, in terms of equality, solidarity and efficiency. However, the general traditional exemption for people who (want to) stay at home for the household work and the education of (young) children will no longer be maintained in the complete combination model. During the process towards the model, this general exemption must be replaced by a specific, temporary exemption due to (very) difficult family situations that prevent one partner from combining professional and family work. This specific exemption can then be combined with a sufficiently high temporary replacement income.

The realisation of the full employment goal needs a fiscal system that is both largely inspired by and sufficiently supportive of the realisation process towards the complete combination model. Therefore it is necessary to thoroughly transform the fiscal system (including social security). A strongly democratic society invests sufficient means in collective services to cope with major societal risks and to support all socially and professionally weaker groups, ranging, for example, from 35%-50% of GDP. The choice for a strong collective financial basis, however, implies an efficient use of the available means, maximally supporting the democratic division of labour at all levels of society. Next, the fiscal pressure on human labour must be systematically diminished, until a good balance is reached between the relative fiscal pressure on human and non-human labour/capital. So, more means can be invested in human-intensive activities in all segments of society, stimulating the creation of new decent jobs for all qualification levels. Additionally, the collective damage of the different activities must be correctly included in the fiscal tariffs, both for prevention and correction. So, hidden inefficiencies can be avoided or corrected and all market actors are confronted much more with the real societal cost and benefit of their activities.

To realise the complete combination model in the long run, the tariff structure of personal income tax and social security contributions should also be transformed. A *possible new tariff system* is presented for all professionally active people, based on a few basic criteria (Figures 6.3 and 6.4). The total professional income of men and women remains the major basis for the calculation of the total fiscal contribution for professional income. An additional criterion is the *average real number of working hours per week*. Around the new norm of the average 35-hours job, a gradual tariff system is possible with increasing tariffs (in percentages), to the extent that the real number of working hours per week of men and women differs from this norm. The third criterion is professional income per working hour, as the expression of the real earning capacity of men and women. Fiscal tariffs slowly increase with *professional income per working hour*. The tariff system is based on a progressive tax rate for total professional income per working hour, expressing the real earning capacity. To encourage the equal division of labour within couple families, the *relative division of professional labour between the two adult partners* can be used as a fourth criterion. The tariffs then increase to the extent that the division of labour between the partners is more unequal.

To answer the needs of families with children, parents can be given a *fiscal time credit*, with full entitlement to security provisions. The fiscal time credit implies that the gradual tariff system starts from a reference job with a lower number of hours (Figure 6.5). The objective is that parents maintain enough working hours per week but also have more time for family, personal and social activities. An additional time credit can be granted for single parents and for adults with a dependent older, ill or disabled person. A negative time credit is possible for specific professional groups with intrinsic long working hours, such as self-employed people or senior managers. So, some variants of the tariff system are possible.

The new tariff system encourages all families and companies to convert (step by step) to a more equal and family-friendly division of professional and family labour. It implies a *dynamic employment policy*, leading to more new suitable jobs in all segments of society. In a democratic market system, both public and private organisations are responsible for stimulating and shaping this process, by broad investment in (new) useful market activities and by a sufficiently equal distribution of the benefits. Good employment is oriented at the employment of all human capital in the daily production process in all segments of society.

The complete combination model aims at minimising *structural unemployment* by breaking the vicious circle of unemployment in a positive way. The right to sufficient income is linked to the responsibility and willingness to perform a useful societal task. Replacement incomes are being used as a collective input for the creation of useful tasks in favour of families and (public and private) organisations. These societal tasks are called 'bridge jobs', that is, largely subsidised jobs that act as a bridge between effective unemployment and a 'normal' job. Every unemployed person can have a 'bridge job' of about 20-25 hours/week in a family or societal organisation and will then receive a decent basic income. Everyone must be able to choose between a few bridge jobs offered, according to their interests, education and capabilities. All organisations can then create a number of bridge jobs for a certain percentage of the total actual number of full-time equivalent jobs, with a very low total labour cost. In general, bridge jobs can be seen as 'basic jobs' that guarantee societal participation and a decent basic income for everyone. Moreover, the organisations are continually encouraged to transform these bridge jobs step by step into 'normal' jobs. At the same time they can develop a number of supporting activities that have so far been postponed or neglected.

Basically, the system of bridge jobs offers an equal treatment of all unemployed people, irrespective of their education level, duration of and reasons for unemployment. People staying at home (mostly housewives) are strongly encouraged to participate, with the same basic rights and duties. All unemployed people taking up a bridge job will receive a higher income and improve their welfare level, at the same time stimulating (local) companies and markets. People who really do not want to have a job, however, must face the social and financial consequences of that free choice.

Such activating labour market policy is more efficient than current policy in most European countries and in the EU as a whole, with unemployment traps largely eliminated. It is also more efficient than the 'basic income' approach (Van Parijs, 1992, 1995; Ackerman et al, 2005) that provides a 'basic income' for all people, with no or only a weak link to societal labour to be performed.

Given the 'normal working time arrangement' (number of hours and days, overtime, shift system, and so on) and high-quality 'shared' education for children, the complete combination model aims at providing an adequate set of leave arrangements to offer all people sufficient time for their personal, family and social activities. The model aims at improving existing family leave arrangements around the time of childbirth, for both mothers and fathers, in order to support personal and family changes during the first months. At the same time, the model wants to encourage a sufficiently equal division of professional and family responsibilities between men and women. This implies that long and complete leave facilities must be reduced to a minimum and can only be used as a last resource when other options prove to be impossible in the short run. So, it is desirable to transform existing long parental leave arrangements into a general flexible system of family leave, to support people combining their jobs and family work, as a permanent challenge and process of learning by doing.

This additional 'family leave' can be realised by means of a time credit, with a fixed basic time credit for all people and a variable time credit, based on professional work performed in the past and to be performed in the future (as a time loan to be paid off afterwards by means of a certain amount of professional work). Sufficiently high financial compensation can be provided that decreases with increasing length and quantity of the leave. As a consequence, many more families would be able to use this family leave.

7.6.3 Adequate provisions for dependent children

The realisation of the complete combination model needs a number of adequate societal provisions for children and young people who are (financially) dependent: a direct collective financial allowance, external daytime education/care for young children, additional childcare facilities for different age groups and democratic secondary and higher education.

A strong democratic society should give sufficient direct financial support to families with children, enabling them to cover part of the daily private costs of children. Following the logic of the complete combination model, it is possible to develop a consistent and fairly simple system of basic child allowances that is fully compatible with collective investment in external education/care for children. The basic idea is to create one large collective fund to give all children a monthly child allowance, until the moment they are financially independent, usually when they start their first full job. Child allowance is an additional support for total family income, to be combined with the professional income of the parents. It increases with the age of the child to cover increasing daily costs of children.

Child allowance offers each generation the necessary extra support for their personal development, irrespective of the success or failure of the parents. The allowance can be seen as a basic income for the 'education work' of children in order to develop their human capital in an optimal way, as the basis for the welfare of future society.

Next, the complete combination model aims at transforming external daycare for the youngest children into a fully-fledged system of daytime education/care for all children from the age of three to six months. The starting point is that all children can enjoy a well-balanced combination of good education/care within both the family and external living arrangements (extended family, families of friends and neighbours, minder family, daycare centre, school, club, and so on). The combined education offers a strong basis for the total development of children and for the daily combination of professional and family work of parents. Of course, the family must play its role as the home basis for education, but at the same time, external education/care for the youngest children is a basic provision to support and enrich education within the family. This approach is fully compatible with the approach to the division of labour between men and women.

This implies that, from the age of three to six months after birth, all children are entitled to complete external education/care as a basic provision that is fully streamlined with basic education/care for older children (nursery and primary school), with respect to pedagogical objectives, organisational setting and financial arrangements. For countries with (almost) free basic education/care for older children, this basic provision should also be (almost) free of charge, financed by general collective means. Daytime education/care then becomes a maximally collective good: (almost) all children effectively use it in a largely equal way, the use of provision by one child does not restrict the use by other children and total use can be planned and limited quite well in order to avoid both over-consumption and social exclusion. At the same time, the complete combination model ensures sufficient availability of parent(s) for their children by restricting both the time that parents spend on professional work and the time that children spend on external education/care.

On a societal level, external daytime education/care combined with education/care at home is much more efficient than full-time care at home by one of the parents. Pedagogically, it offers a strong combination of internal and external sources for the complete development of children. Financially, combined high-quality education/care is much cheaper than full-time education/care at home by one of the partners, due to the much higher productivity of professional external education/care (in small groups).

In addition to daytime education/care for children under the age of 18, sufficient possibilities for *additional external childcare* must be available for all age groups: before and after daytime education/care, during (long) holiday periods, during weekends and periods of illness. These facilities must be fully streamlined with basic provisions for daytime education/care to allow parents to successfully combine their professional and family work. Consequently, it is essential to restrict the daily and weekly number of hours of additional external care to a level that is pedagogically acceptable. This is possible with an income-related contribution, sufficiently supporting lower-income families. Additional (financial) support is also possible for parents who need a lot of extra care due to inevitable special working hours.

Different actors can contribute to a broad supply of additional care: schools, grandparents, extended family, neighbourhood, circle of friends, local clubs (sport, arts, and so on). Companies can offer specific facilities that are necessary and supportive for their personnel, for example evening, night and weekend care for children of parents with a special working time schedule. Companies' investments in specific provisions will then be more efficient. Finally, the government should answer the remaining needs.

The *system of secondary and higher education* must also be improved in order to contribute as much as possible to the realisation of the complete combination model in a democratic society. Both secondary and higher education are an important link in the overall development of the human capital of all young people. Therefore, all young people should be able to participate in secondary and/or higher education, according to their capabilities, interests and efforts, in order to develop their human capital in an optimal way, as the basis for their personal development. For the young people involved it is also a basic provision that has to be financed in the same way as basic education for younger children, in proportion to the total cost. The net return on these investments will be sufficiently high, for the young people themselves, for their family, for organisations and for society as a whole.

7.6.4 Societal provisions for adults

The realisation of the complete combination model also demands a number of *societal provisions* for adults, in line with other policy perspectives.

First, all adults should have sufficient possibilities for additional lifelong learning, to answer education needs during their life course, for their professional, family and social life. The quality and quantity of additional education depends on the actual level of the human capital and future needs for an adequate division of labour. In particular (young) adults with a really inadequate education for one or more of the basic activities must be strongly supported in order to develop a strong and stable division of labour.

Second, *efficient mobility infrastructure* is a permanent element of the daily combination of family and professional life. The central policy challenge here is to control and reduce private travelling by car. A sufficiently large number of people using their car every day must be encouraged to use other transport means. One way of dealing with this is increasing the variable cost of car use, related to a number of factors such as distance, type and age of the car, region, level and frequency of congestion. At the same time, the supply of decent, fast and frequent public transport must be strongly increased (train, tram, buses), especially during rush hour, between and within urban centres. The right prices have to be charged to realise a good balance between demand and supply. Furthermore, systems of carpooling, collective school transport and business transport should be encouraged, together with the use of bicycles and motorbikes for short distances. Finally, more attention needs to be paid to the possibility of working at home, to save time for daily family tasks and to reduce the transport burden.

In general, one could treat the cost of commuter traffic as an integral part of the total production cost of an organisation, encouraging organisations to find the most efficient combination for all employees and for the organisation as a whole. They would probably employ more people who live nearer to the workplace, thereby decreasing the overall cost of commuter traffic.

The complete combination model also aims at encouraging the supply of *household services* allowing all families to buy the services that are most supportive for their specific division of labour and that are also most compatible with the preferences and competences of family members. The model therefore enables great diversity in the concrete combination of internal production and use of external services. In the new fiscal tariff system proposed, these activities enjoy a relatively low tax rate to realise a broad variety of services and to create useful jobs for lower-qualified people.

Furthermore, the model wants to realise *sufficiently flexible opening hours for shops, services and public offices*, maximally respecting the basic need of most employees for 'normal working hours' during the traditional working week. This has to be in balance with their need for flexibility in favour of family life and the need for flexibility in favour of the organisation.

Finally, the complete combination model aims at enabling all older people to receive an adequate combination of professional, family and social care of sufficiently high quality, at an acceptable price. At the same time, older people need to offer sufficient care to other older people in their (immediate) surroundings. This mutual care between older people has enormous potential, because of the large availability of time and competences/experiences. The major policy perspective here is the creation of broad, *integrating 'activity centres' for older people in all local communities,* as a bridge between traditional home care and residential care. These centres must create a broad supply of activities/services in an adequate infrastructure and an efficient organisational setting, combining professional, family and voluntary labour of all generations in an efficient way. The basic goal is that older people remain active in local social life, according to their preferences and capabilities, thereby minimising the risk of social isolation. Efficient social organisations can be established, largely starting from existing associations (for older people) and working together with schools, sporting clubs, artistic clubs, and so on.

7.6.5 Adequate combination policies in professional organisations

The complete combination model also aims at an adequate combination policy in professional organisations. Companies must be encouraged to fit their internal work organisation to the needs of the family life of their employees. A gender- and family-friendly work organisation implies that companies invest more in their employees, the social organisation, the equal position of men and women and in the daily combination of their professional and family life, in the long and short run. In the first place, the government can activate and support scientific research in this field to evaluate the new approaches and strategies with respect to their relevance and feasibility.

An efficient combination policy in and by companies aims at developing and applying the right mix of combination facilities for the different groups of employees, starting from the needs and possibilities of both the employees and the organisation. The main goal is to find sufficient win–win situations as the basis for effective action plans. These facilities refer to working time arrangements, leave arrangements, workplace options and work organisation, different provisions (childcare, commuter traffic, personal and family services and financial arrangements) and aspects of the quality of the job and organisational culture.

To realise such 'combination management', organisations can make use of professional counselling for the application of specialised audit instruments that have been developed during the past years. We refer to the German Work and Family Audit ('Audit Beruf und Familie'; see Leist, 2005), the European Work and Family Audit (Leist, 2005), the instrument 'When work works' (Galinsky, 2005) and the MCC framework (Benko and Weisberg, 2007) that are being applied in the US, and the Flemish 'Family and Business Audit' (FBA) (Danau and Van Dongen, 2002; Van Dongen et al, 2002; Van Dongen, 2005b). Governments can encourage and support companies to apply such instruments as the basis for a new and effective combination policy.

The Flemish FBA was developed during 2000–05 by means of several case studies in Flemish companies. At the end of 2006, two commercial consultancy organisations received a licence from the Flemish government to implement the FBA in Flemish organisations.

The FBA can be used in all sorts of professional organisations and deals with the different aspects of the work organisation. The main goal is to improve the daily combination of professional and family work, both for employees and the organisation. The process and result of the FBA are integrated in the general management process of the organisation.

As well as company-oriented instruments, it is desirable that from the start of their professional career, all employees/families receive sufficient individual support or guidance for the planning/management of their life course and professional career. Different sorts of organisations can offer this kind of guidance.

7.6.6 Adequate data systems and research with respect to the daily life

The realisation in the longer run of an efficient combination policy on the basis of solid empirical and normative models demands adequate integrated data systems with respect to the daily life of men and women within the context of families, companies and associations. In the first place, existing data systems can and should be improved by introducing the combination and life course perspective. In addition, however, European countries need a recurrent integrated survey about the daily life and life course of men and women within families, companies and associations. Such a survey should focus on the daily combination of professional and family work of the professional population, but sufficient attention must also be paid to the daily life of children below the age of 18 and people above the age of 60.

Bibliography

Ackerman, B., Alstott, A. and Van Parijs, P. (2005) *Redesigning distribution. Basic income and stakeholder grants as cornerstones for an egalitarian capitalism*, London: Verso (Real Utopias).

Adam, B. (1990) *Time and social theory*, Cambridge: Polity Press.

Adam, B. (1995) *Timewatch. The social analysis of time*, Cambridge: Polity Press.

Adam, B. (2004) *Time*, Cambridge: Polity Press.

Adler, H.J. and Hawrylyshyn, O. (1978) 'Estimates of the value of household work, Canada 1961 and 1971', *Review of Income and Wealth*, vol 24, no 4, pp 333-55.

Aguiar, M. and Hurst, E. (2006) *Measuring trends in leisure: The allocation of time over five decades*, Working Paper No 06-02, Boston, MA: Federal Reserve Bank of Boston.

Anderson, M. (1999) 'What can the mid-Victorian censuses tell us about patterns of married women's employment?', *Local Population Studies*, no 62, pp 9-30.

Anxo, D. (2004) 'Working time patterns among industrialized countries: a household perspective', in J.C. Messenger (ed) *Working time and workers' preferences in industrialised countries. Finding the balance*, London: Routledge.

Anxo, D. and Boulin, J.-Y. (eds) (2004) *A new organisation of working time throughout working life*, Dublin: European Foundation for the Improvement of Living and Working Conditions.

Anxo, D. and Boulin, J.-Y. (eds) (2005) *Working time options over the life course: Changing social security structures*, Dublin: European Foundation for the Improvement of Living and Working Conditions.

Anxo, D. and Boulin, J.-Y. (eds) (2006a) *Working time options over the life course: New work patterns and company strategies*, Dublin: European Foundation for the Improvement of Living and Working Conditions.

Anxo, D. and Boulin, J.-Y. (2006b) 'The organisation of time over the life course: European trends', *European Societies*, vol 2, no 2, pp 319-41.

Anxo, D. and Ehrel, C. (2004) *Irreversibility of time, reversibility of choices? A transitional labour market approach*, Position paper for the TLM.net conference, Amsterdam, 25-26 November.

Anxo, D., Cebrian, I., Fagan, C., Moreno, G. and Toharia, L. (2004) 'Patterns of labour market integration in Europe: a gender and life course perspective', Paper for the TLM.NET conference, Amsterdam, 25-26 November.

Anxo, D., Fagan, C., Cebrian, I. and Moreno, G. (2006) 'Patterns of labour market integration in Europe: a life course perspective on time policies', *Socio-Economic Review*, vol 5, no 2, pp 230-60.

Arrighi, G. (1994) *The long twentieth century*, London and New York: Verso.

Baeck, L. (1984) *De geschiedenis van het economisch denken*, Leuven: Centrum voor ontwikkelingsplanning, KUL.

Becker, G.S. (1965) 'A theory of the allocation of time', *Economic Journal*, vol 75, no 299, pp 493-517.

Becker, G.S. (1975) *Human capital. A theoretical and empirical analysis with special reference to education*, New York and London: Colombia University Press.

Becker, G.S. (1976) *The economic approach to human behavior*, Chicago, IL: Prentice Hall.

Becker, G.S. (1981) *A treatise on the family*, Cambridge, MA: Harvard University Press.

Becker, U. (1999) *Europese democratieën: Vrijheid, gelijkheid, solidariteit en soevereiniteit in praktijk*, Amsterdam: Het Spinhuis.

Benko, C. and Weisberg, A. (2007) *Mass Career Customization. Aligning the workplace with today's non-traditional workforce*, Boston, MA: Harvard Business School Press.

Bianchi, S.M., Milkie, M.A., Sayer, L.C. and Robinson, J.P. (2000) 'Is anyone doing the housework? Trends in the gender division of household labour', *Social Forces*, September, vol 79, no 1, pp 191-228.

Bianchi, S.M., Robinson, J.P. and Milkie, M.A. (2006) *Changing rhythms of American family life*, New York: Russell Sage Foundation.

Bielenski, B., Bosch, G. and Wagner, A. (2002) *Working time preferences in sixteen European countries*, Dublin: European Foundation for the Improvement of Working Conditions.

Bittman, M., Brown, J. and Craig, L. (2005) 'Part-time work and time for care: the consequences of three policy designs', Paper for the IATUR conference 'Time use in daily life: the content and context of human behaviour', Halifax, Nova Scotia, Canada, 2-4 November.

Bittman, M., Craig, L. and Folbre, N. (2004) 'Packaging care: what happens when children receive nonparental care', in N. Folbre and M. Bittman (eds) *Family time. The social organisation of care*, London and New York: Routledge, pp 133-51.

Bittman, M., Fast, J.E., Fisher, K. and Thomson, K. (2004) 'Making the invisible visible: the life and time(s) of informal caregivers', in N. Folbre and M. Bittman (eds) *Family time. The social organisation of care*, London and New York: Routledge, pp 69-89.

Blau, D.N. (2001) *The child-care problem. An economic analysis*, New York: Russell Sage Foundation.

Blood, R.O. Jr and Wolfe, D.M. (1960) *Husbands and wives: The dynamics of married living*, Glencoe, IL: The Free Press.

Borchorst, A. (2008) 'Women-friendly policy paradoxes? Childcare policies and gender equality visions in Scandinavia', in K Melby, A. Ravn, and C.C. Wetterberg (eds) *Gender equality and welfare politics in Scandinavia. The limits of political ambition?*, Bristol, The Policy Press, pp 27-42.

Bovenberg, L. (2003) *Nieuwe levensloopbenadering*, OSA Discussion paper DISP2003-1, Tilburg and Utrecht: University of Tilburg and Utrecht University.

Breedveld, K. (2007) 'Odd working hours and time pressure', in T. van der Lippe and P. Peeters (eds) *Competing claims in work and family life*, Cheltenham: Edward Elgar, pp 57-72.

Brines, J. (1994) 'Economic dependency, gender and the division of labor at home', *American Journal of Sociology*, vol 100, no 3, pp 652-88.

Bryson, V. (2007) *Gender and the politics of time. Feminist theory and contemporary debates*, Bristol: The Policy Press.

Budig, M.J. and Folbre, N. (2004) 'Activity, proximity, or responsibility? Measuring parental childcare time', in N. Folbre and M. Bittman (eds) *Family time. The social organisation of care*, London and New York: Routledge, pp 51–68.

Cantillon, B. (ed) (1999) *De welvaartsstaat in de kering*, Kapellen: Uitgeverij Pelckmans.

Cantillon, B., de Lathouwer, L. and Thirion, A. (1999) *Financiële vallen in de werkloosheid en de bijstand*, Eindrapport van het gelijknamige onderzoek, in Opdracht van de Vlaamse Minister van Werkgelegenheid en Toerisme in het kader van het VIONA onderzoeksprogramma, Antwerpen: UFSIA, Universiteit Antwerpen.

Cantillon, B., Kerstens, B. and Verbist, G. (2000) 'De verdelingseffecten van het ontwerp van fiscale hervorming (Plan Reynders). Microsimulatieresultaten', *CSB Berichten*, Oktober, Antwerpen: UFSIA, Universiteit Antwerpen.

Cantillon, B., Marx, I. and Van den Bosch, K. (2002) 'The puzzle of egalitarianism. About the relationships between employment, wage inequality, social expenditures and poverty', *CSB Berichten*, December, Antwerpen: Universiteit Antwerpen.

Christiansen, N.F., Petersen, K., Edling, N. and Haave, P. (eds) (2006) *The Nordic model of welfare: A historical reappraisal*, Copenhagen: Museum Tusculanum Press.

Cliquet, R. (ed) (1996) *Gezinnen in de verandering, veranderende gezinnen*, CBGS Monografie, 1996/2, Brussels: CBGS, pp 181–207.

Commissie Dagindeling (1998) *Dagindeling. Tijd voor arbeid en zorg. Eindadvies*, Den Haag: Ministerie van Sociale Zaken en Werkgelegenheid.

Commissie Toekomstscenario's Herverdeling Onbetaalde Arbeid (1995) *Onbetaalde zorg gelijk verdeeld*, Den Haag: Ministerie van Sociale Zaken en Werkgelegenheid.

Creighton, C. (1996) 'The rise of the male breadwinner family: a reappraisal', *Comparative Studies in Society and History*, vol 38, no 2, pp 310–37.

Creighton, C. (1999) 'The rise and decline of the "male breadwinner family" in Britain', *Cambridge Journal of Economics*, vol 23, no 3, pp 519–41.

Crompton, R. (ed) (1999) *Restructuring gender relations and employment: The decline of the male breadwinner*, Oxford: Oxford University Press.

Crompton, R. and Lyonette, C. (2006) 'Work-life balance in Europe', *Acta Sociologica*, December, vol 49, no 4, pp 379–93.

Csani, V. (1989) *Evolutionary systems and society. A general theory of life, mind and culture*, Durham, NC and London: Duke University Press.

Cuvilier, R. (1979), The housewife: an unjustified financial burden on the community, *Journal of Social Policy*, vol 8, no 1, pp 1–26.

Danau, D. and Van Dongen, W. (2002) *Algemeen Eindrapport FBA-project*, (*Final report of the Family and Business Audit project*) Brussels: CBGS, Universiteit Antwerpen and ECWS. De Borger, B. (2005) *Mobiliteit en de prijsstructuur in de transportsector*, Beleidsnota nr 9, Brussels: VKW – Metena.

De Borger, B. and Proost, S. (eds) (2001) *Reforming transport pricing in the European Union: A modelling approach*, Cheltenham: Edward Elgar.

De Ceuster, G. (2004) *Internalisering van externe kosten van wegverkeer in Vlaanderen*, Studie uitgevoerd in opdracht van de Vlaamse Milieumaatschappij, MIRA/2004/04, Leuven: Transport & Mobility Leuven.

Delarue, S., de Winne, L., Gryp, S., Maes, J., Marx, S., Peeters, A., Ramioul, M., Sels, L. and Van Hootegem, G. (2003) *Organisatie in bedrijf – editie 2003. Een overzicht van de resultaten van het PASO Flanders onderzoek*, Leuven: Steunpunt WAV.

De Lathouwer, L. (2004) 'Making work pay, making transitions flexible. The case of Belgium in a comparative perspective', *CSB Berichten*, Antwerpen: CSB, Universiteit Antwerpen, July.

del Boca, D. and Vuri, D. (2006) *The mismatch between employment and child-care in Italy: The impact of rationing*, no 08/2006, University of Turin, CHILD.

Deleeck, H. (2001) *De architectuur van de welvaartsstaat opnieuw bekeken*, Leuven/Leusden: Acco.

den Dulk, L. (2001) *Work–family arrangements in organisations. A cross-national study in the Netherlands, Italy, the United Kingdom and Sweden*, Amsterdam: Rozenberg Publishers.

den Dulk, L., Peper, B. and van Doorne-Huiskes, A. (2005) 'Work and family life in Europe: employment patterns of working parents across welfare states', in B. Peper, A. van Doorne-Huiskes and L. den Dulk (eds) *Flexible working and organisational change. The integration of work and personal life*, Cheltenham and Northampton, MA: Edward Elgar, pp 13–38.

den Dulk, L., van Doorne-Huiskes, A. and Schippers, J. (eds) (1999) *Work–family arrangements in Europe*, Amsterdam: Thela Thesis.

de Ruijter, E. and van der Lippe, T. (2007) 'Household outsourcing: a transaction cost approach', in T. van der Lippe and P. Peeters (eds) *Competing claims in work and family life*, Cheltenham and Northampton, MA: Edward Elgar, pp 195-212.

De Smedt, P. (2005) *Verkennen van de toekomst met scenarios*, Brussels: Studiedienst van de Vlaamse Regering.

Deven, F. and Jacobs, T. (ed) (2006) *Vooruitdenken over zorg in Vlaanderen*, CBGS Publicaties, Antwerpen-Apeldoorn: Garant.

Deven, F. and Moss, P. (2002) 'Leave arrangements for parents: overview and future outlook', *Community, Work & Family*, vol 5, no 3, pp 237-55.

Deven, F. and Moss, P. (2005) *Leave policies and research. Reviews and country notes*, CBGS-Werkdocument, 2005/3, Brussels: CBGS.

de Vries, J. (1994) 'The Industrial Revolution and the Industrious Revolution', *Journal of Economic History*, vol 54, no 2, pp 249-70.

Donaldson, T. and Preston, L. (1995) 'The stakeholder theory of the corporation: concepts, evidence, and implications', *Academy of Management Review*, vol 20, no 1, pp 65-91.

Duxburry, L. and Higgins, C. (2005) *Work–life balance in the new millennium. Where are we? Where do we need to go?*, CPRN Discussion Paper W/12, October (www.cprn.org).

Egerton, M. and Mullen, K. (2004), Gender, Educational Attainment and the Value of Unpaid Helping and Voluntary Work, Paper for the IATUR conference 'Time use: what's new in methodology and application fields?', ISTAT (Italian National Statistical Institute), 27-29 October, Rome.

Elkington, J. (1997, 1999) *Cannibals with forks. The triple bottom line of 21st century business*, Oxford: Capstone.

Esping-Andersen, G. (1990) *The three worlds of welfare capitalism*, New York: Princeton University Press.

Esping-Andersen, G. (1996) *Welfare states in transition: National adaptations in global economies*, London: Sage Publications.

Esping-Andersen, G. (1999) *Social foundations of postindustrial economies*, New York: Oxford University Press.

Ester, P., Muffels, R.J.A. and Schippers, J. (eds) (2006) *Dynamiek en levensloop: De arbeidsmarkt in transitie*, Assen: Koninklijke Van Gorcum.

European Commission (2004) *Structures of the taxation systems in the European Union*, Detailed tables, Brussels: European Commission, Directorate-General Taxation and Customs Union.

European Network Family and Work (1998) *European audits, new ways, 1998/1*, Brussels: European Commission.

Evans, J.M. (2001) *Firms' contribution to the reconciliation between work and family life*, OECD Labour Market and Social Policy Occasional Papers, number 48, New York: OECD Directorate for Employment, Labour and Social Affairs, OECD.

Fagan, C.K. (2006) 'Different models of part-time work in Europe and the question of work-life balance across the life course', Paper for the conference 'Innovating labour market policies', 30 November-1 December, Amsterdam.

Ferber, M.A. and Birnbaum, B.G. (1977) 'The New Home Economics: retrospects and prospects', *Journal of Consumer Research*, vol 4, no 1, pp 23-36.

Ferber, M.A. and Birnbaum, B.G. (1980) 'Housework: priceless or valueless?', *Review of Income and Wealth*, vol 4, no 1, pp 387-400.

Ferrarini, T. (2003) *Parental leave institutions in eighteen post-war welfare states*, Stockholm: Stockholm University, Swedish Institute for Social Research.

Ferre, Z., Piani, G. and Rossi, M. (2004) *El tiempo en el hogar: Parejas desparejas*, Documentos de trabajo, No 18/04, Diciembre, Montevideo: Universidad de la Republica.

Ferree, M.M. (1990) 'Beyond separate spheres: feminism and family research', *Journal of Marriage and the Family*, vol 52, no 4, pp 866-84.

Folbre, N. (1991) 'The unproductive housewife: her evolution in nineteenth-century economic thought', *Signs*, vol 16, no 3, pp 463-84.

Folbre, N. (2004) 'A theory of the misallocation of time', in N. Folbre and M. Bittman (eds) *Family time. The social organisation of care*, London and New York: Routledge, pp 7-24.

Folbre, N. (2006a) 'Rethinking the child-care sector', *Journal of the Community Development Society*, vol 37, no 2, summer, pp 38-52.

Folbre, N. (2006b) 'Measuring care: gender, empowerment and the care economy', *Journal of Human Development*, vol 7, no 2, July, pp 183-99.

Folbre, N. and Bittman, M. (eds) (2004) *Family time. The social organisation of care*, London and New York: Routledge.

Folbre, N. and Goodin, R.E. (2004) 'Revealing altruism', *Review of Social Economy*, vol LXII, no 1, March.

Folbre, N. and Yoon, J. (2005) 'The value of unpaid childcare in the US in 2003', Paper for the IATUR conference 'Time use in daily life: the content and context of human behaviour', Halifax, Nova Scotia, Canada, 2–4 November.

Folbre, N., Yoon, J., Finoff, K. and Fuligni, A.S. (2005) 'By what measure? Family time devoted to children in the United States', *Demography*, vol 42, no 2, May, pp 373–90.

Fraser, N. (1994) 'After the family wage: gender equity and the Welfare State', *Political Theory*, vol 22, no 4, pp 591–618.

Fraser, N. (2006) 'After the family wage: a postindustrial thought experiment', in M.K. Zimmerman, J.S. Litt and C.E. Bose, *Global dimensions of gender and carework*, Stanford, CA: Stanford University Press, pp 305–9.

Fuwa, M. (2004) 'Macro-level gender inequality and the division of household labor in 22 countries', *American Sociological Review*, vol 69, no 6, pp 751–67.

Galinsky, E. (2005) 'The changing workforce in the United States. Making work "work" in today's economy', Presentation for the founding conference of the International Centre for Work and Family (ICWF), IESE Business School, Barcelona, 7–9 July.

Galinsky, E. and Bond, J.T. (1998) *The 1998 business work–life study: A sourcebook*, New York: Families and Work Institute.

Galinsky, E., Friedman, D.E. and Hernandez, C.A. (1991) *The corporate reference guide to work-family program*, New York: Families and Work Institute.

Garhammer, M. (2007) 'Time pressure and quality of life', in T. van der Lippe and P. Peeters (eds) *Competing claims in work and family life*, Cheltenham and Northampton, MA: Edward Elgar, pp 21–40.

Gauthier, A.H. (1996) *The state and the family. A comparative analysis of family policies in industrialized countries*, Oxford: Clarendon Press.

Geist, C. (2005) 'The Welfare State and the home: regime differences in the domestic division of labour', *European Sociological Review*, vol 21, no 1, February, pp 23–41.

Gershuny, J. (1978) *After industrial society?*, London: Macmillan Press Ltd.

Gershuny, J. (2000) *Changing times. Work and leisure in postindustrial society*, Oxford: Oxford University Press.

Gershuny, J. (2005) *Time allocation and the comprehensive accounting of economic activity*, ISER Working Papers, Nr 2005/8, Colchester: ISER, University of Essex.

Gershuny, J. and Robinson, J.P. (1988) 'Historical changes in the household division of labour', *Demography*, vol 25, no 4, November.

Gershuny, J., Godwin, M. and Jones, S. (1994) 'The domestic labour revolution: a process of lagged adaptation?', in M. Anderson, F. Bechhoffer and J. Gershuny, *The social and political economy of the household*, Oxford: Oxford University Press.

Geurts, K. (2002) *Minder gezin, meer arbeid? De arbeidsdeelname van de bevolking naar gezinspositie*, Jaarreeks 2002 – De Arbeidsmarkt in Vlaanderen, Steunpunt Werkgelegenheid, Arbeid en Vorming, Stuurgroep Strategisch Arbeidsmarktonderzoek, Antwerpen: Garant Uitgevers nv.

Ghysels, J. (2004) *Work, family and childcare. An empirical analysis of European households*, Cheltenham and Northampton, MA: Edward Elgar.

Ghysels, J. and Debacker, M. (ed) (2007) *Zorgen voor kinderen in Vlaanderen: Een dagelijkse evenwichtsoefening?*, Leuven/Voorburg: Acco.

Glorieux, I. (1995) *Arbeid als Zingever. Een onderzoek naar de betekenis van arbeid in het leven van mannen en vrouwen*, Brussels: VUB Press.

Glorieux, I. and Moens, M. (2001) 'The 1999 Flemish Time Budget Study. Response, External Validity and Results'. Paper presented at the IATUR conference 'Time Use 2001: New Regions, New Data, New Methods and New Results', Oslo, Norway, October 3-5.

Glorieux, I. and Vandeweyer, J. (2001) *Time Use in Belgium. Results of the TUS 1999 carried out by Statistics Belgium*, Brussels: Statistics Belgium.

Glorieux, I., Koelet, S., Mestdag, I., Moens, M., Minnen, J. and Vandeweyer, J. (2006) *De 24 uur van Vlaanderen. Het dagelijkse leven van minuut tot minuut*, Tielt: LannooCampus.

Glorieux, I., Minnen, J. and van Thielen, I. (2003) *Moeder, wanneer werken wij? Arbeidsmarktconclusies uit het Vlaams Tijdsbestedingsonderzoek 1988-1999*, Brussels: TOR-VUB.

Goldin, C. (2006) 'The quiet revolution that transformed women's employment, education, and family', *American Economic Review, Papers and Proceedings*, vol 96, no 2, pp 1-21.

Goldscheider, F. (2002) 'Non-domestic employment and women's lives: revisiting the roles of supply and demand', Paper presented at the 2002 annual meeting of the Population Association of America, Atlanta, Georgia, 9-11 May.

Goldschmidt-Clermont, L. (1982) *Unpaid work in the household. A review of economic evaluation methods*, Geneva: International Labour Office.

Goldschmidt-Clermont, L. (1983) 'Does housework pay? A product-related microeconomic approach', *Signs*, vol 9, no 1, pp 109-19.

Gordon, B. (1975) *Economic analysis before Adam Smith, Hesiod to Lessius*, London: Macmillan.

Gornick, J.C. and Meyers, M.C. (2003) *Families that work. Policies for reconciling parenthood and employment*, New York: Russell Sage Foundation.

Gornick, J.C. and Meyers, M.C. (2004a) 'Supporting a dual-earner/dual carer society: lessons from abroad', in J. Heymann and C. Beem (eds) *A democracy that works: The public dimensions of the work and family debate*, New York: The New Press.

Gornick, J.C. and Meyers, M.C. (2004b) 'Welfare regimes in relation to paid work and care', in J.Z. Giele and E. Holst (eds) *Changing life patterns in Western industrial societies*, New York: Elsevier Science.

Gratton, L. (2004) *The democratic enterprise. Liberating your business with freedom, flexibility and commitment*, London and New York: Prentice Hall and *Financial Times*.

Gravelle, H. and Rees, R. (1987) *Microeconomics* (7th edn), London and New York: Longman.

Greenstein, T. (1996a) 'Gender ideology and perceptions of the fairness of the division of household labour: effects on marital quality', *Social Forces*, vol 74, no 3, pp 1029-42.

Greenstein, T. (1996b) 'Husbands' participation in domestic labor: interactive effects of wives' and husbands' gender ideologies', *Journal of Marriage and the Family*, vol 58, no 3, pp 585-95.

Greenstein, T. (2000) 'Economic dependency, gender and the division of labor at home: a replication and extension', *Journal of Marriage and the Family*, vol 62, pp 322-335.

Gronau, R. (1973a) 'The intra-family allocation of time: the value of the housewives' time', *American Economic Review*, vol 63, no 6, pp 634-51.

Gronau, R. (1973b) 'Measurement of output of the non-market sector: the evaluation of housewives' time', in M. Moss (ed) *The measurement of economic and social performance*, New York: National Bureau of Economic Research, pp 1163-90.

Gronau, R. (1974), 'The effect of children on the housewife's value of time', in T.W. Schultz (1974), *Economics of the Family*, London: University of Chicago Press, pp 451-88.

Gronau, R. (1977) 'Leisure, home production and work, the theory of the allocation of time revisited', *Journal of Political Economy*, vol 85, no 6, pp 1099-123.

Gronau, R. (1980) 'Home production, a forgotten industry', *Review of Economics and Statistics*, vol 62, no 3, pp 408-16.

Gronau, R. and Hamermesh, D.S. (2002) 'Time versus goods: the value of measuring household production technologies' (www.eco.utexas.edu/faculty/Hamermesh/HPSeriously.prn.pdf).

Gustafsson, B. and Kjulin, U. (1994) 'Time use in child care and housework and the total cost of children', *Journal of Population Economics,* vol 7, no 3, pp 287-306.

Haas, L. (2003) 'Parental leave and gender equality: lessons from the European Union', *Review of Policy Research*, vol 20, no 1, pp 89-114.

Haataja, A. and Nyberg, A. (2005) *Did the dual-earner model become stronger or weaker in Finland and Sweden in the 1990s?*, Luxembourg Income Study Working Paper Series, Working Paper No 414, New York: Maxwell School of Citizenship and Public Affairs, Syracuse University.

Hagenaars, A.J.M. (1988) *De economie van de huishoudelijke sector. Deel I: De tijdsbesteding van huishoudens, Deel II: Inkomen en bestedingen van huishoudens*, Rotterdam: Erasmus Universiteit.

Hagenaars, A.J.M., Homan, M. and van Praag, B.M.S. (1982) *Monetaire waardering van huishoudelijke produktieverschillen tussen één – en tweekostwinnershuishoudens*, Rapport 84, 10, Leiden: Centrum voor Onderzoek van de Economie van de Publieke Sektor, RU.

Hakim, C. (2003) *Models of the family in modern societies. Ideal and realities*, Aldershot: Ashgate Publishing Company.

Hamermesh, D.S. and Pfann, G.A. (eds) (2005) *The economics of time use*, Amsterdam: Elsevier.

Hawrylyshyn, O. (1976) 'The value of household services: a survey of empirical estimates', *Review of Income and Wealth*, vol 22, no 2, pp 101-33.

Hawrylyshyn, O. (1977) 'Towards a definition of non-market activities', *Review of Income and Wealth*, vol 23, no 1, pp 79-96.

Henderickx, E. and De Prins, P. (1998) 'Bedrijfsleven en Gezinsleven. Transformatie van maatschappelijke bouwstenen', in W. Van Dongen, E. Vanhaute and K. Pauwels (eds) *Het kostwinnersmodel voorbij? Naar een nieuw basismodel voor de arbeidsverdeling binnen de gezinnen*, Leuven-Apeldoorn: Garant, pp 137-53.

Higgins, C., Duxburry, L. and Johnson, K.L. (2000) 'Part-time work for women: does it really help balance work and family?', *Human Resource Management*, spring, vol 39, no 1, pp 17-32.

Hillebrink, C., Schippers, J., Peters, P. and van Doorne-Huiskes, A. (2007) 'Trading time and money: explaining employee participation and leave choices in a flexible benefit plan', in T. van der Lippe and P. Peeters (eds) *Competing claims in work and family life*, Cheltenham and Northampton, MA: Edward Elgar, pp 179-94.

Hochschild, A.R. (1989) *The second shift*, New York: Viking Press.

Hook, J. (2004) 'Reconsidering the division of household labour: incorporating volunteer work and informal support', *Journal of Marriage and the Family*, vol 66, no 1, pp 101-17.

Hook, J. (2005a) 'Care in context: men's unpaid work in 20 countries, 1965-1998', Annual Meeting of the American Sociological Association, San Francisco, CA.

Hook, J. (2005b) 'Still specialized? Cross-national trends in the division of household labour, 1965–1998', Annual Meeting of the American Sociological Association, Philadelphia, PA.

Hopkins, T.K. and Wallerstein, I. (eds) (1996) *The age of transition. Trajectory of the world-system*, North Melbourne: Pluto Press.

Horrell, S. and Humphries, J. (1995) 'Women's labor force participation and the transition to the male breadwinner family, 1790–1865', *The Economic History Review*, new series, vol 48, no 1, pp 89-117.

Horrell, S. and Humphries, J. (1997) 'The origins and expansion of the male breadwinner family – the case of nineteenth-century Britain', *International Review of Social History*, vol 42, supplement 5, pp 25-64.

Hues, T. (ed) (1976) *Economics and sociology: Towards integration*, Leiden: Nijhoff Social Sciences.

Hunt, E.K. and Schwartz, F.S. (eds) (1972) *A critique of economic theory*, Harmondsworth: Penguin Books.

Ironmonger, D. (2000a) *Household production and the household economy*, Research Paper No 759:13, Melbourne: Department of Economics, University of Melbourne.

Ironmonger, D. (2000b) 'There are only 24 hours in a day! Solving the problem of simultaneous time', Paper for the 25th IATUR conference on 'Time use research', 17-19 September, Brussels.

Ironmonger, D. (2004) 'Bringing up Betty and Bobby: the inputs and outputs of childcare time, family time', in N. Folbre and M. Bittman (eds) *The social organisation of care*, London and New York: Routledge, pp 93-109.

Janssens, A. (1997) 'The rise and decline of the male breadwinner family? An overview of the debate', *International Review of Social History*, vol 42, supplement 5, pp 1-23.

Jennes, G. and Dierickx, G. (1992) *Het belastingbeleid in 15 OESO-landen (1955-1988). Alternatieve verklaringen*, SESO-rapport 92/267, Universiteit Antwerpen.

Jensen, H. (ed) (2002) *The welfare state. Past, present and future*, Pisa: Edizioni Plus, University of Pisa.

Juster, E. (1973) 'A framework for the measurement of economic and social performance', in M. Moss (ed) *The measurement of economic and social performance*, New York: National Bureau of Economic Research, pp 25–84.

Juster, F.T. and Dow, G.K. (1985) 'Goods, time and well-being: the joint dependence problem', in F.T. Juster and F.P. Stafford (eds) *Time, goods, and well-being*, Michigan, MI: Survey Research Centre, Institute for Social Research, University of Michigan.

Kamerman, S.B., Neuman, M., Waldfogel, J. and Brooks-Gunn, J. (2003) *Social policies, family types and child outcomes in selected OECD countries*, Paris: OECD.

Kerkhofs, M., Chung, H. and Ester, P. (2006) 'Working time flexibility across Europe', Presentation for the conference 'Innovating labour market policies', 30 November–1 December, Amsterdam.

Kirzner, I. (1976) *The economic point of view*, Kansas City, MO: Sherd and Ward Inc.

Kooreman, P. and Wunderink, S. (1996) *The economics of household behaviour*, Houndmills: Macmillan.

Korpi, W. (2000) 'Faces of inequality: gender, class, and patterns of inequalities in different types of welfare states', *Social Politics*, vol 7, no 2, pp 127–91.

Kreps, D.M. (1990) *A course in microeconomic theory*, New York and London: Harvester Wheatsheaf.

Kruithof, J. (1968) *De zingever. Een inleiding tot de studie van de mens als betekenend, waarderend en agerend wezen*, Antwerpen: Standaard Wetenschappelijke Uitgeverij.

Kruithof, J. (1973) *Eticologie, inleiding tot de studie van het morele verschijnsel*, Boom: Meppel.

Kruithof, J. (1980) *Democratie en efficiëntie*, Cursus sociologie van de moraal, Gent: RUG.

Kruithof, J. (1984) *Arbeid en Lust, deel I: Theorie*, Berchem: EPO.

Kruithof, J. (1986) *Arbeid en Lust, deel II: Empirie*, Berchem: EPO.

Kuhn, T.S. (1962) *The structure of scientific revolutions*, Chicago, IL and London: University of Chicago Press.

Kwon, T.H. (2007) 'Economic valuating household work in Korea, 1999 and 2004', Paper for the IATUR conference 'Work vs play: competing models of the proper use of time', Washington, DC: University of Maryland, 17–19 October.

Leist, A. (2005) 'Work and family audit (Audit Beruf und Familie)', Paper for the Founding conference of the International Centre for Work and Family (ICWF), IESE Business School, Barcelona, 7–9 July.

Leitner, A. and Wobrewski, A. (2006) 'Welfare states and work-life balance: can good practices be transferred from the Nordic countries to conservative welfare states?', *European Societies*, vol 8, no 2, pp 295–318.

Lis, C. (1984) 'Gezinsvorming en vrouwenarbeid tijdens een versnellingsfase in de ontwikkeling van het kapitalisme, 1750-1850', *Tijdschrift voor Sociale Geschiedenis*, vol 10, no 4, pp 380–405.

Lundberg, S. and Pollak, R. (1996) 'Bargaining and distribution in marriage', *Journal of Economic Perspectives*, vol 10, no 4, pp 139–58.

Lundqvist, A. (2008) 'Family policies between science and politics', in K Melby, A. Ravn and C.C. Wetterberg (eds) *Gender equality and welfare politics in Scandinavia. The limits of political ambition?*, Bristol, The Policy Press, pp 85–100.

MacInnes, J. (2005) 'Work–life balance in Europe: a response to the baby bust or reward for the baby boomers?', *European Societies Revision*, vol 8, no 2, 11 October.

Madsen, P.K. (2006) 'Flexicurity. A new perspective on labour markets and welfare states in Europe', Paper for the conference 'Innovating labour market policies', 30 November-1 December, Amsterdam.

Malinvaud, E. (1972) *Lectures on micro-economic theory*, New York: North Holland Publishing Company Inc.

Mandel, E. (1977) *Marxist economic theory*, London: Merlin Press.

Manser, M. and Brown, M. (1980) 'Marriage and household decision-making. A bargaining analysis', *International Economic Review*, vol 21, no 1, pp 31-44.

Marx, K. (1974) *Capital, A critique of political economy, Volume III, The process of capitalist production as a whole* (ed Friedrich Engels, 5th edn), London: Lawrence and Wishart.

Matthijs, K. (2003) 'Demographic and sociological indicators of privatisation of marriage in the nineteenth century in Flanders', *European Journal of Population*, vol 19, no 4, pp 375-412.

Melby, K., Ravn, A. and Wetterberg, C.C. (eds) (2008) *Gender equality and welfare politics in Scandinavia. The limits of political ambition?*, Bristol, The Policy Press.

Michelle, J.B. and Folbre, N. (2004) 'Measuring parental childcare time', in N. Folbre and M. Bittman (eds) *Family time. The social organisation of care*, London and New York: Routledge, pp 51-68.

Ministerie van Sociale Zaken en Werkgelegenheid (1997) *Kansen op combineren. Arbeid, zorg en economische zelfstandigheid*, Den Haag: Ministerie van Sociale Zaken en Werkgelegenheid, Directie Voorlichting, Bibliotheek en Documentatie.

Ministerie van Sociale Zaken en Werkgelegenheid (1999a) *Op weg naar een nieuw evenwicht tussen arbeid en zorg. Nota deel 1*, Den Haag: Ministerie van Sociale Zaken en Werkgelegenheid, Directie Voorlichting, Bibliotheek en Documentatie.

Ministerie van Sociale Zaken en Werkgelegenheid (1999b) *Op weg naar een nieuw evenwicht tussen arbeid en zorg. Nota deel 2 + bijlagen*, Den Haag: Ministerie van Sociale Zaken en Werkgelegenheid, Directie Voorlichting, Bibliotheek en Documentatie.

Ministerie van Sociale Zaken en Werkgelegenheid (2000) *Van vrouwenstrijd naar vanzelfsprekendheid. Meerjarennota Emancipatiebeleid: achtergronddeel*, Den Haag: Ministerie van Sociale Zaken en Werkgelegenheid, Directie Coördinatie Emancipatiebeleid.

Mirowsky, P. (1984) 'Physics and the marginalist revolution', *Cambridge Journal of Economics*, vol 75, no 2, pp 361-79.

Mortimer, J.T. (2003) *The handbook of the life course*, New York: Kluwer Academic/Plenum Publishers.

Muffels, R.J.A. (2006) 'Het Transitionele arbeidsmarktmodel: theorie, empirie en beleid', in Ester, P., Muffels, R.J.A. and Schippers, J. (eds) *Dynamiek en levensloop: De arbeidsmarkt in transitie*, Assen: Koninklijke Van Gorcum, pp 9-36.

Muffels, R.J.A. and Ester, P. (2004) *De transitionele arbeidsmarkt. Naar een nieuwe sociale en economische dynamiek*, Tilburg: OSA.

Muffels, R.J.A., Wilthagen, T. and van den Heuvel, N. (2002) *Labour market transitions and employment regimes: Evidence on the flexibility–security nexus in transitional labour markets*, WZB-discussion papers (Ext rep FS I 02-20), Berlin: WZB, Wissenschaftszentrum Berlin für Sozialforschung.

Murphy, M. (1976) 'The value of time spent in home production', *American Journal of Economics and Sociology*, vol 35, no 2, pp 191-7.

Murphy, M. (1978) 'The value of non-market household production: opportunity cost versus market cost estimates', *Review of Income and Wealth*, vol 17, no 3, pp 243-55.

Murphy, M. (1982) 'Comparative estimates of the value of household work in the US for 1976', *Review of Income and Wealth*, vol 28, no 1, pp 29-43.

Neuberg, L.G. (1989) *Conceptual anomalies in economics and statistics. Lessons from the social experiments*, Cambridge: Cambridge University Press.

Nicolis, G. and Prigogine, I. (1989) *Exploring complexity*, New York: W.H. Freeman.

OECD (Organisation for Economic Co-operation and Development) (2003) *Revenue statistics of OECD member countries, 1965-2002*, New York: OECD.

OECD (2005) *Revenue statistics of OECD member countries, 1965-2004*, New York: OECD.

Osterman, P. (1995) 'Work/family programs and the employment relationship', *Administrative Science Quarterly*, vol 40, no 4, pp 681-700.

Peper, B., van Doorne-Huiskes, A. and den Dulk, L. (eds) (2005) *Flexible working and organisational change. The integration of work and personal life*, Cheltenham and Northampton, MA: Edward Elgar.

Perrons, D., Fagan, C., McDowell, L., Ray, K. and Ward, K. (eds) (2006) *Gender divisions and working time in the new economy: Public policy and changing patterns of work in Europe and North America*, Cheltenham and Northampton, MA: Edward Elgar.

Peters, P. and van der Lippe, T. (2007) 'Access to home-based telework: a multi-level and multi-actor perspective', in T. van der Lippe and P. Peeters (eds) *Competing claims in work and family life*, Cheltenham and Northampton, MA: Edward Elgar, pp 233-48.

Plantenga, J. and Schippers, J. (2000) 'Arbeid, zorg en inkomen', in Ministerie van Sociale Zaken en Werkgelegenheid, *Van vrouwenstrijd naar vanzelfsprekendheid. Meerjarennota Emancipatiebeleid: achtergronddeel*, Den Haag: Ministerie van Sociale Zaken en Werkgelegenheid, Directie Coördinatie Emancipatiebeleid, pp 7-31.

Poelmans, S. (2001) *Family-friendly policies. A concern for Spanish companies?*, Technical note, June, Barcelona: IESE.

Poelmans, S. and Chinchilla, M. (2001) *The adoption of family-friendly HRM policies. Competing for scarce resources in the labour market*, Research Paper no 438, June, Barcelona: IESE.

Poelmans, S., Spector, P., Cooper, L., Allen, T., O'Driscoll, M. and Sanchez, J. (2003) 'A cross-national comparative study of work/family demands and resources', *International Journal of Cross Cultural Management*, vol 3, no 3, pp 275-88.

Polanyi, K. (ed) (1957) *Trade and market in the early empires: Economics in history and theory*, Glencoe, IL: The Free Press and the Falcon's Wing Press.

Polanyi, K. (1977) *The livelihood of man*, New York, San Francisco, London: Academic Press.

Pollak, R.A. and Wachter, M.L. (1975) 'The relevance of the household production function and its implications for the allocation of time', *Journal of Political Economy*, vol 83, no 2, 255-277.

Pott-Buter, H. (1993) *Facts and fairy tales about female labour, family and fertility. A seven-country comparison 1850-1990*, Amsterdam: Amsterdam University Press.

Prigogine, I. (1980) *From being to becoming. Time and the complexity in the physical sciences*, San Francisco: CA: W.H. Freeman.

Prigogine, I. (1996a) 'The laws of chaos', *Review*, vol XIX, no 1, winter, pp 1-11.

Prigogine, I. (1996b) *Het einde van de zekerheden*, Tielt: Lanno.

Prigogine, I. and Stengers, I. (1984) *Order out of chaos. Man's new dialogue with nature*, London: Heinemann.

Ravn, A. (2008) 'Married women's right to pay taxes: debates on gender, economic citizenship and tax law reform in Denmark, 1945–83', in K Melby, A. Ravn, and C.C. Wetterberg (eds) *Gender equality and welfare politics in Scandinavia. The limits of political ambition?*, Bristol, The Policy Press, pp 63-84.

Reamer, F.G. (1993) *The philosophical foundations of social work*, New York: Columbia University Press.

Reid, M. (1934) *Economics of household production*, New York: John Wiley and Sons.

Reid, M. (1977) 'How new is the New Home Economics?', *Journal of Consumer Research*, vol 4, no 3, pp 181-3.

Reynaert, E. (1998) *Handleiding Social Auditing. Een stapsgewijze ontwikkeling naar duurzaam ondernemen*, Leuven/Amersfoort: Acco.

Riedman, A., Bielinski, H., Szczurowska, T. and Wagner, A. (2006) *Working time and work–life balance in European companies. Establishment survey on working time, 2004-2005*, Dublin: European Foundation for the Improvement of Living and Working Conditions.

Risseuw, C., Palriwala, R. and Ganesh, K. (2005) *Care, culture and citizenship. Revisiting the politics of the Dutch welfare state*, Amsterdam: Het Spinhuis.

Rohrlich, F. (1987) *From paradox to reality. Our new concept of the physical world*, Cambridge and New York: Cambridge University Press.

Roman, A. (2006) *Deviating from the standard: Effects on labor continuity and career patterns*, Amsterdam: Dutch University Press.

Roman, A., Schippers, J. and Heylen, L. (2006) 'Diverging career paths: mind your step!', Paper for the conference 'Innovating labour market policies', 30 November–1 December, Amsterdam.

Ruuskanen, O.P. (2005) 'Taking the fun out of housework: the effect of including secondary activities in the valuation of unpaid housework', Paper for the IATUR conference 'Time use in daily life: the content and context of human behaviour', Halifax, Nova Scotia, Canada, 2-4 November.

Sanchis, A.G. (2007) 'Economic theories about the allocation of time. A survey of the literature throughout time and some contributions', Master thesis for the Degree of Environmental and Development Economics, Department of Economics, University of Oslo.

Sayer, L. (2005) 'Gender, time and inquality. Trends in women's and men's paid work, unpaid work and free time', *Social Forces*, vol 84, no 1, September, pp 285-303.

Schippers, J. (2006a) 'Labour markets and life courses: theory, empiricism and policy', in N. van den Heuvel, P. van der Hallen, T. van der Lippe and J. Schippers, *Diversity in life courses: Consequences for the labour market*, Tilburg: OSA, pp 19-42.

Schippers, J. (2006b) 'The life course approach to the labour market: a new challenge', in N. van den Heuvel, P. van der Hallen, T. van der Lippe and J. Schippers, *Diversity in life courses: Consequences for the labour market*, Tilburg: OSA, pp 191-200.

Schmid, G. (1997) *The Dutch employment miracle. A comparison of employment systems in the Netherlands and Germany*, Discussion paper, ISSN 1011-9523, Berlin: Wissenschaftszentrum Berlin für Sozialforschung.

Schmid, G. (1998) *Transitional labour markets: A new European employment strategy*, Discussion paper FSI98-206, ISSN 1011-9523, Berlin: Wissenschaftszentrum Berlin für Sozialforschung.

Schmid, G. (2002a) 'Towards a theory of transitional labour markets', in G. Schmid and B. Gazier (eds) *The dynamics of full employment. Social integration through transitional labour markets*, Cheltenham and Northampton, MA: Edward Elgar, pp 151-95.

Schmid, G. (2002b) 'Transitional labour markets and the European social model: towards a new employment compact', in G. Schmid and B. Gazier (eds) *The dynamics of full employment. Social integration through transitional labour markets*, Cheltenham and Northampton, MA: Edward Elgar, pp 393-435.

Schmid, G. and Gazier, B. (eds) (2002) *The dynamics of full employment. Social integration through transitional labour markets*, Cheltenham and Northampton, MA: Edward Elgar.

Schmid, G. and Schomann, K. (2004) *Managing social risks through transitional labour markets: Towards a European social model*, Working paper for the TLM.NET conference, 25-26 November, Amsterdam: SISWO.

Schmidt, A. (2005) 'Vrouwenarbeid in de vroegmoderne tijd in Nederland', *Tijdschrift voor Economische en Sociale Geschiedenis*, vol 2, no 3, pp 2-21.

Schultz, T.W. (1974) *Economics of the family*, London: University of Chicago Press.

Schwartz, J.G. (1977) *The subtle anatomy of capitalism*, Santa Monica, CA: Goodyear Publishing Company.

Seccombe, W. (1992) *A millennium of family change. Feudalism to capitalism in northwestern Europe*, London and New York: Verso.

Seccombe, W. (1993) *Weathering the storm. Working-class families from the industrial revolution to the fertility decline*, London and New York: Verso.

Segalen, M. (1986) 'La révolution industrielle: du prolétaire au bourgeois', in J. Goody (ed) *Histoire de la famille*, vol 2, Paris: Armand Colin.

Sen, A. (1985) 'The moral standing of the market', *Social Philosophy and Policy*, vol 2, no 2, spring.

Shapiro, G., Valbjorn, L. and Olgiati, E. (1998) *Developing innovative work organisation with equal opportunities: Self-assessment diagnostic tool, including company examples*, Brighton: University of Brighton.

Smith, J. and Wallerstein, I. (eds) (1992) *Creating and transforming households. The constraints of the world-economy*, Cambridge and Paris: Cambridge University Press.

Solow, R.M. (1985) 'Economic history and economics', *American Economic Review*, vol 75, no 2, pp 328-31.

Souza-Poza, A., Schmid, H. and Widmer, R. (2001) 'The allocation and value of time assigned to housework and child-care: an analysis for Switzerland', *Journal of Population Economics*, vol 14, no 4, pp 599-618.

Sullerot, E. (1979) *Geschiedenis en sociologie van de vrouwenarbeid*, Nijmegen: SUN.

Szalai, A. (ed) (1972) *The use of time*, The Hague and Paris: Mouton Press.

Tijdens, K. (2007) 'Employees' preferences for longer or shorter working hours', in T. van der Lippe and P. Peeters (eds) *Competing claims in work and family life*, Cheltenham and Northampton, MA: Edward Elgar, pp 109-24.

Tijdens, K., van Doorne-Huiskes, A. and Willemsen, T. (1997) *Time allocation and gender. The relationship between paid labour and household work*, Tilburg: Tilburg University Press.

Van Bavel, J. (2004) 'Beroepsarbeid van vrouwen en de daling van de vruchtbaarheid in het Westen, 1850–2000. Is er een oorzakelijk verband?', *Bevolking en Gezin*, vol 33, no 1, pp 61-90.

Vandenbroeck, M. (2003) 'De kinderopvang als opvoedingsmilieu tussen gezin en samenleving. Onderzoek naar een eigentijds sociaal-pedagogisch concept voor de kinderopvang', PhD thesis, Ghent: University of Ghent.

Vandenbroucke, F. (1999) 'Social justice and individual ethics in an open society. Equality, responsibility and incentives', Doctoral thesis, Oxford: Oxford University.

Vandenbroucke, F. (2001) 'The active welfare state: a European ambition', Speech given at the Commission for Social Development of the United Nations, 13 February, New York, *Documentatieblad*, Ministerie van Financiën, 61 jaargang, nr 3, May-June, pp 3-16.

van den Heuvel, N., Holderbeke, F. and Wielers, R. (2001) *De transitionele arbeidsmarkt. Contouren van een actief arbeidsmarktbeleid*, Den Haag: Elsevier bedrijfsinformatie.

van den Heuvel, N., van der Hallen, P., van der Lippe, T. and Schippers, J. (2006) *Diversity in life courses: Consequences for the labour market*, Tilburg: OSA.

van der Lippe, T. (1997) 'Time allocated to paid work by women in Western and Eastern European countries', in K. Tijdens, A. van Doorne-Huiskes and T. Willemsen, *Time allocation and gender. The relationship between paid labour and household work*, Tilburg: Tilburg University Press, pp 123-43.

van der Lippe, T. and Peeters, P. (eds) (2007) *Competing claims in work and family life*, Cheltenham and Northampton, MA: Edward Elgar.

Van Dongen, W. (1990) 'Een geïntegreerde analyse van de individuele en maatschappelijke arbeidsverdeling. Toepassing: theoretisch, empirisch en beleidsgericht onderzoek van de combinatie van de betaalde arbeid en de gezinsarbeid van de vrouwen in Vlaanderen', Doctoraal proefschrift, Gent: RUG.

Van Dongen, W. (1992a) 'An integrated analysis of the internal and external division of labour of the family. Theory and operationalisation', *Population and Family in the Low Countries 1992: Family and labour*.

Van Dongen, W. (1992b) 'A positive culture towards external day nursery: a dynamic and integrated infrastructure on a local scale', *Population and Family in the Low Countries 1992: Family and labour.*

Van Dongen, W. (1993) *Nieuwe krijtlijnen voor gezin, Markt en maatschappij. Een geïntegreerde benadering* (*New perspectives for the family, the market and society. An integrated approach*), Leuven-Apeldoorn: Garant.

Van Dongen, W. (1997) 'The double day's duty of married men and women in Flanders', *Population and Family in the Low Countries 1996/97*, pp 141-69.

Van Dongen, W. (2004a) 'Van een vrije markt naar een democratische markt?' ('From a free market to a democratic market?'), *Ethiek en Maatschappij*, 1 trimester, jaargang 7, nr 1, maart.

Van Dongen, W. (2004b) *Het combinatiemodel in Vlaamse organisaties. Beschikbare regelingen voor de werknemers* (*The combination model in Flemish companies: Available facilities for employees*), CBGS-Werkdocument 2004/1, Brussels: CBGS.

Van Dongen, W. (2004c) *Kinderopvang als basisvoorziening in een democratische samenleving. Toekomstscenario's voor de dagopvang van kinderen jonger dan drie jaar in Vlaanderen* (*Childcare as a basic provision in a democratic society. From daycare to full daytime education for children younger than three years*), CBGS-document 2004/4, Brussels: CBGS.

Van Dongen, W. (2004d) 'From day care to fully-fledged daytime education for children under the age of three as a basic facility for children, parents and companies in Flanders?', Paper voor Sociaal Wetenschappelijke Studiedagen, SISWO, 22-23 April, Amsterdam.

Van Dongen, W. (2004e) 'Time use research as the basis for policy models in a democratic society. The case of Flanders', Paper for the IATUR conference 'Time use: what's new in methodology and application fields?', ISTAT (Italian National Statistical Institute), 27-29 October, Rome.

Van Dongen, W. (2005a) 'Development of the combination model in EU countries and the combination policies in organisations', Paper for the TLM.NET conference 'Managing social risks through transitional labour markets', 19-21 May, Budapest.

Van Dongen, W. (2005b) 'The combination model in EU countries: actual development, policy models and the Family & Business Audit for organisations', Paper for the Founding conference of the International Centre for Work and Family (ICWF), IESE Business School, Barcelona, 7-9 July.

Van Dongen, W. (2005c) 'Democracy of daily life. The development of the combination model in Western countries for the reconciliation of professional and family life', Paper for the IATUR conference 'Time use in daily life: the content and context of human behaviour', Halifax, Nova Scotia, Canada, 2-4 November.

Van Dongen, W. (2006a) 'Democracy of daily life in the Western world: conceptual approach and actual development', Paper for the IATUR conference 'Time use in daily life: the content and context of human behaviour', Copenhagen, 16-18 August.

Van Dongen, W. (2006b) 'Democracy of daily life in the Western world: the complete combination model as the basis for an integrated policy', Paper for the IATUR conference 'Time use in daily life: the content and context of human behaviour', Copenhagen, 16-18 August.

Van Dongen, W. (2006c) 'Analysemodel en instrumenten voor een doelmatige dienstverlening in een democratische samenleving' ('Analysis and instruments for efficient public services in a democratic society'), in F. Deven and T. Jacobs (eds) *Vooruitdenken over Zorg in Vlaanderen* (*Discussing care in Flanders*), Antwerpen–Apeldoorn: Garant, pp 151–77.

Van Dongen, W. (2008) *Naar een democratische arbeidsverdeling? Het Combinatiemodel als basis voor een geïntegreerd beleid in Vlaanderen en Europa*, SVR-Studie, 2008–1, Brussels: Studiedienst van de Vlaamse Regering.

Van Dongen, W. and Beck, M. (eds) (1999) *Gezinsleven en beroepsleven. Uitdagingen, modellen en perspectieven*, Platformtekst van de rondetafelconferentie 'Gezinsleven en bedrijfsleven', Brussels: CBGS.

Van Dongen, W. and Danau, D. (2003) *Maatschappelijke gelijkheid als basiswaarde van de democratie. Actualisering van het Combinatiemodel inzake tijds- en inkomensverdeling van mannen en vrouwen, als basis voor een geïntegreerd beleid* (*Societal equality as a basic value of democracy. Updating the combination model regarding the division of labour and income, as basis for an integrated policy*), Brussels: Gelijke Kansen in Vlaanderen.

Van Dongen, W. and Franken, M. (1999) 'Gender equality as a basic value of democracy. An integrated approach', Paper for the conference of the Council of Europe: 'Gender mainstreaming: a step into the 21st century', Athens, 16–18 September.

Van Dongen, W. and Pauwels, K. (1996) 'Gezinnen, arbeid en inkomen', in R. Cliquet (ed) *Gezinnen in de verandering, veranderende gezinnen*, CBGS Monografie, 1996/2, Brussels, pp 155–79.

Van Dongen, W., Beck, M. and Vanhaute, E. (eds) (2001) *Gezinsleven en beroepsleven. Het combinatiemodel als motor voor de actieve welvaartsstaat?* (*Professional and family life. The combination model as a motor for an active welfare state?*), CBGS Publicaties, Leuven–Apeldoorn: Garant.

Van Dongen, W., Danau, D. and Vloeberghs, D. (2002) *FBA-project. Summary of the final report*, Brussels: CBGS, Universiteit Antwerpen and ECWS.

Van Dongen, W., Deschamps, L. and Pauwels, K. (1987a) *De waarde van huishoudelijke arbeid. Deel 1: Beschrijving en praktische toepasbaarheid van de economische methoden voor de waardebepaling*, CBGS-Werkdocument, nr 39, Brussels: CBGS.

Van Dongen, W., Deschamps, L. and Pauwels, K. (1987b) *De waarde van huishoudelijke arbeid. Deel 2: Theorie van de waardevorming en de fundamentele problemen van de economische methoden voor de waardebepaling*, CBGS-Werkdocument, nr 41, Brussels: CBGS.

Van Dongen, W., Deschamps, L. and Pauwels, K. (1987c) '(Hoe) kan de waarde van huishoudelijke arbeid worden gemeten?', *Bevolking en Gezin*, 1987/1, pp 31–64.

Van Dongen, W., Malfait, D. and Pauwels, K. (1995) *De dagelijkse puzzel 'gezin en arbeid'. Feiten, wensen en problemen inzake de combinatie van beroeps- en gezinsarbeid in Vlaanderen* (*The daily puzzle 'Family and work'. Facts, preferences and problems with respect to the combination of professional and family work in Flanders*), CBGS-Monografie 1995/2, Brussels: CBGS.

Van Dongen, W., Vanhaute, E. and Pauwels, K. (eds) (1998) *Het kostwinnersmodel voorbij? Naar een nieuw basismodel voor de arbeidsverdeling binnen de gezinnen* (*Beyond the breadwinner model? Towards a new basic model for the division of labour in families*), Leuven-Apeldoorn: Garant.

van Echtelt, P., Glebbeek, A.C., Wielers, R. and Lindenberg, S. (2007) 'The puzzle of unpaid overtime: can the time greediness of post-Fordist work be explained?', in T. van der Lippe and P. Peeters (eds) *Competing claims in work and family life*, Cheltenham and Northampton, MA: Edward Elgar, pp 125-42.

Vanhaute, E. (1992) *Heiboeren. Bevolking, arbeid en inkomen in de 19de eeuwse Kempen*, Brussels: VUB-Press.

Vanhaute, E. (1997a) 'Labour markets and family strategies in Flanders, 1750-1990. A long-term perspective', *Population and Family in the Low Countries 1996/1997*, Selected current issues, pp 171-90.

Vanhaute, E. (1997b) 'Between patterns and processes: measuring labour markets and family strategies in Flanders, 1750-1990', *History of the Family. An International Quarterly*, vol 2, no 4, pp 527-45.

Vanhaute, E. (2002) 'Breadwinner models and historical models. Transitions in labour relations and labour markets in Belgium', in H. Jensen (ed) *The welfare state. Past, present and future*, Pisa: University of Pisa, Edizioni Plus, pp 59-76.

Van Hootegem, G. (2000), *De draaglijke traagheid van het management. Tendenzen in het productie- en personeelsbeleid*, Leuven: Acco.

Van Parijs, P. (ed) (1992) *Arguing for basic income. Ethical foundations for a radical reform*, London and New York: Verso.

Van Parijs, P. (1995) *Real freedom for all. What (if anything) can justify capitalism?*, Oxford: Oxford University Press.

van Poppel, F.W.A., van Dalen, H.P. and Walhout, E. (2006) *Diffusion of a social norm: Tracing the emergence of the housewife in the Netherlands, 1812-1922*, Discussion Paper, TI 2006-107/1, Rotterdam: Tinbergen Institute, University of Rotterdam.

van Velzen, S. (1997) 'Economics, strategic behaviour and the intrahousehold division of labour', in K. Tijdens, A. van Doorne-Huiskes and T. Willemsen, *Time allocation and gender. The relationship between paid labour and household work*, Tilburg: Tilburg University Press, pp 61-78.

Vlasblom, J.D. and Schippers, J. (2004) 'The dynamics of female employment around childbirth', Paper for the TLM.net conference, 25-26 November.

Wallerstein, I. (1991) *Geopolitics and geoculture. Essays on the changing world-system*, Cambridge: Cambridge University Press.

Wallin, S. (2006) 'Monitoring families and their management of time and space in everyday life', Paper for the workshop 'Patterns in everyday life: understandings of everyday contexts', Linköping University, Linköping, Sweden, 11-12 September.

Wilson, J. (2000) 'Volunteering', *Annual Review of Sociology*, vol 26, pp 215-40.

Wilson, J. and Musick, M. (1997) 'Who cares? Toward an integrated theory of volunteer work', *American Sociological Review*, vol 62, no 5, October, pp 694-713.

Index